Bob Feller

Also by JOHN SICKELS

The STATS Minor League Scouting Notebook (since 1996)
The Baseball Prospect Book 2003

Bob Feller

ACE OF THE GREATEST GENERATION

John Sickels

BRASSEY'S, INC.
Washington, D.C.

Library of Congress Cataloging-in-Publication Data

Sickels, John.
    Bob Feller : ace of the greatest generation / John Sickels.—1st ed.
        p.   cm.
    Includes bibliographical references and index.
    ISBN 1-57488-441-7 (alk. paper)
    1. Feller, Bob, 1918–   2. Baseball players—United States—Biography.
I. Title.
GV865.F4S53   2003
796.357'092—dc22   2003023088

Printed in the United States of America on acid-free paper that meets the American National Standards Institute Z39–48 Standard.

Brassey's, Inc.
22841 Quicksilver Drive
Dulles, Virginia 20166

First Edition

10 9 8 7 6 5 4 3 2 1

For Joe Sickels,
my father and my friend

CONTENTS

List of Tables

ACKNOWLEDGMENTS

BOOKS HAVE MANY AUTHORS, not just the name on the front page. The writing and production of this book could not have been done without the hard work, cooperation, and input of the following individuals.

I must thank—

My wife, Jeri Sickels, who is my best friend and my soulmate. She is also the most patient, loving, and supportive spouse that any person could have. She encouraged me when I was discouraged. She supported the project through thick and thin, even when it took me away from her for weeks at a time. I am not an easy person to live with when under stress, but she remains the rock on which any success I have is based. Finding words to express exactly how appreciative I am for her love is impossible.

My son, Nicholas, who is the best son any father could ask for. He didn't always understand why Dad couldn't play, but like his mother, he cheered me up when I was down.

My parents, Joe and Hilda Sickels, and my sister, Lisa.

My in-laws, Marsh and Gwen Jackson, and the entire Jackson family.

My mentor, Bill James, not only for his friendship, but for the easy access to and use of his extensive baseball library.

My editor, Chris Kahrl, exemplar of patience, and a good friend.

Kevin Cuddihy and Teresa Metcalfe at Brassey's, whose fine work was instrumental in getting this book to press.

Mr. Bob Feller himself, the subject of this book, who gave several hours of his valuable time to answer my questions, even though this was not an "authorized" biography.

John Kelling, former curator of the Bob Feller Museum, who

kept me in touch with Bob and provided access to the materials of the museum.

Steven P. Gietschier and James R. Meier of the Sporting News Research Center, who let me graze through their vast resources in search of material that proved invaluable.

The staffs of the University of Kansas Library system, the Lawrence Public Library, the State Historical Society of Iowa, the Iowa Historical Archive, and the Ohio Historical Society.

I'm certainly forgetting someone important; my memory is not what it once was. For this I apologize.

Finally, I must emphasize that any and all errors of fact or interpretation in this book are my responsibility alone.

JOHN SICKELS
Lawrence, Kansas

INTRODUCTION

WHEN I FIRST EXHIBITED an interest in baseball at the age of 7, my father began taking me to minor league games, to see the Triple-A Iowa Oaks play at Sec Taylor Stadium in Des Moines. My favorite player quickly became Oaks first baseman Mike Squires, who hit a home run in the first professional game I ever attended. I don't remember exactly when it happened, but at some point I asked my dad who his favorite player had been when he was growing up. "Bob Feller" was his reply. This made perfect sense, since my father grew up in rural Iowa during the 1930s and 1940s, when Feller was in his heyday. Following Feller, wanting to imitate him and his improbable storybook rise to the majors, was an obsession with tens of thousands of young boys throughout the Midwest and across the country. Hollywood could not have done it better.

But now 50 years have gone by, and to a great extent, something of the Feller mystique has been lost. Ask the casual baseball fan of today who the greatest stars of 50 years ago were, and you'll likely hear about Joe DiMaggio and Ted Williams. But while serious fans of the sport know about Bob Feller, his position in the knowledge base of the average fan has declined, declined to a much greater extent than the observers of 50 years ago would have thought possible.

In his own day, Feller was as big a star as DiMaggio or Williams, and definitely the biggest star outside of the Eastern cities. He had the most endorsements; he was the highest-paid player for several years; he was the biggest gate attraction. But while the average fan of today may identify Feller's name under the mental category of "great pitcher," in his own day he was far more than that. To his contemporaries, he was both the personification of pitching greatness and the epitome of the all-American story. To today's casual fan, Feller is just some guy who threw really hard, struck some people out, and served in one of those wars.

The baseball bookshelf reflects this phenomenon. There are two autobiographies of Feller, *Strikeout Story*, published in 1948, and *Now Pitching: Bob Feller*, published in 1990. Another autobiographical production, this one filled with a combination of pithy observations and crankiness, *Bob Feller's Book of Baseball Wisdom*, was published in 2001. But despite Feller's undoubted importance in baseball history, there are only two *biographies* of the man. *Bob Feller: Hall of Fame Strikeout Star* came out in 1962, the year of Feller's induction into the Hall of Fame, but is hard to find nowadays. An offering in the Baseball Legends series of biographies for children and adolescents, *Bob Feller*, was published in 1990. Both of these bios are good for what they are: relatively straightforward accounts of Feller's life and career. But neither book can be regarded as analytical, about the man himself or his era. And considering the voluminous tomes that have been written about other stars of his time, Feller has been almost ignored by the baseball press.

So why the dearth of retrospection and the decline in the historical consciousness of Feller?

Feller himself is something of an enigmatic figure. He is an extremely intelligent man, and can be engaging, friendly, and very gracious. He can also be testy, obtuse, and self-centered. Those who know him seem to either love him or hate him. In the course of researching this book, I came into contact with numerous people, inside the baseball world and outside of it, who've known Feller or had dealings with him over the years. The number of "he's one of the best people I've ever met" comments was about equal to the number of "he's a lousy human being" comments. Clearly, there is more to Feller than just the all-American boy story put forward in his two brief biographies.

Of course, being a complex personality didn't prevent Ted Williams from being the focus of huge amounts of media attention. Williams' complexities even seemed to encourage observation, to draw writers into the personality of the man. Williams often had lousy press when he was a player, but as he aged and mellowed, the media attention devoted to him became more nuanced, more intricate, and ultimately more fair. But the opposite seemed to happen with Feller. Most (but far from all) of his press attention while playing was positive, especially early in his career. But at the height of his prowess as a player, many in the press turned against him. After his retirement, coverage of Feller lessened and at times took on a more negative tone. How and why this happened is one of the themes of this book.

My purpose in writing this book is not just to present a new biography of Bob Feller, but rather to examine and re-create his impact as a player, to show how important Feller was in the history of the game—worthy of far more attention than he's received in recent years.

I will present a biographical chronology of his career, of course, with particular attention to his record during the Second World War. The basic outline of Feller's career is fairly well known, but he was much more than just a great ballplayer. Feller's impact was felt on issues such as race relations and baseball economics, but much of this information is scattered through various sources in the baseball library. I want to bring those strands together.

I will also look at his career statistically, using some of the breakthroughs in sabermetric baseball analysis developed over the last 20 years. How dominant, exactly, was Feller? What did his service in the Second World War cost him? Looking at his statistical accomplishments within the context of their time is the key to developing an understanding of how good Feller was.

In addition, I will look at the various ways Feller has been viewed over the years. Feller's personality seems to be dichotomous, lending itself to both positive and negative images. Both stereotypes of Feller, the All-American Boy and the Cranky Old Man, contain elements of truth about his personality, but neither view is complete.

Ultimately, I view this book as an attempt to bring Feller's career and life alive once again. Bob Feller was one of the absolutely crucial figures in baseball history, both on and off the field. I wish to present him to a generation of fans that may have only a limited appreciation or understanding of his impact on the game.

1

From the Banks of the Raccoon

[W]hat kid wouldn't enjoy the life I led in Iowa? Baseball
and farming, and I had the best of both worlds.
—Bob Feller, *Now Pitching: Bob Feller*, p. 32

A bout 15 miles west of Des Moines, Iowa, in the floodplain
of the Raccoon River, lies the town of Van Meter. Straddling
Dallas County Road R16, the burg sits about a mile south of
the interchange with Interstate 80. Don't be deceived by the
term "county road." It isn't the gravel-topped track that the
term "county road" conjures up in the minds of people who don't
know the Midwest. R16 is wider and in better condition than many
thoroughfares that pass for U.S. highways in some states. Good
roads are the arteries of rural commerce, and have been a major
focus of development in Iowa since the 1920s.

On the surface, there is little to distinguish Van Meter from the
hundreds of similar communities that dot the state. The town fea-
tures a Casey's General Store and a Wells Fargo Bank branch, along
with several local businesses. The 2000 U.S. Census puts the population at 866, about a hundred people more than were recorded in
the 1990 census. The Des Moines metropolitan area is growing rap-
idly, and many of the small hamlets surrounding it are becoming
bedroom communities. Suburbanites who work in Des Moines and
its environs during the day migrate to the smaller towns at night,
seeking a quieter life, less-crowded classrooms for their children,
and the trappings, if not the reality, of small-town living. In this
respect, Van Meter is exactly like sister towns Granger, Grimes, De

Soto, and Adel: caught up in a gradual population migration from the big city that is making Dallas County the fastest-growing county in the state.

There is one critical way in which Van Meter differs from these other communities. No one outside of Central Iowa has ever heard of Dallas Center, Perry, Redfield, or Dexter. But if you have a knowledge of or an interest in baseball history, there is a very good chance that you've heard of Van Meter. And 50 years ago, even the very casual baseball fan knew of Van Meter and her most famous product—Bob Feller.

The Feller family roots run deep in Van Meter. The first European settlers arrived in Dallas County sometime in the late 1840s. Originally inhabited by Native Americans of the Sac and Fox tribes, the area had been "cleared" for European settlement just before Iowa joined the Union in 1846. Van Meter itself was laid out in 1869, though not incorporated until 1877.[1] The town was originally named Tracy, but was soon rechristened Van Meter to honor one of the earliest settlers. The first Fellers arrived in the area about this time; county militia records from the early 1870s list military-age males named "Feller" and "Fellers."[2]

Like most Iowans in this period, the Fellers were farmers. Agriculture was the focus of life in Van Meter, centered around the grain elevator. Three general stores, two drugstores, and two meat markets catered to the surrounding farmsteads. The railroad came through the town in the 1870s. An enterprising local businessman, eyeing the nearby woods, set up a woodcutting business, and Van Meter became a leading supplier of railroad ties. Methodist and United Brethren churches were organized, providing for the spiritual well-being of the townsfolk. Two saloons provided other forms of well-being, at least until the advent of Prohibition. The discovery of coal led to the development of a mine and a brickyard, and by the early 1890s the town supported a bustling population of well over a thousand. The coal mine was exhausted by the turn of the century, however, crippling the local economy. The population of Van Meter quickly dropped to a little less than 500 by 1920, where it hovered for decades.

Politically, Iowa had been a Republican state since the Civil

War, and rural Dallas County during this period reflected this. Iowa went for Republicans in every election between the Civil War and the Great Depression, except in 1912. That year, Theodore Roosevelt and William Howard Taft split the GOP vote, which allowed Woodrow Wilson to win the state and contributed to his winning the presidency. Only since 1988 has Iowa moved consistently into the Democratic column. Politics in Iowa has always been a unique mixture of conservatism and progressivism, and this remains true today. There are more registered Republicans than Democrats in Iowa even now, but the rightward shift of the national GOP over the last 20 years has helped swing Iowa's electoral votes toward the Democratic party.

Even at the height of the Great Depression, when the national Republican Party was in disarray, the GOP was the dominant political force in Van Meter and Dallas County. The local newspaper, the *Dallas County News*, featured a strongly pro-GOP tilt in both its editorials and news stories. On April 9th, 1930, the editorial page inveighed, "President Hoover's record has been assailed by the democratic congressional leaders, charging lack of leadership and a failure to secure results . . . so far as these claims are justified by facts, the blame belongs, not with President Hoover, but with the coalition between democratic senators and the small bunch of republican deserters, who have united with them in opposing his efforts." The 1932 presidential election saw Van Meter go for FDR by just four votes: 175 for Roosevelt to 171 for Hoover. Every other slot on the ballot that year went for the GOP candidate.[3] Temperance was another major issue of the day. Van Meter was a "dry" stronghold in the county, and a special election in June of 1933 saw the good citizens of Van Meter vote 179 to 120 to remain so.[4]

A look through the newspapers of the day reveals Van Meter and Dallas County to be typically rural in viewpoint. National stories intruded into the local paper only rarely. The news was filled with stories about local business conditions, happenings at the school, regional sports, births and deaths, visits from relatives. A few examples give us an idea about the tenor of rural life in this period. The Van Meter Methodist church put on a "temperance drama" about the evils of alcohol in April of 1930. Paving of country roads was a frequent topic of discussion and news interest. The proposed establishment of a state income tax in 1930 caused great controversy. Exciting events occurred occasionally. "The coal in the bin at the [Van Meter] schoolhouse was discovered to be on fire by Mr. Johnson, custodian, on Saturday evening," the October 5th, 1932, edition of the *Dallas County News* tells us. "It was necessary to remove the coal. No damage was done." Sometimes, tragedies could not be prevented. A boy named Clifton Orahood, age 12, drowned in a river south of Adel in May 1930. Bob Feller was 11 at the time. February of 1933 saw the death of Henry C. Clayton, the last Van Meter veteran of the Civil War. A "colored boy" killed his stepfather in Adel in June 1930.

Race relations in Iowa were far from ideal, though not particularly awful when compared with other areas of the country at the time. Iowan African Americans lived primarily in the urban areas of the state. The 1930 U.S. Census counted 17,380 "Negroes" in Iowa, of which only 2,195 lived in rural areas.[5] Occasional mention was made in local papers of "coloreds" visiting from Des Moines, often in connection with sporting events. The newspapers in Des Moines were somewhat more enlightened than their rural counterparts, usually referring to African Americans as "Negroes" rather than "coloreds."

Segregation in Iowa was not formal; the state had one of the most progressive civil rights statutes on the books in the United States, dating back to the 1870s. Public schools were integrated across the state. But the civil rights ordinance was enforced only erratically, especially when private enterprise was involved. Some restaurants had segregated lunch counters, for example, though this was at the behest of private ownership, not by the laws of the state. Peaceful demonstrations and civil disobedience, by both African Americans and white supporters, against such prejudice were common in the larger cities by the 1940s. When civil rights cases were actually prosecuted, convictions often resulted, even when the jury was all-white, although enforcement was sporadic and depended on the specific attitude of local officials.[6]

Iowa's progressivism in race relations was only relative. Crimes committed by "Negroes" were often front-page news, even if the crime in question was quite minor. Some towns were considerably less "enlightened" than others; blacks could be comfortable and accepted in some areas, but badly harassed in others. Even news stories and commentary laudatory toward African Americans are jarring to read from our perspective today. Take this item from the October 15th, 1928, issue of the *Des Moines Tribune-Capital*. "Critics Praise Young Violinist: Negro Youth Credited with Splendid Tone," reads the headline.

> Bernard Mason, Negro violinist, has been called by musical authorities the best violinist in any high school of Iowa. Although he has the remarkable sense of rhythm peculiar to his race, Bernard has something more, critics say. He has the most vital quality in violin playing—tone . . . [I]n Des Moines, he has played with the Bankers Life trio over the radio, for the library association, for the Rotary Club, and for the services of the Plymouth Congregational Church. . . . Bernard's ambition, when he is graduated, is to become professor of music in one of the finer Negro colleges—Fisk, Hamilton Institute, or Howard.

There are some intriguing issues here to reflect on. Mason attended an integrated high school, and played before both white and black audiences. Those facts by themselves show that Iowa was out in front on race relations compared with the South or even most of the Midwest. Mason's photo appeared in the most important newspaper in the state, an unusual occurrence for a young Negro of this era not involved in a crime, and again not something that was very common in much of the country in this period. Despite the racial stereotype about the "peculiar sense of rhythm," the article does nothing but praise his abilities. Yet there is no sense here that Mason could do anything *but* attend a historically black college, no hint that he might attend the University of Iowa, for example. His options were limited, despite his talent.

Bernard Mason went on to become a professor of music at Howard University.

It was in this economic and social environment that the Feller family made their living. Bob's father, William Andrew Feller, lived his entire life in Dallas County, inheriting the 360-acre family farm about two miles northeast of Van Meter from his own father.

Of French and Swiss stock, Bill Feller had been a baseball fan and player from an early age, but at the age of nine had given up his dreams of the game to work the family farm following his father's death. He did this very well; Bill was respected in the community for his business skill. Through a combination of hard work, astute farm management, and good luck, he weathered the serious economic storms that battered American agriculture in the early 20th century. But he never gave up his devotion to the diamond game.

Bill Feller married Lena Forret. A registered nurse and schoolteacher, Lena was the daughter of Edward Forret, a local farmer who also happened to be a very successful Iowa semipro pitcher in the 1870s and 1880s. He worked his fields during the week, but lit up the local diamonds on the weekends.[7] Ed Forret was renowned in Iowa amateur circles for his strong fastball, and old-timers were fond of saying that he could have pitched professionally if he'd just been able to develop a curve.[8] Despite his talent, his baseball activities were something of an embarrassment to the Forret females. "My grandmother had the same fondness for baseball that she had for a corn borer," Bob wrote in his first autobiography.[9] In any event, baseball interest and skill ran on both sides of the Feller/Forret family.

Robert William Andrew Feller was the first fruit of the union between Bill and Lena. Born in the Feller farmhouse on November 3d, 1918, "Bobby" was a healthy, vigorous, and active child. In the age before antibiotics, this was far more of a blessing than modern readers may realize. Childhood deaths from polio, pneumonia, measles, and a variety of other scourges were very common. In 1918–19, a horrendous influenza epidemic ravaged the globe, killing millions, adding an extra premium to the misery already suffered by the world during the Great War.

Young Robert got through this gauntlet of childhood diseases without misfortune. He demonstrated an interest in baseball from an early age, playing frequent games of catch with a rubber ball with his father at age 5, even inside the house during the long winters.[10] His maternal grandfather, Ed Forret, also did much to encourage a love of baseball in his grandson. In this, of course, young Bob was little different from tens of thousands of other farm youngsters. Baseball was considerably more popular than basket-ball or football. Almost every small and medium-sized town in rural Iowa had a semipro baseball team, in some cases more than one. Baseball interest ran deep and wide.

Generally, Robert's early childhood was typical of that of an Iowa farm boy in the 1920s: lots of chores. In his autobiographies and numerous newspaper articles, Feller recalls this period of his life fondly. Milking cows, hauling hay, cleaning out the barn, help-ing his father with the planting and harvesting, these were the rhythms of daily life for Bobby Feller. His family raised cattle, hogs, horses, and chickens. They planted corn, wheat, and alfalfa. A vegetable garden and fruit orchard provided plenty of extras for the supper table.[11] They made their own soap, and did their own slaughtering. Their homestead was a "full-functioning farm," in Feller's words.[12]

The Feller home was a white frame house, typical in that part of Iowa. It lacked running water or indoor plumbing; again, this was nothing unusual at the time. They did have telephone service, sharing a party line with 16 other families.[13] A wind charger and home generator provided electricity, but the family often used ker-osene lamps to provide illumination.[14]

The Feller land was fertile, some of the most productive in this part of the state. The farm itself lies near the Raccoon River, from which the Fellers would draw water for their cattle. Hauling water up the hill to the farm in buckets was one of young Robert's most common chores. Feller would later credit these duties for helping to develop his arm and tremendous overall athleticism. "Some-times, when I have been asked how I developed my fast ball, I have been tempted to answer: 'Carrying water for cattle from the Rac-coon River.'"[15] The products of the Feller farm were diverse, as Bill Feller was a creative businessman. His son inherited and/or learned these traits from his father, as we shall see.

Not all of the Feller family neighbors were as fortunate. The rural economy of Iowa missed out on the prosperity of the "Roar-ing 20s," as stagnation in farm prices helped set the stage for the economic dislocations that led to the Great Depression. The birth of Bob's sister, Marguerite, when he was 10 years old added another mouth to the family, but also another pair of hands to help with chores. Despite the intractable problems of low farm prices, economic chaos, and drought, the Feller farm was prosperous, producing enough to keep the family fed and clothed, plus enough extra income to support the intense obsession that Bill Feller and his son were developing with baseball.

Physically, Bill Feller did not fit the modern stereotype of a burly early-20th-century farmer. Standing about six-foot, wiry-strong, Bill Feller was rather thin. His eyes were deep-set, and he was a bit gaunt by the time his son reached adolescence. Lena was several inches shorter than her husband, not as thin, with a stronger jaw and fuller body. Bobby inherited his father's high cheekbones, nose, and forehead. But his jaw, highlighted by a dimple, was stronger than his father's, his torso more powerful, his shoulders broader. Measuring 6 feet and 180 pounds by the age of 18, Bob was a blend of both parents. His size doesn't sound great by today's standards, but contemporary accounts consistently refer to the young Feller as "husky." Athleticism and strength ran on both sides of the family tree.

Brainpower did as well. Running a successful farm as Bill Feller did takes intelligence and business acumen as well as brawn. Lena Feller was a nurse and schoolteacher. Bob wasn't a spectacular student, but he was a diligent one, and generally did well in school. O. E. Lester, superintendent of the Van Meter school during Bob's youth, rated Feller's "native ability" as "10 points above normal."[16] "His average in school has never been below 80. That's his high school average. His grade school average was better than that," Lester told the *Des Moines Tribune*.[17] In high school at least, Feller preferred history and government courses. He also did well in English, but had the most trouble in physics.

The relationship between Bill and Lena Feller and their son was a close, though not overtly emotional, one. "There was no tearful parting. Mother and dad aren't very faint-hearted," Feller told the *Chicago Herald-Examiner* in 1937, describing his leaving home to join the Indians.[18] Nevertheless, by all accounts, the Feller home was a happy one, and Robert had strong relationships with both parents. While most accounts of Feller's life emphasize (quite rightly) his friendship with his father, Lena Feller also had a strong impact on her son.

> My mother was always there when I came home. In all of the years until I left high school, I don't think my mother missed greeting me five times. . . . Mom was always there to meet me. It meant the world to me. . . . My mother gave me something, as did my father, that was better than money or the keys to the car: quality time.[19]

Lena had given up her nursing and teaching jobs when Bob was a young child, in order to stay home and help prepare him for school. Her main desire, like any good mother, was for her son to get an education and lead a happy life. She was not opposed to his interest in baseball: Lena would tell Bob, "with a mixture of pride and shame," about the diamond exploits of her father.[20] But at least early in his life, she did not take Bob's interest as seriously as his father did, and was sometimes annoyed that her men were more interested in playing catch when the chores were done than in coming into the house for supper.

You can eat anytime, they would tell her, but you can't play catch when it is too dark outside.[21]

While Lena Feller may have had mixed feelings about baseball, Bill Feller did not. Although he'd given up his own baseball ambitions as a child (his main athletic activity by the time Bob was born was horseshoes), he remained interested in the game. The birth of a son presented him with an opportunity to live his baseball dream vicariously. The Little League parent achieving a dream through the offspring is not just a modern phenomenon. Bill Feller was fortunate, however, in that his son had both interest and aptitude in baseball. He did not rebel against his father, or feel excess pressure to succeed in something that he didn't care about. Many father–son relationships have been consumed by such pressure. This one was not. In just about any book or article you can find by or about Bob Feller, or even when you talk with him yourself, Bob's love and respect for his father comes through strongly. "All of these backyard games represented the time my dad spent with me and the love and support he gave me to pursue my career in professional baseball."[22]

The elder Feller's solid approach to handling his young son was at least partially responsible for their strong relationship. Even from an early age, he explained things, rather than just bossing his son around or pushing him into it. "I reason everything out with Bob," he told *The Saturday Evening Post*, "he's easy to handle if you talk to him. I never tell him to do this or not to do that. I explain what it's all about."[23] Bill Feller's patient, explanatory approach meshed perfectly with Bob's personality. "Dad reasoned things out with me . . . he didn't make me a ball player, he made me want to become one."[24] "From the age of nine," said Feller in 2002, "I knew I wanted to be a major league player. It was all I ever wanted to do."[25]

Although the young Feller was not exactly shy, he was rather quiet and thoughtful. He was reasonably popular in school, but not a "joiner." He had few close friends as a child. "It isn't that Bob is high-hat exclusive," said Superintendent Lester, "he just is, well, he's just independent, that's all."[26]

This independence from peers was also a family trait. Bill Feller was respected in the community for his business acumen. But it is also true that after the birth of his son, many of the townsfolk thought that Bill Feller had gone somewhat crazy and "did the strangest things" when it came to playing baseball with his son.[27] Playing catch behind the barn was nothing unusual, of course. Many fathers did that. But few fathers rigged the second floor of their barn up as a makeshift baseball throwing range for use during the winter, and few fathers altered their business practices to leave more time for baseball. When it became obvious that Bob had natural talent, his father stopped planting corn. He switched to wheat, which required less labor, thus freeing more time for baseball.[28] If the disapproval of friends and neighbors bothered the independent Bill Feller, he never showed it.

Baseball training for young Bob began in his infancy. His favorite toy during his "creeping days" was a baseball.[29] He would use a rubber ball inside the house during the cold winter. From the age of 4 on, games of catch between father and son were an everyday occurrence when weather permitted, and sometimes even when it didn't. Bill recognized early on that Bob had more than just a passing fancy for the game. He even quit his beloved games of horse-shoes to have more time to play catch with his son. It became the bond that cemented their relationship.

Bob was more of a baseball player than a fanatical devotee of the distant major leagues. "I didn't follow the big leagues much in the newspapers. I didn't worship the heroes of the diamond, as most kids do. I spent all my time practicing throwing and fielding and hitting."[30] Even his time in school was spent thinking about baseball. At the age of seven, young Bob wrote the following composition:

> When I was a tree, and my brothers and sisters, there were many of us there but there is not many of us now. Many of us have been cut down and made into lumber and it came my turn and they cut me down and made me into a big board. And Mister Stucke's manual training boys got me and made me into a home plate for the baseball diamond. And that's the end.[31]

By the age of nine, Bob was able to throw a ball more than 270 feet.

It was about this time that the baseball education of Bob Feller took a new turn. One day in the spring of 1928, Bill Feller came home with several packages. One contained a Rogers Hornsby glove, another a Ray Schalk catching mitt. Completing the bounty was a mail-order uniform, a pair of spikes, baseball stockings, a bat, and several "good baseballs, not the nickel rocket kind."[32] The hard-hitting but mercurial Hornsby quickly became Feller's favorite player. Excited by his new toys, Bob even went so far as to wear his new uniform to school.

The year 1928 also brought Bob's first personal exposure to major league players. Barnstorming was a common way for major league players to make extra money after the season was over. Babe Ruth and Lou Gehrig made a swing through the Midwest that October, and one of their stops was Des Moines. The Thursday, October 25th issue of the *Des Moines Tribune-Capital* featured a front-page item about the upcoming visit of the New York sluggers. Sandwiched between an item about a 16-year-old shooting his best friend in an argument over a girl ("Lovesick Council Bluffs Youth Runs Amuck in Jealous Frenzy"), and an article about the "Monoplane" *Yankee Doodle* making a cross-country flight, was a photograph of Lee Keyser, president of the Des Moines Demons of the Western League.[33] Keyser was pictured in front of a basket of 120 baseballs to be autographed by Ruth and Gehrig. Said balls would be sold for $5 apiece, the money raised to be donated to local charity.

When he learned of the upcoming visit, Bob (a month short of his 10th birthday) knew he had to have one of those baseballs. His father, of course, could probably have just given or loaned him the money. The Fellers were successful enough to own a 1927 Rickenbacker Sedan, not a cheap automobile by the standards of the day. But the Fellers believed in hard work, and Bob would have to earn the money if he wanted the ball. He devised a creative way to do so.

Dallas County had a gopher problem. The animals were rampant, and did a fine job of sabotaging crops and seriously annoying farmers. To combat the gopher menace, the county government established a bounty system: kill a gopher, bring in the front claws, and the county would give you 10 cents a pair. For an enterprising young man, this was the perfect opportunity.

> I recruited my pal and neighbor, Paul Atkins, and gave him a gunny sack and told him to hold it over the gopher holes in our alfalfa field. Then I ran a hose from the gopher's mound to the exhaust of Dad's 1922 Dodge truck, turned the engine on, and pulled the choke knob all the way out. I was careful not to use up all the gas. After all, it cost Dad 6 cents a gallon—9 cents minus a three-cent rebate if you used it for agricultural purposes.[34]

Bob and Paul's experiment in chemical warfare netted 50 dead gophers: exactly enough to bring the $5 he needed for the baseball. The precise body count makes the story sound apocryphal, though Feller stands by the veracity of the tale. They needed 50 gophers, so they killed 50.

The exhibition went ahead as scheduled the following Monday, October 29th. The crowd at Des Moines' League Park was a small one, estimated at only 500 or so by the newspaper the next day. They did see an exciting contest, with the "Larrupin' Lous" defeating the "Bustin' Babes" by a 15–4 score.[35] Both Ruth and Gehrig hit home runs, Gehrig's being an inside-the-park job. Ruth pitched the final four innings for his club, allowing no runs. Interestingly, Gehrig pitched as well, hurling three-and-a-third innings of relief, and giving up two runs.

It must have been an extraordinary event for a nine-year-old baseball fan. Best of all, of course, was the fact that Feller got his autographed baseball. He still has it today, on display in his museum. Seventy-four years after the fact, Feller still recalls the memory of this day as one of the greatest moments of his life.

By the age of 10, then, Bob Feller was a confirmed baseball maniac, playing the game constantly, and increasingly interested in the professional aspect of it. "Hot Stove" talk became common around the Feller farm during the cold winter months. It was the main connection between father and son. Even the birth of his sister in 1928 did not quench this early-20th-century version of baseball family fever. Bill and Bob would try to turn Marguerite into a baseball player—alas, with little success. She did, however, show great proficiency in basketball and table tennis.[36] She eventually earned honors as the Iowa Ping-Pong Champion. Marguerite later followed her mother into nursing. Like her brother, she inherited both intelligence and athleticism from her parents.

At some point when his offspring was between the ages of eight and 10, Bill Feller became convinced that his son had a professional future as a pitcher. "I knew it by the way he stood on the mound out there behind the barn and threw," Bill explained to the *Saturday Evening Post*, "Bob had it all—rhythm, timing, follow-through, and form—a little crude, but he had it all."[37] To this point, Bob was more fond of hitting than pitching, emulating his idol Hornsby in the batters box and in the makeshift batting cage his father built during this time. But in the back of his mind, Bill Feller knew that his son's professional future would be on the mound, not in the field or with the bat.

Bob still needed to be convinced, however. Bill Feller took a cautious approach, gradually shifting his son's focus to pitching, rather than ordering him into it. During the summer of 1930, the Van Meter high school played a series of games against the elementary school. Bob, now 11, threw harder than anyone on the field, and was able to overpower most of the older hitters when he took the mound. On the strength of his right arm, the grade school won six of seven contests against the high schoolers.[38]

The next year, during the spring and summer of 1931, Bob began playing for the American Legion team in Adel, the county seat. He rebelled against this at first, being painfully shy and almost afraid of strangers.[39] It helped that the Legion club was managed by Lester Chance, the local rural mailman, a familiar face. It also helped that Bill Feller acted as a coach for the team, and Bob got over his initial hesitation quickly. Again, he was obviously the most talented person on the field, but he spent most of his time playing shortstop or the outfield. He still wanted to emulate Rogers Hornsby. While he was a solid fielder and decent country hitter, his skills in those areas were less impressive than his throwing arm. That summer, Bill Feller continued to guide Bob toward pitching, talking more and more often about how major league pitchers like "Tommy Bridges, Mel Harder, Lefty Grove, and Wes Ferrell" went about their business.[40] Finally, by the end of the summer, father had convinced son that his future was on the mound.

With Bob's long-term position decided, Bill Feller knew that his son required careful handling if he was to reach his full potential. He didn't want someone teaching Bob bad habits, overworking his arm, or mishandling him psychologically. During the winter of 1931–32, he conceived an ambitious plan to ensure that his son remained under his careful guidance during his formative years, while simultaneously showcasing his burgeoning talent.

They would build their own ballpark.

2

Oak View and the Field of Dreams

There wasn't anything my dad wouldn't do for me.

—Bob Feller, *Bob Feller's Little Black Book of Baseball Wisdom*, p. 5

Sometime in the fall of 1931, Bill Feller took young Bob aside and asked him a question he'd been considering for several weeks. Would Bob like it if they built their own ballpark, right there on the farm? The idea was not a unique one; grandfather Forret had built a diamond on his land during his playing days, and some of Bob's earliest ball was played there.[1] But Bill Feller had more in mind than just simply their own ball diamond: they would form their own team as well. Bob said yes, of course; no 13-year-old could turn something like that down. But building your own ballpark—that would be quite a task. To do it right would require tremendous effort, but the Fellers were nothing if not hardworking.

They began work that fall. First, they cleared some oak trees in a field about half a mile from the main farmstead. Using an old crosscut saw, Bill and Bob felled about 20 oaks. Work resumed the next spring after the frozen ground melted. They disked the field, flattened the surface, and cut a diamond in the pasture, in a spot formally used by an assemblage of turkeys as a meeting ground.[2] A backstop was built using chicken wire and lumber; fences extended some 150 feet down each base line. A pitching mound was built up. An old wooden plank from the barn was split in two, and fashioned into the pitcher's rubber and home plate. Seats for spectators were constructed down each baseline, using more old lumber. A scoreboard was fabricated, as well as a rudimentary concession stand. Construction of the diamond and the primitive ballpark took several weeks, but by the end of spring things were ready to go. Bill and Bob decided on the name "Oak View Park," due to the large number of oak trees in the area, centerpieces of the beautiful rural scenery.

Recruiting a team came next. Bill Feller purchased 12 uniforms for his club, to be called the "Oakviews." There was no shortage of players, or opponents, for the team. Local semipros and talented high schoolers were enlisted to fill the roster, and games were scheduled between the Oakviews and various local clubs. Besides Bob, two Oakview players were of particular note. A cousin from nearby Waukee, Hal Manders, was a year older than Bob and a talented player in his own right. Hal didn't throw quite as hard as his younger cousin, but his velocity was still good, and he had solid control. Manders would reach the major leagues with Detroit in 1941, though his professional career was not nearly as successful as Bob's.[3] Another local youngster, Max England, probably also had major league potential. Later, no less an authority than Bob Feller would say that, as adolescents, England threw as hard as he did, perhaps harder. England, not Feller, would be Oakview's main pitcher in 1932.[4]

It should also be noted that Bill Feller had no hesitation about recruiting African-American players to fill out the Oakview roster and to provide opponents. "Playing against black players and having them on my own team was nothing new or special to me. Dad recruited black players for our own Oakview team back on the farm."[5] Although the African-American population of Iowa was less than 1 percent at this time, there were several black semipro clubs that made the rounds of the local diamonds, both urban and rural.

Oakview won their first six contests in the summer of 1932. Although Bill Feller had determined that Bob's future was on the mound, and Bob had reluctantly agreed, his son still spent most of his time at shortstop or in the outfield. The quality of baseball played by Oakview steadily improved, and word spread throughout the area about the "Field of Dreams" that Bill Feller had built. Even today, Bob Feller takes pride in pointing out that the idea of putting a baseball diamond in the middle of an Iowa farm field predates W. P. Kinsella's story and Kevin Costner's feature film by some 50 years. The Fellers charged 25 cents' admission for Oakview games (35 cents for a doubleheader), though the family didn't turn a profit. Most of the money went for tending the field, maintaining equipment, purchasing baseballs, and providing food and transportation for the players. The remainder of the purse went to pay semipro players that Mr. Feller occasionally hired to fill out the roster when there weren't enough local boys available. Mrs. Feller spent most of her time on game days cooking meals for the players. At times, crowds of nearly 1,000 people made their way to Bill Feller's pasture to watch baseball.[6] Many families brought picnic lunches. By 1933, Oakview contests were mentioned in the *Dallas County News* along with other semipro games on a regular basis, though formal box scores were not printed.

Oakview was Bob Feller's self-described incubator: it was here that he played in an intensely competitive environment for the first time, though still under the watchful eye of his father, and still in a familiar setting. The team continued playing in 1933, and Bob occasionally played for an American Legion team in Des Moines as well. He hit .321 for the Oakviews in '33, still mostly playing shortstop.

The shared Oakview experience cemented the bond between father and son. "I knew my dad had confidence in me and that was his way of displaying it."[7] How many children wish their fathers simply had enough time to play catch with them? Remember that rural life in 1930s Iowa was not a "nine to five" job for the average farmer. Hard work from dawn to dusk was the norm, with usually only Saturday evening and Sunday afternoon reserved for recreation. The Feller farm still functioned through the Oakview years; just keeping it running during the Depression must have been physically and psychologically exhausting for the Fellers. But Bill and Lena somehow found the time not only to run the farm, but to operate a baseball team on the side. It is no wonder that Bob Feller, some 60 to 70 years after the fact, still discusses his parents in reverent tones.

In 1934, 15-year-old Bobby Feller took another step out of the incubator. The occasion was an early spring game between Oakview and Winterset; the exact date is lost to history. Oakview's starting pitcher had gotten into trouble in the third inning. With a man on third and no one out, Feller came in to pitch.

His first pitch was a swinging strike, the hitter unable to catch up with Feller's fastball. The second pitch was a ball, well outside the strike zone. With his father watching intently from the dugout, Feller took a moment to collect himself, then fired another fastball down the middle. Another swinging strike. Realizing that the hitter couldn't catch up with his velocity, he threw another heater for strike three. The next batter suffered a similar fate, striking out on three pitches. The one after that was promptly down in the count 0–2, when the runner on third (perhaps realizing that his compatriots had no chance against this 15-year-old kid with a blazing fastball) broke for home in an attempted steal. Feller kept his composure and fired a strike to the catcher, who tagged the runner out on a clean play.

Feller finished the game strongly, then made relief outings in Oakview's next two games, allowing no runs. With his son warming up to the challenge of pitching, and obviously able to handle the competition, Bill Feller decided the time was finally right to make Bobby into Oakview's main starting pitcher. The contest chosen was a July game against the town team of Waukee, Iowa, another small town near Des Moines. Bobby (standing about 5 feet, 9 inches, and weighing 140 pounds) was pitching against the best players from Waukee, most of whom were several years older than he was. He was wild, unable to throw his rudimentary curveball for strikes, and walking "quite a few."[8] But he was able to fire his fastball past most of the competition. He threw a complete game, allowed just two hits, fanned 15, and won the contest by a 9–2 score.[9] It was a highly impressive debut.

It didn't take long for word to get around the local baseball grapevine about this new young pitcher. Oakview's next opponent was Valley Junction, another nearby small town. Valley Junction later became a suburb of Des Moines as the larger city grew, and is now known as West Des Moines. The Valley Junction Terminals manager, looking to boost his gate, suggested to Bill Feller that visiting Oakview start Bobby, hoping to attract some extra buzz to what would otherwise just be another midsummer town ball contest. Bill readily agreed, and started his son in a game that attracted nearly 2,000 spectators.[10] Again, Bob was pitching against older competition, and again he did very well. He won the game 9–1, allowing just one hit, while fanning 20. He walked several, the lone Valley Junction run scored on a passed ball that Bobby himself believed should have been scored a wild pitch.

Oakview now had a genuine ace. Bobby Feller had two starts to his credit, with at least 35 strikeouts in 18 innings and only three runs allowed. Not bad, not bad at all. But not everyone was willing to buy into the hype.

The manager of Oakview's next opponent, De Soto, decided to take on the precocious youngster directly. He contacted Bill Feller, and told him that his son couldn't possibly be as good as everyone said, and that the De Soto team would take him down without difficulty. When game time arrived, Oakview found that De Soto had brought in numerous "stringers" from Des Moines to take on Bobby Feller. Only two of De Soto's regular players were in the lineup that day; the rest were more experienced, more talented imports.[11] The game was at De Soto, adding to the pressure. To top it off, Bobby wanted to prove to everyone, especially himself, that his father was no braggart, and that his outings against the other clubs were no fluke. Fortunately, Bill Feller understood the pressure his son was under, and tried to assuage it.

> While the umpire was announcing the batteries, he [Bill Feller] walked over to me and quietly cautioned me against trying too hard. He advised me to relax and just go out there and pitch as though he and I were out west of the barn, playing catch, just as we had been hundreds of times.[12]

This was the biggest game of Bobby Feller's life to that point, and he rose to the occasion. His stuff was excellent that day, and the "enhanced" De Soto team managed just one hit, a single in the ninth inning. Feller fanned 15, leading the Oakview club to a 2–0 victory, and thwarting the designs of the De Soto manager to cut the burgeoning "phenom" down a peg.

The next step out came again that summer. Feller began pitching regularly for the American Legion team in Adel, to give him extra innings against good competition. He still pitched for Oakview (winning two more starts, fanning 18 and 17, respectively), but Legion ball gave him another avenue for mound experience. As he had in the past, he still played shortstop and outfield for Adel in addition to his occasional pitching duties. In approximately 40 innings for the Adel Legion team, Feller recorded 79 strikeouts.[13] Feller's battery mate was often Adel native Nile Kinnick, who later became an All-American quarterback at the University of Iowa. Kinnick was a tremendous all-around athlete; he hit leadoff for the Adel Legion club, not what you normally expect from a catcher. The two best athletes in Iowa history grew up within 20 miles of each other, and played together.

As he had done with the proposal to build Oakview back in the fall of '31, Bill Feller sprung a surprise on Bob during the autumn of '34. The St. Louis Cardinals had won the National League pennant by two games over the New York Giants, and would face the Detroit Tigers in the World Series. Bill Feller asked his son if he would like to attend the St. Louis games in the series. You can imagine what his answer was.

However, the neighbors weren't sure it was a good idea, advising Bill not to take his son to see the games. They felt Bobby would get discouraged by watching professional players in action.[14] Bill and Bob went anyway, originally intending to stay in a hotel in St. Louis, but opting instead for a tourist camp on the outskirts of town, apparently at Bob's insistence. He wanted to be able to play catch in the evenings, rather than spend their time in a stuffy hotel lobby.

Feller and Feller took in games four and five of the seven-game series. Game four was a slugfest, as the Tigers pounded five Cardinal hurlers in a 10–4 victory. St. Louis came back the next day with a 3–1 win on the strength of Dizzy Dean's right arm. The World

Series experience had the opposite effect of what the Feller neighbors feared. Rather than discouraging young Bob from a career in baseball, it actually convinced him that he had what it took to pitch professionally. "I can do that," Bob Feller thought to himself while watching the games in Sportsman's Park.[15] Referring to game four, Bill Feller said, "The Cardinals used everybody but Branch Rickey and the bat boy on the hill, and Bob said he was sure he could go in and stop those Detroit hitters better than that."[16] His father agreed. Bobby's amateur success wasn't an illusion generated by poor competition. He really did have what it took to succeed professionally. The drive back to Iowa was consumed with baseball conversation, Feller and son discussing plans for the future. He would be a major league pitcher; there was no longer any doubt.

The winter of 1934–35 was spent like all the other winters: school, chores, games of catch outside when the weather permitted, games of catch in the barn when it did not. Influenced by what he'd seen in St. Louis, Bob altered his mechanics during his throwing sessions that winter, while also working to improve his curveball. He also played for the Van Meter high school basketball team, to help stay in good condition. Feller wasn't as good at hoops as he was on the diamond, but he was a sufficiently gifted natural athlete to be the starting center.

Winter turned to spring again, and as the 1935 baseball season began, Bill Feller was looking ahead at the next steps in his son's development. Both Bob and Bill knew that 1935 was the "year which might find me attracting the attention of some professional team's manager or scout."[17] Bob did his part by staying in shape and working to refine his game. Bill did his by arranging new competition for his son. While the Oakview team continued to play, Bob pitched some games for Van Meter high school in the spring, then spent most of his time that summer pitching for Farmers Union, a semipro team based in Des Moines. The competition was better in the big city, and certainly, more professional scouts made their way to Des Moines than to Van Meter.

At age 16, Feller was once again pitching to players who were for the most part older and more experienced. Again, he did quite well. Exact statistics for Feller's Farmers Union tenure are hard to pin down. Numbers kept by Bill Feller showed Bob pitching 157 innings that summer, with 361 strikeouts, only 42 hits allowed, and an ERA less than 1.00.[18] The numbers sound exaggerated, and are impossible to completely confirm, but the box scores that do exist show that Feller was pitching baseball of this magnitude. Some examples:

July 4, 1935   Farmers Union played a doubleheader against the Texas Black Spiders, a touring Negro team. Feller pitched the second game, throwing hitless baseball for six innings. Tiring in the July heat, he gave up seven hits and four runs in the seventh and eighth inning, losing the game 9–7. He fanned 19.[19]

July 25   Pitching in the city semipro championship tournament, Feller fired a 2–0 shutout for Farmers Union against Potosi Beer. His strikeout total is not given in the box score, but he allowed just one hit.[20]

July 29   Feller led Farmers Union to the "City Ball Crown," defeating Des Moines Steel by an 8–3 margin. No strikeout total was given, but he gave up just five hits. A crowd of about 1,000 watched the contest.[21]

August 8   Feller made a relief appearance, coming in to bail out Hal Manders in a 4–3 defeat to Chappy's Independents of Colfax. Feller pitched 4.2 innings, allowing one run. He struck out nine, but took the loss.[22]

August 24   Playing in the Iowa State Fair semipro baseball tourney, Feller led Farmers Union to a 10–1 win over the Burlington Chevrolets. He scattered seven hits, walked two, and fanned 18. The newspaper account headlined him as "Bobby Fellers, youthful mound sensation."[23]

August 25   In the final game of the state fair tourney, just 24 hours after his previous start, Feller pitched Farmers Union to a 4–2 win over the Cascade Reds. He walked four, allowed six hits, and fanned 13. He also went 3-for-4 with an RBI to help himself. The victory put Farmers Union into the national semipro tournament, to be held in Dayton, Ohio, in September.

In these six games, Feller pitched a total of 48.2 innings, allowing 11 runs. That comes to a 2.05 runs-allowed average, not accounting for unearned runs. Four of the 11 runs came in one game, the July 4 contest. He allowed 26 hits. We have a record of 59 strikeouts, but in two games the strikeout number was not recorded in the newspaper account. Dropping the 18 innings pitched in those two contests, we end up with 59 strikeouts in 30.2 innings, a rate of 17.3 strikeouts per nine innings. This is lower than the 20.7 mark recorded by his father for that season, but is still incredibly impressive, especially when you consider that Bob was doing it against competition that was older and more experienced. The numbers we have are enough for us to believe that, while the statistics recorded by Bill Feller were possibly exaggerated, they were not exaggerated by very much. A few additional high-strikeout games would push the numbers toward Bill Feller's figure.

We have anecdotal evidence from three additional Farmers Union games, though no actual box scores. In a May game against Slater, Iowa, Bob punched out 17 in a 2–1 contest.[24] On May 26th, Feller fanned 22 in a no-hitter against Yale, Iowa.[25] A few days later, Feller gave up three hits in a 1–0 triumph against St. Mary's, fanning 19 in the process.[26] These games add 58 strikeouts and 27 innings to our database, giving us 115 strikeouts and 57.2 innings. This pushes his strikeout rate per nine innings to nearly 18. Since these three contests lack box scores and the information is anecdotal, I didn't want to count them formally. But they do not differ much from the games we do have solid information about, and they move us closer toward believing Bill Feller's figures.[27]

The bottom line is that Bob Feller was clearly the best high-school–age pitcher in Iowa, and possibly the best in the country. At the age of 16, he was dominating players several years older than he was, with a fastball that was already major league caliber, and growing faster every year.

In early September, Farmers Union traveled to Dayton, Ohio, for the national amateur baseball tournament. The first game was against Battle Creek, Michigan, and as you would expect, the Iowa club went with its ace, Bob Feller. He pitched very creditably, fanning 18 and allowing just two hits.[28] But he lost the contest by a 1–0 score. The game was lost on a dropped fly ball by the center fielder, sending Farmers Union back to Iowa with a first-round tourney defeat. It wouldn't be the first time that Feller failed to be the victor in a critical postseason contest he pitched well enough to win.

There was more going on at Dayton than just a semipro baseball tourney. Word had gotten out about this young Iowa farm boy with the blazing fastball, and several scouts were in attendance to check him out on a national stage. There were at least eight scouts in Dayton with Robert Feller on their agendas, including some relatively famous scouting names like Steve O'Rourke of the Detroit Tigers, Bill Bradley of the Cleveland Indians, and Frank Rickey of the St. Louis Cardinals.[29]

All were very impressed with Feller's performance in the Dayton game, and were soon swarming Bill Feller with offers for his son's services.

Steve O'Rourke offered a bonus of upwards of $9,000, plus an expense-paid trip to the World Series for the Feller family. Frank Rickey beat that offer, matching the money and the Series trip, while throwing in a free appendectomy should Feller ever need one. Cleveland scout Bradley raised the ante, telling Bill Feller that the Indians would beat any offer from another team. Red Sox scout Fred Hunter contacted his front office, asking them to wire a large sum of money so that he could take Bill and Bob for a long drive: to the East Coast and Boston.

The efforts of the scouts were for naught, for Bill and Bob had a secret. They kept it close to the vest as long as they could, but suspicion arose soon enough. Bill Feller asked O'Rourke if taking the World Series trip would obligate the Fellers to sign with Detroit. Dubious about Bill's question, O'Rourke contacted William G. Bramham, head of the National Association and the minor league equivalent of Commissioner Kenesaw Mountain Landis, and asked him if Feller was already under contract to another club. The answer came back: yes. Bramham's records showed that Bob Feller was already the property of the Cleveland Indians, his contract having been assigned to their minor league affiliate in Fargo-Moorhead for 1936.[30]

The next day, O'Rourke ran into Indians scout Bill Bradley in a hotel lobby, who asked him what the latest news was about Feller. "O'Rourke said afterward that he was never nearer to murder," commented the *Saturday Evening Post*. He thought that Bradley was stringing him along, but this was not the case. The news that Feller was already Cleveland property came as a great surprise to Bradley. He had been dispatched by the Cleveland front office to scout Feller, without being informed by his own team that the Indians already owned him.

Like so much in Bob Feller's life, the story of how he signed with the Indians sounds like something out of a movie. The ending was happy, though it could very well have turned out differently.

Sometime during the spring of 1935, while Feller was pitching for Farmers Union, someone tipped off the Cleveland Indians about him. There are two different stories about who did the tipping. The official story for years was that a Des Moines semipro umpire named John J. McMahon contacted C. C. "Cy" Slapnicka, Indians superscout and future general manager.[31] Slapnicka had signed Hal Trosky and Mel Harder, and would later be responsible for signing Herb Score and Lou Boudreau. According to this version, McMahon told Slapnicka about Feller's blazing fastball and domination of older opponents, encouraging him to scout the youngster as soon as possible.

The second version of the story was that the Indians had been tipped by a different Des Moines semipro umpire, a former major leaguer named Pat Donahue. According to this account, Donahue informed Billy Evans, general manager of the Indians in 1935, about Feller. Evans then dispatched Slapnicka to observe Feller and sign him if he was as good as advertised. For years, Donahue carried on a campaign to get the baseball world to acknowledge that it was he, rather than McMahon and Slapnicka, who was most responsible for "finding" Feller. Although Slapnicka always maintained that it was McMahon who'd tipped him off, and that Donahue was merely trying to shake down the club, Donahue eventually produced a letter from Evans acknowledging that it was Donahue who first informed the Tribe about Feller. "I get a laugh when I read Slapnicka unearthed Cleveland's great pitcher. That's the whole story Pat. All the glory belongs to you," wrote Evans in

1946, then serving as president of the Southern Association.[32] Both Donahue and McMahon would have had opportunity to see Feller as an amateur. Feller himself backs up the account given by McMahon and Slapnicka, dismissing Evans' letter in support of Donahue as an attempt to help a friend.

Whoever did the original tipping, it remains true that Slapnicka was the man who signed Feller to a contract. An Iowa native, Slapnicka made frequent trips back to his home state for scouting purposes. In late July, he made a trip to Des Moines to scout a talented local pitcher named Claude Passeau, who ended up signing with the Pirates. Passeau went on to have a successful major league career for the Pirates, Phillies, and Cubs, posting a 162–150 W-L (won-loss) record, and a 3.32 ERA in 2,718 innings. Slapnicka decided to check out this Feller kid while he was in the area. On July 21st, he drove from Des Moines to the Feller farm near Van Meter, where he found Bill and Bob combining wheat in their fields. Bob was driving a tractor as he saw Slapnicka approach.

> As the tractor climbed a slight rise, I could see the figure of a man coming towards us, threading his way through the wheat. Like my father he was tall and thin. As he came closer, I decided that they looked a great deal alike.
>
> "Howdy," he said, and my father nodded.
>
> "I'm Cyril Slapnicka," he continued, "of the Cleveland Indians. That the boy they tell me is quite a pitcher?"
>
> As I remember it now, I don't believe my father thought Slapnicka's reference to me was respectful enough.
>
> "That's Bob, all right," he answered. "I've heard of you, Mr. Slapnicka. You're an Iowa man yourself aren't you?"
>
> "Cedar Rapids. Mr. Feller, I'd like to see your boy pitch. When will he pitch again and where?"
>
> "He'll pitch in Des Moines for the Farmers Union day after tomorrow, Mr. Slapnicka. Figure to be there?"
>
> "Believe I will. Fellow named Claude Passeau pitching in Des Moines, too. Want to look at him?" Slapnicka turned to me and gave me the kind of uneasy smile adults use on precocious kids.
>
> "Do you like baseball, son?" he asked.
>
> I nodded. It was too big a moment for talking. Slapnicka's uneasiness seemed to grow.
>
> "Well, see you in Des Moines," he said, and started back.[33]

The dialogue may be apocryphal, but it captures what would end up being a key factor in the relationship between the Fellers and Slapnicka: Iowa roots. The fact that Slapnicka was from Iowa, and understood the state and its rhythms, gave him instant credibility with Bill Feller, credibility that someone from another background may not have had. In addition, despite the "uneasy" beginning in the wheat field, Cy Slapnicka and Bob Feller developed a very close relationship, with a strong "father–son" component.

Slapnicka resembled Bill Feller not just physically, but psychologically as well. Both were patient men, not overtly emotional, but nurturing in their own quiet way. Both knew how to handle Bob and teach him what he needed to know, on and off the field, to make the most of his natural talent. Both were shrewd businessmen. It was a perfect match.

After Slapnicka watched Feller pitch for himself, he knew that he had more than just an average prospect on his hands. He drove back to the Feller farm, and got Bob (and Bill's) signature on a contract, Bill's being necessary because Bob was still a minor. The contract called for a bonus of $1, and an autographed Cleveland Indians baseball. The baseball and a copy of the contract are still on display today at Feller's museum in Van Meter. Feller was technically assigned to Fargo-Moorhead, a Class D team and the lowest rung in the Indians farm system ladder. He would receive a salary of $500 for the 1936 season.

By signing a pro contract, Bob had taken his biggest step toward his dream of pitching in the major leagues. There were still forces that could derail it, however, as the legalities and procedures governing major and minor league contracts in this era were both confusing and frequently bypassed. As we shall see, the contract signed by the Fellers and Slapnicka would eventually become a source of national controversy, threatening to throw the arcane universe of baseball contracts into chaos.

3

Coming to Cleveland

Gentlemen, I've found the greatest young pitcher I ever saw. I suppose this sounds like the same old stuff to you, but I want you to believe me. This boy I found out in Iowa will be the greatest pitcher the world has ever known.

—Cy Slapnicka, speaking to the Indians Board of Directors, spring 1936. Quoted in *The Cleveland Indians*, by Franklin Lewis, p. 190

Bob Feller turned 17 in November of 1935. Now a high school junior, he spent the winter of 1935–36 as he had spent the previous winter: playing catch with his dad, attending school, working on the farm, and playing center for the high school basketball team. He may have had a professional contract in his pocket, but on the surface his life had not changed.

In March of '36, the Van Meter basketball team made the state finals, although they lost in the first round to Logan by a 28–25 score.[1] There was some controversy, however. An opposing team claimed that Bob, having signed a professional baseball contract, was not eligible to play *any* high school sport, even basketball. Van Meter would have to forfeit all games in which Feller had appeared if a ruling by a state sports commission went against them. The commission ruled in favor of Feller and Van Meter, noting that Feller had yet to receive any money from Cleveland, and had not pitched for any professional club yet.[2] Apparently the $1 bonus was ignored. It was clear, however, that once Bob actually threw a professional pitch or accepted his salary money from Fargo-Moorhead, his eligibility for all high school sports would end.

It was not certain at this time, however, that Bob would actually *throw* a professional pitch. A potentially major problem arose. His arm was sore; he had a "sharp pain" below his shoulder. The exact cause was uncertain. He felt he might have injured the shoulder during a basketball game, or perhaps while helping his father plough the fields in preparation for spring planting. The pain was serious enough that Bob "began to wonder if my career was over before it had begun."[3] Despite his workload over the years, this was the first time that Bob had experienced anything more serious than mild soreness or stiffness. One might imagine that there were second thoughts in the Feller family about the $1 bonus, especially in comparison to the various offers tendered by other clubs at Dayton the previous summer.

Worried about his son, Bill Feller wrote to Cy Slapnicka in Cleveland, suggesting that it might not be a good idea for Bob to report to Fargo-Moorhead as scheduled because of his sore arm. Slapnicka has been promoted from scout and now held the position of "Special Assistant" to Indians president Alva Bradley. His responsibilities were equivalent to a modern general manager. Slapnicka wrote back, telling Bill to keep Bob at home and to avoid pitching. He said he would tell the Fellers later where Bob was supposed to report, once the high school semester had ended.

Around this time, the Indians transferred Feller's contract from Fargo-Moorhead to New Orleans of the Southern League. When the professional baseball season began, Feller was placed on New Orleans' "voluntarily retired" list, to enable him to finish the high school semester. These contract shenanigans clearly violated the spirit of the bylaws governing the relationship between the major and minor leagues. Major league teams were forbidden to sign players directly from the "sandlots." Only college players could go directly to a major league roster without first signing with a minor league team and serving a minor league apprenticeship. Such violations were extremely common, of course; every team was guilty of furtive contract manipulations, especially where hot prospects were involved. As it was, baseball fans in neither Fargo nor New Orleans were destined to see Bob Feller pitch for their hometown clubs.

In early June, Slapnicka asked Feller to come to Cleveland, ostensibly to work in the concession department at League Park, though in reality Slapnicka wanted to make sure Feller's arm was sound. It also seems likely that he didn't want to entrust his young prodigy to an unsupervised minor league coach somewhere in the boondocks. Just as Bill Feller built a ballpark so he could monitor his son's progress closely, Cy Slapnicka wanted Bob Feller under his own direct supervision.

Riding the train from Des Moines to Cleveland, Feller found that his thoughts "kept racing back and forth between the pasture where dad and I played hundreds of games of catch, and the place I pictured as the Cleveland baseball park."[4] No doubt this was true. What else would he have thought about? Fame and fortune? Perhaps. By all accounts, Feller was a remarkably sober young man, utterly devoted to baseball, and relatively indifferent to the temptations that would soon come his way. He thought girls were "all right, but time enough for them later on."[5] A date with a female Van Meter friend every few weeks was enough. He didn't smoke. He didn't drink. He didn't even use chewing tobacco. The future for young Bob Feller did not center around fast cars or faster women. He was focused solely on success on the diamond. It is not an exaggeration to say that Feller had a "professional" mindset years before he actually became a professional player.

The biggest adjustment that Bob would have to make was being on his own. For the first time in his career, his father would not be there to monitor his progress, to provide coaching tips, to boost his morale when things threatened to go wrong. The absence of his dad, as well as worry about the condition of his arm, must have weighed on his mind during that train trip, however confident he appeared outwardly.

In retrospect, Feller observed that upon his arrival in Cleveland:

> I walked into his office in old League Park in early June, 1936. I know now that I looked exactly like what I was. A somewhat fat faced country boy of 17, with an awkward manner and an odd, rolling walk. I looked at the pictures on the walls of Tris Speaker and the World Champion Indians of 1920, of Larry Lajoie and other great Cleveland players of the past. I felt small and unimportant. My arm hurt.[6]

Slapnicka took Feller out of his office and onto the League Park field. The young man was deeply impressed by his first footsteps upon a major league diamond. He was bothered a bit by the short right field porch, just 290 feet down the line, a fine target for southpaw sluggers. It wouldn't be a problem, Slapnicka assured him, "if you pitch carefully to left-handed hitters."[7]

The Indians were on the road at the time, so Slapnicka had Feller work out with Bruce Campbell, a Tribe outfielder trying to recover from a difficult bout with spinal meningitis. Feller worked out nearly every day with Campbell, playing catch, running sprints, spending time in the sun, generally getting the feel for his environment. The soreness in Feller's shoulder gradually eased. When the Indians returned from their road trip, trainer Max "Lefty" Weisman began treating Feller's arm with daily rubs. "Careful workouts and careful massage" from Weisman eliminated the remaining tenderness, and by late June Feller was ready to pitch.[8]

Feller was still under contract to New Orleans, but Slapnicka wasn't interested in sending the young man to the minors just yet. He wanted him to stay in Cleveland, but there was clearly the need to get Feller some innings to shake the rust off. Slapnicka arranged for Feller to sign with the Rosenblums, a Cleveland amateur team sponsored by a local clothing store. The Rosenblums played in a highly competitive Ohio semipro league, the level of competition being about equivalent to professional Class C, one level above Feller's initial contract assignment at Class D Fargo-Moorhead.[9]

Feller's first start was against a semipro club from Akron. He lost the contest 3–2, but pitched credibly, allowing five hits in eight innings, while fanning nine. His second start was more impressive: nine innings, four hits, and 16 strikeouts in a 3–2 victory.[10] These two semipro outings proved that Feller's arm was sound; his stuff was especially good in the second contest. Rosenblum manager Art Heiden supposedly advised Feller to alter his release point when using his curveball, resulting in much better command of the pitch in the second game.[11] It seems unlikely that a semipro manager would have made such a change without the knowledge or approval of the Indians, if it was in fact Heiden who suggested the change.

After these two starts for the Rosenblums, it was abundantly clear that semipro competition was no challenge for Feller. The Indians brain trust was now faced with another decision: should they send the young right-hander to New Orleans? The Southern League club did technically own his contract, after all, and his arm was obviously healthy again. They were running out of excuses. Slapnicka and Indians manager Steve O'Neill decided to stall a bit longer. They had neither the intention nor the desire to send him to New Orleans; again, they wanted him under their direct supervision, not entrusted to a minor league manager. But they also wanted to give Feller some innings against the best competition possible. Was it possible that he was ready to handle major league competition, someone suggested? They decided to pitch him in an All-Star Break exhibition contest, on July 6th, against the illustrious St. Louis Cardinals.

About 10,000 fans showed up for the exhibition between the Cardinals and Indians on July 6th. The Cleveland starter was George Uhle, a curveball artist who had first pitched for the Indians in 1919. Uhle had last seen big league action as a reserve pitcher for the Yankees back in '34, and was currently employed as a coach by the Indians. He wanted to make a comeback, and had talked Slapnicka and O'Neill into letting him start the contest. He would pitch the first three innings, then give way to Feller in the fourth. Uhle threw well in the outing, showing a better fastball than expected, while snapping off his trademark curve with relative ease. He was activated by the Indians a few days later, and used as a mop-up pitcher down the stretch.

Reflecting shades of Bill Feller's advice before another critical game two years before, Slapnicka advised a nervous Feller before the game to "just forget who they are and throw. Don't be afraid of them."[12] The presence on the field of Indians manager O'Neill, who decided to catch the young fireballer himself, was also a steadying influence that day. It was O'Neill who decided to avoid using the still-erratic curveball against the Cardinals. Feller would get by on his fastball, or nothing.

The game was a 1–1 tie when Feller came out to the mound to start the fourth inning. As he warmed up, both teams paused to "watch in wide-eyed fascination," according to *Cleveland Plain Dealer* sportswriter Gordon Cobbledick.[13] Feller's windmill-like delivery was extremely unusual, his velocity mind-boggling. The first hitter was Bruce Ogrodowski, a rookie catcher. O'Neill signaled for a fastball . . . called strike one. The success of his first pitch apparently calmed Feller's nerves. Ogrodowski bunted the next pitch, and was thrown out by third baseman Sammy Hale on a close play at first. The next hitter was Leo Durocher, the Cardinals' starting shortstop and future legendary manager. "Keep the ball in the park, busher," he yelled to the rookie.[14] His attempt at intimidation failed; Durocher struck out swinging on three fastballs. The same fate awaited the third hitter of the inning, Arthur Garibaldi, a reserve infielder.

Returning to the dugout, Feller was a bit disappointed that the fans gave him only tepid applause. The crowd wasn't especially impressed by his performance, since Ogrodowski, Durocher, and Garibaldi were far from the best the Cardinals had to offer. His disappointment faded quickly once catcher/manager O'Neill gave his opinion. " 'I'm not as spry as I used to be,' grinned Steve, 'and you might kill me with that fast ball before we're through. But you're great, Kid.' That more than made up for the apathy of the crowd."[15]

Cleveland scored a run in the bottom of the fourth, giving Feller a one-run lead when he returned to the mound in the fifth. Feller easily fanned Cardinals pitcher Les Munns, but leadoff hitter Terry Moore (the best hitter Feller had faced thus far in his entire life) lined a fastball for a sharp single to left field. Rattled by giving up his first hit, Feller walked number-two hitter Stu Martin.

At this point in his life, Feller hadn't worked much on a move to first base, since it had seldom been necessary. Moore and Martin decided to take advantage of Feller's exaggerated leg kick and lack of a polished pickoff move. Trying to unnerve the rookie, they pulled a double steal on the first pitch to the next hitter, Pepper Martin. Distracted, O'Neill let the pitch go by for a passed ball, allowing Moore to score and putting Stu Martin safely on third base. To his credit, Feller quickly got his composure back, and threw three hot fastballs past Pepper Martin for a swinging strikeout. The next hitter, cleanup man Ripper Collins, struck out on three pitches.

In the top of the sixth, Feller allowed a leadoff bloop double to Ogrodowski, but bore down to strike out Durocher, new third baseman Charlie Gelbert, and pitcher Munns, all swinging on fastballs. His work done for the day, Feller turned the game over to another rookie pitcher, Paul Kardow, in the top of the seventh. The Indians went on to win the contest by a 7–6 score.

Feller's performance was electrifying. He was wild, yes. He didn't use his curve, and his inability to hold base runners was painfully obvious. But his velocity was exceptional, his fastball immediately drawing comparisons to that of legendary hurler Walter Johnson. He'd fanned eight hitters in three innings, including talented and experienced batsmen like Pepper Martin and Ripper Collins. Certainly, it had been an exhibition game, but it was clear to any objective observer that his performance was no fluke. Asked to pose with Feller after the game by a photographer, Cardinals ace pitcher Dizzy Dean responded, "If it's all right with him, it's all right with me. After what he did today, he's the guy to say."[16] Young Bob grinned with pride. As he put it, "[P]raise from Dizzy Dean was approval from the baseball gods."[17] Dean wasn't the only one impressed. Home plate umpire Brick Owens, a veteran of nearly 20 years in baseball, told a Philadelphia reporter that Feller "had more stuff than any pitcher he had ever seen."[18]

The Cleveland press was quite excited about Feller's performance, though Uhle's credible comeback outing also drew attention. Back home in Iowa, both Des Moines newspapers featured stories about Feller's feat. In the countryside, the front page of the *Dallas County News* headlined with a two-column article entitled "Bob Feller Gets Chance in Big League Company: Van Meter High School Boy Strikes Out Pepper Martin and Other Hot Shots."[19] Bill Feller must have beamed with quiet joy. Bill Feller had been right about Bob, not the gossiping neighbors, nor the De Soto manager, nor any of the other doubters.

Six days later, Feller made another appearance, this time for the

Rosenblums. This caused an outcry of controversy from the other teams in the Cleveland amateur league: surely, someone like Feller, who'd pitched in a major league exhibition game and was clearly property of the Indians, wouldn't qualify for semipro action. Slapnicka and the Rosenblums management maintained that since Bob wasn't taking any money from the Rosenblums, and hadn't pitched in an official game for the Indians, that he was still technically eligible. However, they agreed that he would leave the amateur team if a majority of the other clubs voted that he wasn't truly eligible. The vote hadn't yet taken place when Feller took the mound against the Poschke Barbecues on July 12th. He lost a 3–2 contest, undone by his control, but he did fan 15.

The vote was likely to go against them, but it became irrelevant the next day, when Slapnicka announced that Feller's contract would be "purchased" from New Orleans, and that he'd report to the major league club immediately. "I could send you to New Orleans," Slapnicka told Feller, "and there isn't any doubt you need the experience. But I want you in the most capable hands. With the right kind of help, you're ready to win for us."[20] The fact that the Indians were in a pennant race with the Yankees, White Sox, and Tigers, along with the desire to closely supervise Feller's development, finally trumped any thought of sending the farm boy to the minor leagues. O'Neill wanted to keep an eye on the kid himself, and apparently foresaw late-inning, rally-killing use of his tremendous fastball.

The Indians were on an East Coast road swing at the time, so Feller boarded a train the next day, heading toward Philadelphia to join his teammates. He'd made it; he was now a major league pitcher.

He was not, however, a high school graduate, or a daily shaver, or a consistent thrower of strikes. He'd made the major leagues on the strength of his incredible right arm, his physical stamina, and his work ethic. The question now was, how would he fare in games that counted in the standings?

Getting to Philadelphia itself was a challenge. "The club auditor, upon presenting him [Feller] with his railroad tickets, was informed that Feller didn't know how to travel. Train berths were a mystery to him."[21] But Feller was a quick learner. "It didn't take him long to learn the ropes," said Indians president Bradley. Within a month, Feller was "the best-dressed fellow on the club," poised and comfortable on trains, automobiles, and eventually aircraft.

Fine clothing and good grooming would matter little, of course, if Feller didn't pitch well. Arriving in Philadelphia, Feller found that Indians coach Wally Schang had been assigned as his roommate.[22] An excellent defensive catcher and a solid hitter in his playing days, Schang was a perfect guide for Feller at this stage of his career. Schang knew the hitters; he'd been in and around the game of baseball for decades, playing with and against the best players of his generation. He knew the cities, the temptations that places like Philadelphia or Washington or New York City would present to a young ballplayer, and he could be trusted to steer Feller away from trouble. "He was my buffer," says Feller.[23] Feller also became friends with Fred Weisman, Cleveland's batboy. "We were about equals intellectually, so we became friends right away," recalled Weisman.[24] Weisman noticed that, for all of his talent, Feller was usually modest. "My hat's too large," complained Feller when he got his uniform. "Make sure it stays that way," replied the clubhouse man. Weisman was impressed by the fact that Feller usually got to the ballpark an hour and a half before the other players, a sign that his head stayed the proper size.

The Indians swept the three-game series from the Philadelphia Athletics, getting solid pitching performances from Mel Harder, Johnny Allen, and Denny Galehouse. Feller watched all three contests from the bench, observing the games with Schang at his side, studying the strengths and weaknesses of the hitters. The team had now won five in a row, and though they trailed the Yankees by 9.5 games, they were in third place and only a half game behind the Tigers.

The next stop was Washington. The Indians won the first contest on Saturday, July 18, then settled in for a doubleheader on Sunday. Feller remained stationed in the dugout in game one, Lefty Lee pitching the Tribe to a snappy 11–3 win over the Senators. But George Blaeholder struggled early in the second game, giving up five runs in six innings. Johnny Allen came in from the bullpen to pitch the seventh inning, giving up a run and not looking very sharp. When he got in trouble again to start the eighth inning, O'Neill decided that Bob Feller's time had come. He ordered the youngster out to the bullpen to warm up.

Feller entered the contest with no one on base and nobody out; Allen had allowed three runs, and the game was clearly out of hand by a 9–2 score. It was a perfect no-pressure spot for a rookie's major league debut. Feller hit the first batter, shortstop Red Kress, with a wild curveball. He decided to ditch the curve and go with nothing but fastballs. He walked the next hitter, but retired the following three batsmen on a strikeout and two infield pop-ups, ali of the outs coming on fastballs. His first official major league outing was a success: one inning, one walk, one hit batsman, one strikeout, no hits. The *Plain Dealer* account of the game mentions the debut performance of the "schoolboy pitcher from Iowa" only in passing, concentrating instead on the pleasant results of a successful 10–2 road trip, which pushed the Indians back into second place.[25]

Extra press attention for Feller would come soon enough. Returning to Cleveland, the club found fans tremendously enthusiastic, thanks to the strong road trip performance and the revival of pennant hopes. Ticket sales increased, and there was a buzz of success about the club. In addition, the press began paying closer attention to Feller. The *Plain Dealer* featured him, along with rookie outfielder Roy Weatherly (another Slapnicka protégé) on a front-page spread July 21st. The article was mostly about Weatherly, understandable considering his hot hitting during the road trip. The 21-year-old outfielder from Texas hit .335 in 84 games for the Indians that year, though in the long run his career would be marred by injuries and inconsistency. A photo of Feller, featuring his trademark broad smile, also graced the paper. Feller and Weatherly became roommates, sharing a room in a local hotel, safely away from the Cleveland downtown district with its many potential distractions.

Two quick Indian victories over the Boston Red Sox, combined with two Yankee losses in St. Louis, cut the New York lead over

Cleveland to seven games, further heightening pennant fever along the Cuyahoga. Feller didn't pitch in the series against the Red Sox, though Cy Slapnicka did call young Feller into his office to advise him to stay patient and "keep in condition."[26]

His next chance arrived when the Philadelphia Athletics came to town on the 24th, following the conclusion of the Boston series. The Tribe, behind the strong pitching of Denny Galehouse, took a 15–2 lead into the eighth inning of the first game, when O'Neill decided to put Feller in to close out the contest. He was wild, walking two, hitting Athletics star Bob Johnson and scrub Al Niemiec with pitches, and being touched for two hits. But he also fanned two, and survived his two-inning outing with just one run given up. His velocity was impressive, even if his command was not.

His next outing came two days later, again against Philadelphia. Relieving Oral Hildebrand in the ninth inning of a 13–0 loss, Feller gave up one walk, three hits, and two runs. He also failed to strike out a batter. It was probably one of the worst games so far in his young life, and interestingly he failed to mention it in either of his biographies, even though it was just the third game of his professional career. The outing was eminently forgettable, but the Indians did not overreact by sending Feller to the minor leagues, or by hitting him with undue criticism.

Cy Slapnicka had earned his job as "assistant to the president" not just because of his undoubted scouting prowess, but because of his business sense as well. In this respect, as in others, he again resembled Bill Feller. "There's one thing about Slapnicka—he knows how to make money," Alva Bradley told the Cleveland press.[27] Slapnicka had a knack for promotion. The Yankees came into town for an important series in early August. To help boost the gate for August 2nd, Slapnicka set up an "exhibition of baseball skill" before the game, with throwing, running, and hitting contests, featuring Indians and Yankees players.

An "accurate pitching contest" was part of the event, with five Indians pitchers competing to see who had the best control. A paper hoop was placed inside of a frame at home plate. Each contestant would get five throws, the winner being the pitcher who threw the most strikes through the hoop. The prize was $20. The

Indians entrants were veterans Denny Galehouse, Mel Harder, George Blaeholder, George Uhle . . . and Bob Feller, entered into the contest at Slapnicka's insistence. Bob was "dismayed" that Slapnicka had put his name into the fray; he felt it must have been a joke.[28]

It seems possible that Slap was challenging Feller, although Bob emphasizes the "joke" aspect of the event nowadays. The crowd of nearly 65,000—to accommodate the huge crowd, this game was being held at cavernous Municipal Stadium rather than League Park—laughed when Feller came to the mound. They thought it must have been a joke, too, the idea that this wild 17-year-old thrower could compete with four veteran pitchers in a control contest. No one laughed, though, when Feller (somewhat to his own surprise) fired five straight strikes through the hoop. It was, he said, the proudest moment of his life up to that point. The fact that he was the only pitcher to throw all five pitches for strikes must have added to his pride. The Cleveland press was much impressed, the *Plain Dealer* commenting that "the Iowa pitcher proved stage fright is unknown to him."[29]

The Indians lost two of three games to the Yankees on their home stand, pushing them back to nine games out, and in danger of losing second place to the Tigers. The Tribe went to Detroit to start a critical road swing on August 3d. Mel Harder pitched the first game but was ineffective, giving up five runs in six innings. Feller was brought in to pitch the seventh and eighth innings against the Tigers. He pitched a blank frame in the seventh, but a single by Schoolboy Rowe and a double by Gerald Walker scored a run for Detroit, Walker going to third on an error by outfielder Joe Vosmik.

> But there, with a fast man on third and nobody out, with the top of the batting order coming up, the seventeen-year-old wonder turned on the juice.
> He walked Jack Burns, but then he got Charlie Gehringer on a short fly, and then he fanned Goose Goslin and Al Simmons, famous fastball hitters, on fast balls that boomed into Billy Sullivan's glove almost before they could get their bats off their shoulders.[30]

Feller's confidence was growing.

His next two appearances were relief outings, against St. Louis on August 14th and again on August 16th, allowing one run in a combined two innings of work, with two strikeouts to his credit.

As August wound down, the Indians found themselves falling far behind the Yankees, but still fighting the Tigers, the surging White Sox, and the improving Senators in a battle for second place. The pitching staff was tired. Mel Harder's arm was sore, and he was increasingly ineffective. Johnny Allen was pitching well, but Galehouse, Hildenbrand, and Blaeholder were all struggling, their ERAs creeping closer to 5.00 with each start. The Midwest was sweltering, suffering under the worst heat wave of the century, and the Tribe pitching staff seemed to be wilting as the dog days dragged on.

Something needed to be done.

The St. Louis Browns were in town the weekend of August 21–23. The Browns were fielding their usual weak team, and the Indians regular starting pitchers needed a rest. To Cy Slapnicka and Steve O'Neill, Sunday, August 23d, was the perfect time to see exactly what Bob Feller could do.

> There were newspapermen in the dugout before the game and I heard them talking to O'Neill.
>
> "Does this mean that you're giving up on the pennant?" one asked, "starting this kid today?"
>
> O'Neill seemed annoyed.
>
> "We've got to start him some time," he said, "and this is as good a spot as any. The Browns are in seventh place and aren't hitting too well. We're 11½ games behind the Yankees and the season hasn't much more than a month to go. Anyhow, who's more liable to win, outside of Allen?"[31]

It was a blistering day, 90 degrees at game time, with high humidity and not much wind. There had been little advance publicity about Feller's start, and the League Park crowd was only about 10,000. Feller's battery mate was Charlie "The Greek" George, a rookie just called up from New Orleans to take the place of injured backstop Frankie Pytlak. Feller and George hit it off well. O'Neill had veteran Denny Galehouse warming up at the start of the game, ready to enter immediately should Feller come unglued on the mound.

Galehouse would not be needed.

Leadoff hitter Lyn Lary, the Browns shortstop, struck out on three fastballs. Harlond Clift, St. Louis' third baseman and a very patient hitter, followed with a single to right-center field. But Moose Solters, the number three hitter, and Beau Bell, the cleanup man, were unable to drive him in, both veterans striking out on fastballs.

The contest was a pitching duel, as St. Louis starter Earl Caldwell blanked the Indians through the first five innings. But while Caldwell was effective, Feller was almost unhittable, overpowering the St. Louis lineup, hitter after hitter. Those who did not strike out and managed to make contact still didn't hit the ball well, making out for the most part on weak fly balls to the outfield. The exception came in the top of the sixth, when the Browns scored a run with a pair of hard-hit doubles from Lary and Bell. But Feller got out of the jam by striking out Sammy West and Jim Bottomley, stranding Bell at second base. The Indians scored three runs off Caldwell in the bottom of the sixth, and followed with another in the bottom of the seventh. It was all Feller would need.

Despite the sweltering heat, Feller was throwing as hard at the end of the game as he was at the beginning. When all was said and done, the 17-year-old rookie pitcher had struck out 15 Browns, one short of the American League record set by Rube Waddell back in 1908, and two short of the major league record set by Dizzy Dean in 1933. Feller walked four, and gave up a total of six hits. It was a stunning achievement.

Feller's performance was front-page news in Ohio and Iowa. He shared the front page of the August 24th *Plain Dealer* with updates from the Spanish Civil War, as well as the news that Soviet ex-leaders Zinoviev and Kamenev had been found guilty of treason as part of Stalin's purge of the Communist Party and ordered shot. The *Des Moines Tribune* contributed a front-page biography of Feller and a family profile. The only negative for Bob was that when he called Van Meter to tell his father of his accomplishment, he found that his dad was in Des Moines, seeing a doctor in order to have his tonsils removed.

Feller lost three pounds pitching in the August heat that day, and found that he was "hungrier than I had ever been in my life."[32] That was saying something, since Feller had always been a serious trencherman. He celebrated his performance by going out and having a steak with Roy Weatherly.

As the Indians prepared to depart for another East Coast road trip, Steve O'Neill announced that Feller was now a full-time starting pitcher, and would pitch about once a week.[33] They would pick his spots carefully to avoid overworking him. As the Indians arrived in Washington on the 25th, Feller found that he was now a "nation-wide sensation," mobbed by reporters, photographers, autograph-seeking and advice-giving fans.[34] Everyone wanted to know his life's story. The Indians did their best to shield Feller from unwanted attention as much as possible, but the story was simply too good to pass up. Indeed, how he would handle his sudden fame would be the next test for Feller. Would he let his newfound celebrity get to him?

Feller's next pitching performance was in Boston, on August 30th. He started the second game of a doubleheader against the Red Sox, his mound opponent being 37-year-old veteran lefty Rube Walberg. Played before 25,000 fans in Fenway Park (the Boston and Cleveland papers gave partial credit for the large crowd to Feller), the contest was a contrast in styles between a fireballing phenom and a crafty southpaw old enough to be Feller's father. Walberg was brilliant, taking a no-hitter into the eighth inning, before settling for a three-hitter. Feller's velocity was as good as it had been against St. Louis, but his command wasn't nearly as sharp. He lasted five innings, fanning five, granting the Red Sox three walks, six hits, and four runs, and taking the defeat in a 5–1 loss. He was behind in the count frequently, then would come in and make pitches that were "too good" in order to avoid walks.[35] The Red Sox had won both games of the doubleheader, further dampening Cleveland's pennant hopes.

Command was the problem again in Feller's next game, on September 3d against the Yankees. In front of 11,000 fans and a bushel of photographers and reporters in Yankee Stadium, Feller fanned the first hitter, shortstop Frank Crosetti. But he came unglued after that, walking three men, including one with the bases loaded. He was knocked for five hits, a balk, and five runs total, before being mercifully removed by O'Neill; Galehouse went in to pitch the second inning. The *Plain Dealer* blamed Feller's poor performance on the plate umpire, claiming that George Moriarty was squeezing the strike zone, calling pitches balls that were actually strikes.[36] The *New York Times* disagreed, observing that Feller was "palpably nervous" and pitched "too carefully" to Lou Gehrig.[37] *Times* reporter John Drebinger did praise Feller's "blinding speed" and "sharp breaking curve," but pointed out that his delivery looked "a bit cramped" and somewhat awkward. In this case at least, the *Times* was likely more objective, though one wonders if it were possible to pitch "too carefully" to Lou Gehrig.

When Feller returned to Cleveland, he found that his father had taken the train out from Iowa to see him, to cheer him up after the debacle in Yankee Stadium. Feller had three major league starts to his credit, one a tremendous success, one mediocre, and one a disaster. The Indians were now clearly out of the pennant chase, and had no reason to pull him from the rotation. He made his next start as scheduled, on September 7th in St. Louis against the Browns, in the second game of another doubleheader. Again, he had St. Louis' number, pitching a complete game seven-hitter, allowing one run and three walks, while fanning ten. Gordon Cobbledick in the *Plain Dealer* wrote that Feller was actually more impressive in this game than he'd been in his 15-strikeout affair, since his command was better.[38] Feller also appeared more confident in his curveball, mixing it in more often with his fastball. The negative for the day was that the Indians lost the first game of the double-dip, putting the Yankees within one game of clinching the American League pennant.

Yet there were still some doubters. The only team Feller had truly dominated to this point was the St. Louis Browns, one of the perennial also-rans in the American League. Any doubts were erased, however, after his next game, on September 13th against the Philadelphia Athletics. Connie Mack's team was even worse than the Browns, but Feller's performance against them was so good that even the most hard-boiled baseball cynic could no longer ignore him.

The crowd was small, just 6,000, a result of the death of Cleveland's pennant hopes, plus the weak competition afforded by last-place Philadelphia. Feller decided to use his curveball even more in this start than he'd done in the previous outing against St. Louis.[39] The curve had great break that day, but his fastball was even better than the bender. He had more "stuff" against the Athletics than in any of his previous games, and it showed. He gave up just two hits, neither of them hard-hit. On the other hand, his control was awful. He walked nine. The Athletics stole nine bases, due to his inability to hold runners. But despite the walks and steals, Feller got away with allowing only two runs in a 5–2 win. The velocity of his fastball and the movement of his curve were simply unbelievable. As a result, he fanned 17, setting a new American League record and tying Dean's major league mark. And best of all from Bob's perspective, he pitched this game with his father in the stands.

Feller made three more starts for the Indians as the season wound down to its conclusion. His next game, on September 17th, was against the Tigers in Detroit. His curveball wasn't working well, forcing him to use mainly his heater, which was also not quite as good as it usually was. The Tigers knocked him for five runs in six innings, exploiting four walks and seven hits. He did fan five, but was outpitched by flamethrowing Detroit ace Tommy Bridges in a 6–3 final score.[40] Feller's next start was September 23d, in a League Park doubleheader against the White Sox. His stuff was better in this game, as he pitched a 17–2 complete game, fanning 10.[41] His final outing of the year was against the Tigers in the last game of the season, on September 27th. He got revenge for his weak start from 10 days before, pitching the Tribe to a 9–1 win, fanning six in a game shortened to six innings by rain.[42]

All told, Bob Feller pitched 62 innings for the Indians in 1936, appearing in 14 games, eight of which were starts. He posted a 5–3 record, fanned 76, walked 47, and allowed 52 hits. Five of his starts were complete games. His ERA of 3.34 was the best on the entire

Indians staff. He ranked third on the team with 76 strikeouts, despite ranking only ninth in innings pitched.

Many informed observers already considered Feller the owner of the world's best fastball. If he refined his curve further, and learned how to hold runners, he might be the world's best pitcher. In a postseason interview, Browns manager Rogers Hornsby declared Feller "the fastest pitcher he has ever seen."[43] Hornsby went on that Feller "may become one of the greatest pitchers of all time and rate along with Walter Johnson, Cy Young, Lefty Grove, and all the rest of baseball's famous stars. Feller will get faster. He is not fully developed and will add more speed as he adds weight. And he will gain control with more work. I wish I were a young fellow with his future."[44]

Heady stuff for anyone, let alone a 17-year-old farm kid who once worshipped Hornsby as a hero. As 1936 closed out, and as Bob Feller returned home to Iowa to accolades, it appeared that nothing except injury could stop him from becoming one of the greatest pitchers in history. But whether Feller would do this for the Cleveland Indians or for another team had suddenly come into question. Judge Kenesaw Mountain Landis, Commissioner of Baseball, had taken notice of the young phenom, not because of his pitching, but because of the contract irregularities surrounding his signing with the Indians.

4

The Commissioner

You'd think a kid in my position couldn't have a worry in
the world, but I did.

—Bob Feller, *Now Pitching Bob Feller*, p. 41

"Tribe Owners Face Tough Building Task," wrote Gordon Cobbledick in the *Plain Dealer* on September 13, 1936. On their way to an 80–74 record and disappointing fifth-place finish, the Indians had been over .500 since 1934. There was considerable talent on the roster, and the farm system was strong. But the Indians had been unable to truly challenge for the pennant, finishing no better than third place and 12 games out. The Yankees and Tigers were the class of the league.

Indians fans were full of ideas on how to remedy the situation. The *Plain Dealer* sports department received considerable mail from Tribe supporters, proposing various trades to improve the club. "Oh, how you would throw the money around," Cobbledick chided the letter writers.[1] Then, as now, no team had unlimited resources, something fans often failed to consider in the midst of Hot Stove speculation.

Cobbledick's analysis of the situation was reasonable. "Doing anything to strengthen the Indians is going to be no easy task. Their inferior ball players won't tempt anybody in a trade, and their superior men must be retained as a nucleus of next year's team,"[2] he wrote. Cleveland's hitting attack was strong. They tied for second in the league in runs scored in '36, leading the circuit in batting average. Sluggers Hal Trosky (first base) and Earl Averill (center field) were among the best players in the game, while other regulars like Roy Hughes (second base), Bill Knickerbocker (short-stop), and Odell Hale (third base) were solid contributors. Rookie outfielder Roy Weatherly had hit .335 in 84 games and had the look of a future superstar. Catching was a weakness, but the biggest room for improvement was on the pitching staff. Ace Johnny Allen was one of the best pitchers in the league, but the health of Mel Harder's arm was in question. The rest of the staff was mediocre, and had worn down badly during the blistering summer of '36.

Cobbledick concluded that, while the Indians were not "an all-star aggregation," it would be difficult to improve the club drasti-cally, given a realistic assessment of the trade market. "The players that are unmistakably better than Cleveland's aren't obtainable, and the others would be as likely to weaken as to strengthen the tribe" was his diagnosis. The team would have to rely on bringing players up from the farm system. The trade market had little to offer, and relying on retread veterans who might be released by other teams was never a good idea. Without modern free agency, those were the only avenues for improvement.

Interestingly, Cobbledick's analysis of the Tribe's immediate future failed to mention Bob Feller, despite the fact that the 17-year-old had outpitched nearly everyone on the staff but Allen. Cobbledick's nonmention of Feller may have had something to do with the fact that it was far from certain that Bob Feller would even *be* a Cleveland Indian for 1937.

Judge Kenesaw Mountain Landis, Commissioner of Baseball. Savior of the Game following the Black Sox scandal of 1919. Exem-plar of Fair Play. To modern fans, those words evoke an image of a grizzled old man, sitting high upon a gray tower overlooking the green baseball world, running the game with an iron fist, saving it from self-destruction. In reality, Landis held reign over a fractious conglomeration of owners, every bit as self-aggrandizing and shortsighted as our modern-day ownership idiots. Despite the image of Landis, the reality was that he didn't always get what he wanted. He long fought a defensive and ultimately futile campaign to prevent the major leagues from completely controlling their minor league counterparts, for example.

The Byzantine set of rules and regulations governing the structure of organized baseball was designed to prevent big league clubs from monopolizing the distribution of talent. But in practice, major league organizations, led by the St. Louis Cardinals under Branch Rickey, controlled the fate of hundreds of minor league players through the "farm system" set of affiliations and player "recommendations." The rules as they were at the beginning of 1936 stated that no player could be signed directly "off the sandlots," or out of high school by a major league team. Local minor league teams were supposed to have access to local talent first, which they could then sell to major league teams as the opportunity presented itself. Theoretically, someone like Bob Feller should have signed first with the Des Moines Demons of the Western League (or any other minor league club). The Demons (or whoever) would then be free to sell him to one of the major league teams at some point. Most teams found ways around these regulations, however, and the Indians were especially creative in their methods.

The Indians had tried to get around the rules by signing Feller to a Fargo-Moorhead contract. If Feller had actually reported to Fargo at some point, the controversy would likely not have occurred at all. Landis himself later admitted this. But the fact that he never pitched for Fargo, or New Orleans, and that the Indians had seemingly gone out of their way to keep him from doing so, led quickly to charges of "cover-up," hiding a player from the prying eyes of minor league teams who, theoretically, should have had first call on Feller's services. The fact that Cy Slapnicka had fallen afoul of Commissioner Landis on other occasions for similar infractions only added to the dispute. The standard remedy in such cases was for the player in question to be made a free agent, and the offending team prohibited from re-signing him.

Feller's contract status had been a bone of contention during the spring of '36 in Iowa, and again in early summer during his time with the amateur Rosenblums. At some point, it came to the attention of Landis. The initial complaint was filed by E. Lee

Keyser, owner of the Des Moines Demons, the closest minor league club to Van Meter and the one that, supposedly, should have been most likely to sign him initially. Keyser charged that the Indians had clearly violated the Major-Minor League Agreement regarding contracts. He claimed that the Demons had tried to sign Feller to a contract worth $7,500 in 1935, not knowing that the Indians had already "recommended" him to Fargo-Moorhead.[3]

The first public mention of the issue in Cleveland was apparently a September 23d article in the *Cleveland News*, revealing that Landis was looking into Keyser's charges.[4] *News* writer Ed McAuley had actually been tipped off about the controversy by Slapnicka as early as late July, but had agreed not to divulge any information in his column until the incident had been "straightened out."[5] When it became obvious that a formal investigation was under way and rumors about Feller's contract irregularities were starting to spread back in Iowa, McAuley told Slapnicka that he could no longer hold off on publishing the story. After consulting with Indians president Alva Bradley, Slap told McAuley to "shoot the works" and run the scoop.

The *Plain Dealer* confirmed the *News* report two days later, with a note that L. M. Peet, the business manager of the Farmers Union club back in Des Moines, had wired Landis with information about "details concerning Feller's original negotiation with Cleveland."[6] Peet had no doubt that "baseball rules were violated" in regard to Feller's contract, and offered to tell Landis everything he knew.

Feller first became aware of Landis' interest in him just after his 17-strikeout performance against Philadelphia on September 13th. "We're having trouble with Judge Landis," his father had told him over dinner following the game.[7] One can imagine how this must have shaken the young Feller. Just hours after the greatest triumph in his life thus far, he was told that the Commissioner of Baseball had taken an interest in him, but not for his pitching. On the advice of Bill Feller and Slapnicka, Bob tried to put the burgeoning controversy out of his mind and concentrate on his pitching. He did this fairly successfully at first, until the *News* got hold of the story later that month.

Once the matter became public, Bob had trouble sleeping. He

"was filled with a strange sense of shame and guilt."[8] None of this was his fault, of course. The senior Feller and Slapnicka were the ones responsible, though Bob felt that they clearly had the best of motives. His father in particular was only looking out for his son's best interest, or so the 17-year-old must have told himself over and over again on those sleepless nights.

Just before the end of the season, Bob went into Slapnicka's office and asked him about the situation. What, exactly, would happen if he were declared a free agent, he asked Slapnicka.

"If this should happen, would that mean that I couldn't sign again with Cleveland?" I asked. He nodded.

"You would be lost to us," he said.

"I don't want that to happen," I told him.

"I don't either," he answered grimly.[9]

Feller had decided that he wanted to stay with Cleveland, despite the fact that, if he were indeed made a free agent, he would command an immense sum on the open market. Rumors that the richer clubs would offer Feller hundreds of thousands of dollars to sign were already rampant by early October. The Yankees and Red Sox were said to be especially interested; New York owner Jake Rupert going so far as to say that Feller "should be worth a million dollars" and that the Yankees would make "a big offer" to sign the youngster.[10] Red Sox officials were told by owner Tom Yawkey to "spare no expense" in landing Feller. A Boston scout was allegedly stationed in a Des Moines hotel, equipped with a blank check, ready to rush off to Van Meter at a moment's notice. The Red Sox also approached Sec Taylor, legendary sports editor of the *Des Moines Register-Tribune*, asking him to act as a go-between for their club.[11] The Sox were apparently unaware that Taylor and the Fellers did not get along. Taylor felt that Bill Feller's dealings with Cleveland violated baseball rules (which of course they did). Every team in baseball coveted Feller's right arm, though only a handful could afford to match whatever New York and Boston were prepared to offer.

But Bob was comfortable in Cleveland, and the Feller family felt that they'd been treated fairly by the organization. The respectful relationship between Slapnicka and Bill Feller was another factor, as was the fact that Bob related to the Indians general manager as a father figure. Cleveland was a big city, but it was certainly more like Des Moines than New York or Boston. Ohio, with its mixture of urban and rural settings, was similar to Iowa in many ways. Bob had found a comfort zone, and it must have been highly distressing for him to consider being forced out of it, through no fault of his own, even if the money would be better.

Shortly after the end of the season, the Fellers were called to Commissioner Landis' office in Chicago. The gray-haired eminence, the "symbol of fair play and honesty in baseball" in Feller's words, wanted to hear from the farm boy and his father in person before ruling on the case.

In his 1998 biography of Judge Landis, author David Pietrusza points out that Feller's two biographies differ in their descriptions of young Bob's reaction while meeting Landis for the first time.[12] In *Strikeout Story*, Feller recalls being somewhat intimidated by Landis at first, feeling as if he'd "been called into the office of my school principal." In *Now Pitching: Bob Feller*, the pitcher denied being anxious, responding to Landis' questions with "straight-from-the-shoulder answers."[13] It seems to this author that the earlier recollection is more likely to be accurate, though the shifting sands of memory make it impossible to be certain either way.

In any event, the commissioner and the Fellers got down to business soon enough. Landis was polite, but firm and clear about the seriousness of the situation. "I intend to get to the bottom of it . . . I intend to get the complete truth," he said.[14] He listened to the Fellers' story, and was apparently "dubious" about some of what he heard from Bob and Bill.[15] The Fellers tried to keep their story consistent with what Landis had already heard from Indians president Alva Bradley and Cy Slapnicka. In other words, they lied. "Slap lied to the commissioner . . . he said Knight [Fargo's manager] signed me. So did my dad," Feller recalled years later.[16]

But Landis already knew the truth.

He'd been in touch with Sec Taylor, the man who knew everything there was to know about sports in Central Iowa, including the details of the illegal signing by Cleveland. Landis also had the information provided by L. M. Peet. He had the complaint from

Des Moines owner Lee Keyser. After listening to the Fellers, Landis was apparently convinced that the rules had, indeed, been violated, in both letter and spirit.

But there was more to it than this. Despite the large amount of money that the richer clubs were prepared to throw at him, Feller didn't *want* to become a free agent. "I don't want to play anyplace else. I want to play for Cleveland," the 17-year-old "blurted" to the 69-year-old commissioner.[17] Bill Feller followed Bob's emotionalism with a more legalistic approach: he threatened a civil suit against baseball if Bob were freed and prevented from re-signing with Cleveland. "It's our intention for him to play with Cleveland . . . if you don't permit that, then we're going to sue you in civil court . . . to see if baseball law supersedes civil law."[18]

It's not hard to see Landis' dilemma. He knew that the Indians were in violation of the agreement, and that the appropriate course of action would be to free Feller from his Cleveland contract. But while this would clearly be the "correct" verdict, on practical grounds it presented four serious problems. It would invite a civil suit from the Fellers, with all the accordant negative publicity, which baseball certainly didn't need or want. It would cause a massive bidding war for Feller's services, which would have a disruptive impact on the game. Freeing Feller would force similar verdicts in dozens, if not hundreds, of similar cases, potentially setting off contractual chaos throughout organized baseball. Finally, while Landis did much to cultivate his outwardly gruff reputation, his sentimental streak was not unaffected by Feller's plea to stay with Cleveland. Forcing Feller out of an Indians uniform might make a hard point to Slapnicka and the Cleveland front office, but it would also unfairly punish a 17-year-old boy who wanted to stay in that uniform. It would be unjust to penalize him for the transgressions of the adults around him, especially when there were undoubtedly other serious violations of the rules by other clubs that had gone undisclosed.

Landis kept his thoughts to himself. While the baseball world waited on Landis' decision, Bob Feller returned home to Iowa once Cleveland's season was completed. He found central Iowa alive with interest in him, dwarfing what local fame he'd previously earned during his amateur days. Feller arrived in Des Moines on October 4th, and answered questions for reporters from the local papers. Gayle Hayes in the *Des Moines Tribune* described him as "modest, unassuming, and even bashful."[19]

> I really don't try to strike out every hitter. I try to keep them from hitting and I throw my fast ball most of the time. . . . All I know is that I may be a free agent or may still belong to Cleveland . . . but the Cleveland club gave me my first chance and I like to play for O'Neill. . . . I don't know a lot about the hitters on any team. . . . All the hitters look alike up there at the plate, and of course they are all dangerous. I'm just lucky against some of them I guess.[20]

Two days later, Feller pitched in an exhibition game in Des Moines. A barnstorming tour of major league players, including Rogers Hornsby and Johnny Mize, was coming through the Midwest, stopping in Des Moines to play a game against the "Negro National League All Stars" on October 7th.[21] Feller started the game for the major leaguers, pitching the first three innings. He earned $300 for his appearance, a very large sum considering that his entire 1936 contract with Cleveland was worth just $500. Feller faced ten batters, fanning eight and giving up just one hit. His mound opponent was Satchel Paige, whom Feller would later face in numerous other barnstorming adventures. Paige also pitched three scoreless innings, fanning seven. The "Negroes" eventually won the game by a 4–2 score. A crowd of over 5,000 filled Des Moines' League Park that evening, the local press giving Feller most of the credit for the strong turnout.

On October 9th, Feller returned home to Van Meter, amidst great fanfare. Franklin Delano Roosevelt was also in Iowa that day, speaking at a campaign rally in Creston, some 40 miles south of Van Meter. The president of the United States shared the front page of the October 10th issue of the *Tribune* with the Van Meter prodigy; the photograph of Feller hitting baseballs to some Oak View players during warm-ups was actually larger than the photo of FDR giving his stump speech. Some wondered if sharing the front page with the president of the United States would go to Feller's head. "It could have, but my parents taught me to keep things in perspective," Feller said years later. "My mom and dad always told me, 'no one is immortal. Don't get full of yourself.'"[22]

Feller was focused less on baseball at this point, and more on catching up with his high school classmates, already in school for a month. "I'm going to make it up a week at a time and take tests," he told the *Tribune*. "Physics is going to be tough. But I don't expect them to just sign my diploma and let me do as I please."[23] For his senior year, Feller enrolled in physics, English literature, American history, and government. He decided against enrolling in "advanced manual training" for fear of hurting his arm. The image of a major league pitcher taking high school gym class is rather amusing.

As autumn fell, Feller resumed his usual farm chores, milking cows, feeding the horses, rounding up cattle, though avoiding more strenuous activities that might hurt his arm. He talked the Hot Stove with his father, though now in much greater detail, and with emphasis on what the Indians were doing. He rode the bus to school. He tried as much as possible to fit in with the rest of his classmates, though this wasn't always doable, especially when grade school kids wanted autographs or tips on pitching. Bob had never been much of a joiner, and the distance between himself and his peers widened according to some, understandably, though others insisted that Bob hadn't changed a bit. Bob and Bill took a hunting trip to South Dakota in mid-October, but otherwise their life that fall and winter was just as it had always been, at least on the surface.

The same could not be said for the baseball world.

The Feller case was an obsession in the national baseball media, especially after the end of the World Series and the beginning of the winter gossip season. Judge Landis took a fishing trip to northern Michigan in mid-October, to relax and ponder the Feller case in relative privacy.[24] He returned to his office in Chicago on the 19th, then told several reporters by telephone that he was still examining the evidence and was not close to a decision. The story would pop up every few days in the Cleveland and Des Moines press, usually with a general restatement of the issues and a mention that "several" clubs would offer Feller upward of $100,000 if he were freed from Cleveland. Papers from all the major cities were on the story, usually recycling the same information from the wire services. The Yankees and Red Sox were almost always mentioned in these rumors.

The first break from mere speculation came in mid-November, when two minor league players in the Cincinnati Reds farm system, outfielder Lee Handley and catcher Johnny Peacock, were freed by Landis due to contract irregularities.[25] It seemed likely that Feller would follow, though Indians officials were outwardly optimistic and said that the issues involved were very different. "The Cincinnati club was accused of hindering the progress of the two players . . . into the National League," said Alva Bradley. "We certainly can't be similarly accused in the Feller case."[26]

Many reporters were less sanguine than Bradley, Steve Snider in the *Des Moines Tribune* pointing out that the Handley and Peacock cases set a precedent for Feller. Snider quoted the decision itself, which stated that Cincinnati "at all times completely dominated and controlled Toronto's attitude . . . and disposition of these players and their contracts."[27] The basis of the ruling was not so much that the Reds were preventing Handley and Peacock from reaching the major leagues, as Bradley claimed, but rather that it was clear that it was the Reds, not the Toronto front office, that controlled the fate of the players. The same could be said for the Feller case: the Indians always controlled his fate, not Fargo or New Orleans. "The Feller case reportedly hinges on whether Bullet Bob was signed legally by a minor league club, or by a Cleveland scout . . . many baseball observers believe Landis may set him free on the same grounds as Handley and Peacock."[28]

By the first of December, it seemed clear that Landis would announce his decision on the Feller case during the yearly meeting of the National Association, to be held in Montreal that week. On December 4th, the NA voted to nullify the rule preventing major league clubs from signing players off the sandlots. This would prevent future Feller-type cases, but was not retroactive. When Landis stalled on issuing his ruling in the Feller case, further rumors began spreading. Some felt that Landis would resign his post, fed up with the recriminations and infighting of organized baseball. Others felt that the owners would fire Landis if he ruled against Cleveland, fearing the bidding war it would set off for the youngster, as well as other players in similar situations. The NA meeting ended with no decision from Landis, though more rumors were afoot that Slapnicka and Landis had held a "secret meeting" of some sort to work out a solution to the case.

Attention shifted to New York, where the major league clubs opened their own meetings the following week. The meeting began on Tuesday, December 8th. Ordinary issues dominated the gathering for two days, and the press openly speculated that Landis would delay his decision until the spring. Finally, on Thursday, the decision was announced. Cleveland would pay the Des Moines Demons $7,500 for damages (the amount the Demons had been prepared to offer Feller before he signed with Cleveland), but would retain the rights to Feller. The decision was front-page news (along with the abdication of King Edward VIII in England) in most of the nation's major newspapers the next day. Some relevant excerpts:

> The case has been thoroughly investigated. It turns out that, in reality, Fargo-Moorhead had nothing whatsoever to do with the signing of Feller, which was done by the Cleveland club, its agent, Cyril Slapnicka, using for that purpose a minor league contract because he could not sign him to a Cleveland contract.

> This legislation must be regarded as construing the covenant of the majors not to sign sandlotters as fulfilled if the player first signs a minor league contract notwithstanding he was in fact signed by or for a major league club. . . . Under this rule, had Cleveland taken the precaution to become owner of the Fargo-Moorhead club, and to have Slapnicka designated as vice president of the Fargo-Moorhead club, but had signed Feller, there would never have been a Feller case, because the minors adopted the foregoing rule with full knowledge that it enabled major league clubs to sign sandlot players if they merely had them signed to contracts of their own minor league clubs by persons designated as officials of such clubs . . . this legislation must be regarded as construing that the covenant of the majors not to sign sandlotters as fulfilled if the player first signs a minor league contract. That construction of the covenant . . . binds the commis-

sioner. Consequently the commissioner is precluded from entering an order invalidating the Cleveland-Feller contract.

Landis also discussed the whole process of "recommendation," and acknowledged that the practice was widespread. He further mentioned that both Feller and his father "zealously sought" to stay with the Cleveland organization. This was not a case of a player who felt abused or misled by his controlling organization, as so many other similar cases were. Finally, Landis pointed out that the Des Moines Demons, whose rights had apparently been violated by Cleveland, would not benefit if Feller was made a free agent, since he would obviously sign with a major league club immediately and not with them.

While Landis' legal reasoning was questioned, the justness of his verdict was widely hailed. Feller could stay with Cleveland, as he wished. There would not be a destabilizing bidding war for his services. The lid would not be blown off of dozens of similar cases that would have impacted nearly every club. The Demons would receive financial compensation, Des Moines owner Lee Keyser being "well pleased" with the verdict.[29]

Indians fans were, of course, ecstatic. This was not the last run-in between Landis and Slapnicka over player contracts, however. He freed Tommy Henrich, the Indians' best outfield prospect and a future All-Star with the Yankees, in 1937 after a contract dispute. Landis struck again in 1938, freeing two additional prospects (Myron McCormick and Charles Stanceu) and forbidding Cleveland from re-signing them. Both were journeymen and no great loss in the long run, but the divestiture of Henrich possibly cost the Indians a pennant or two. There were plenty of similar cases, but Landis seemed to have it in for Slapnicka and the rest of the Tribe front office, possibly coming down on them extra hard to make up for his relative leniency in the Feller case. The only team that drew his ire even more than Cleveland was the St. Louis Cardinals, run by Landis' nemesis, Branch Rickey.[30]

The bottom line was that Feller was still an Indian, and that baseball had avoided the circus atmosphere of a massive bidding war. The next step for Bob would be signing a contract for the 1937 season. He did not lack for confidence, predicting rather brashly to the press that he could win 25 games in a full season.[31] He publicly asked for a salary of $20,000, though he didn't "plan to hold out for that amount." Feller did express irritation that Des Moines had been awarded $7,500 by Landis ("Des Moines had no claim on me at all"), but was looking forward to signing with the Indians. When Slapnicka heard that Feller wanted $20,000 to sign, he told reporters that the young man was "out of line" and that Cleveland's offer would be considerably less than that.

Despite this initial disagreement, negotiations were private and reasonably smooth. The main sticking point was over Feller's desire to be a "guest coach" (i.e., drawing card) at Ray Doan's baseball school in Arkansas just before spring training.[32] The Indians didn't like the idea and resisted. Feller and the Indians settled on a $10,000 contract in early January. It wasn't 20 grand, but it still made Feller the highest-paid rookie in the history of baseball to that point. The Doan issue was resolved by having Indians coach Wally Schang accompany Feller, to ensure that everything at Doan's school was handled properly, and that their prodigy was not overworked in any way.

Feller left Van Meter and his classmates behind in late February, going down to Doan's school in Hot Springs for a week, before heading to New Orleans for spring training. To continue his schooling, the Indians and the Van Meter school principal arranged for a private tutor to help Bob prepare for spring finals. Principal Lester agreed that Feller could graduate with the rest of his class, provided that Bob "could pass the usual tests."[33] It seems likely that some of his classmates resented the special treatment being given to Feller, and indeed, Feller admits that his "standing with the senior class was impaired by my early freedom from the daily grind of studies."[34]

If it bothered him, it didn't show. The $10,000 man was on his way.

5

The $10,000 Boy

The class motto was, "The higher we rise . . . the better the view." I thought that one over on the way home. I wondered if I had already used up my view.

—Bob Feller, *Strikeout Story*, p. 77

ob Feller and Wally Schang reported to New Orleans for spring training in late February. Early training involved running, frequent games of pepper, and light throwing. Before the modern days of year-round strength training, most players used the spring to actually "train" and get in baseball shape. Most players had off-season jobs in nonbaseball professions. Spring training was critical to bring arms and legs into athletic condition, especially for the older players.

The Indians team that reported in late February and early March was very similar to the one that had finished 22.5 games out in '36. There had been two major trades. Outfielder Joe Vosmik, pitcher Oral Hildebrand, and shortstop Bill Knickerbocker had been traded to the St. Louis Browns in exchange for outfielder Moose Solters, pitcher Ivy Andrews, and shortstop Lyn Lary. This was pretty much a "running in place" trade, as all the players involved were comparable. The other transaction was with the Chicago White Sox, who had sent southpaw starter Earl Whitehill to Cleveland in exchange for Thornton Lee. Whitehill was a distinguished pitcher, with a better overall record than Lee, but on the downside of his career at age 37. As Gordon Cobbledick had predicted in his autumn *Plain Dealer* article, the trades the Indians were able to make really didn't bolster the club. If 1937 was to be any better than 1936, the incumbents would have to improve. Outwardly, the front office was confident. Cy Slapnicka told the Associated Press on January 24th that the Indians were ready to compete with the Yankees on an even basis, thanks to the trades, expected improvements from the incumbents, and "the law of averages."

As Feller settled into the spring training routine, he sampled New Orleans life in small tidbits, exploring the French Quarter, doing some sightseeing, trying Cajun food for the first time. He found that, other than the menu at the Hotel Roosevelt, New Orleans food was "a trifle rich" for his taste, accustomed as he was to traditional Iowa farm fare.[1] Exploring Cajun cuisine and the local landmarks were the extent of his extracurricular endeavors. Feller remained immune to the more zestful enchantments of New Orleans night life.

Feller began throwing in early March, under the close supervision of O'Neill, Schang, coach George Uhle, and veteran Indians pitcher Mel Harder. Feller's fastball was back in mid-season form quickly, so the focus was on refining his curveball and improving his changeup. While O'Neill, Schang, and Uhle worked on the change, Harder helped with the curve. There was talk of also trying to cut down on Feller's leg kick, although O'Neill felt it was too early in his career to make serious adjustments to his pitching style. Harder also worked with helping Bob hold runners on base, which remained the biggest weakness in his game. Harder noted that Feller "was very easy to work with because he was anxious to learn and to try anything."[2] Feller's curve continued to improve. But despite all efforts, his change remained mediocre, not that he needed it very often at this point in his career.

All was not harmonious in the Cleveland camp. Cleveland's two best players were outfielder Earl Averill and pitcher Johnny Allen. Neither was present; both were holdouts for larger salaries. In both cases, but especially Allen's, the $10,000 contract that Cleveland had given Feller was a cause of irritation. "They're paying Feller $10,000 and they're offering me $11,000. It isn't fair. I won 20 games last year," complained the fiery right-hander.[3] Allen had been paid $10,500 in '36; a raise of just $500 after a strong season was insulting. Feller later said he agreed with Allen's complaint, though "silently." For his part, Averill (who'd made $13,500 in '36), wanted a raise to $16,000.[4] The Indians countered with an offer for $15,000, which the star outfielder rejected. At one point, negotiations became so acrimonious that Averill requested a trade, offering to negotiate with other clubs and set up the trade himself if the Indians were unable to find a trade partner.[5] Cy Slapnicka gave him permission to do so, but Averill (not surprisingly) was rebuffed by the other clubs. The Indians eventually agreed to Averill's $16,000 request on March 14th.

Allen and the Indians settled for $18,500 the following day. This made him the third-highest-paid pitcher in the game, behind Dizzy Dean and Carl Hubbell, with Dodgers Ace Van Lingle Mungo (settling his own contract dispute on March 12th) ranking fourth at $15,000.[6] Joe DiMaggio, who had made $8,500 as a rookie in '36, signed for $17,000 on March 13th. While Feller's $10,000 made him the best-paid rookie in the history of the game, it wasn't out of line compared with what DiMaggio (who'd played 138 games for the Yanks in '36) received. Feller was a pitcher, of course, more prone to injury and uncertainty than a hitter, and he had less major league experience than DiMaggio. In that sense, the $10,000 was a potential bargain, assuming that Feller's arm held up. But Cleveland wasn't Feller's only source of income: he'd quickly signed endorsement deals with several companies, including a candy bar to be produced in the Cleveland area. "He should be financially independent by the time he casts his first vote," noted Jack Miley in the *New York Daily News*.[7] The only products he refused to endorse were alcohol and tobacco, a concession to clean living noted with some admiration by the press.

The national media followed Feller closely during spring training. An Associated Press photo and caption that appeared in several national papers in late February praised the "schoolboy wonder" and compared him to "Johnson, Mathewson, Grove, Waddell, and Alexander." Another AP photo issued on March 2d showed several New Orleans schoolchildren obtaining autographs from a smiling Feller, the "game's latest sensation." Feller took the

time to cultivate relations with the Cleveland newspapermen following the club in spring training, developing good relations with
most of them. "Never lie to a newspaperman," a veteran *Cleveland
Press* editor advised Feller.[8] He took the advice to heart . . . perhaps
too closely at times, for Feller quickly developed a reputation for
straight-shooting, a trait that would get him in trouble in the future.

By late March, the Indians were ready to play. Spring training
in the 1930s was structured differently from the way it is today.
Teams trained in widely scattered locations throughout the South
and West, unlike today when all teams are concentrated either in
Florida or Arizona. Exhibition play didn't begin until very late in
March, often with a pair of clubs touring on the road, rather than
playing in fixed spring training facilities. The Indians paired off
with the New York Giants, beginning a tour through the old Con-
federacy, on March 29th. Feller opened the tour against Giants ace
Carl Hubbell in Vicksburg, Mississippi. Feller pitched three innings, fanning six, while walking just one and not allowing a hit or
run.

The New York journalists were uniformly impressed, as were
most of the Giants. One batsman who refused to kowtow to the
growing Feller phenomenon was Giants shortstop Dick Bartell.
Bartell fanned on three pitches. "I didn't say I saw them. I looked
at them," wrote Bartell years later.[9] Bartell came back to the Giants
bench, claiming implausibly that the young phenom didn't really
throw that hard, certainly not as hard as some National Leaguers
like Van Mungo. This became an inside joke over the years, Feller
striking Bartell out, Bartell returning to the bench to inform his
teammates that Feller "hasn't got a thing."

Those not trying to save face, boost their teammates psychologically, or just make fun of the situation were more impressed. Plate
umpire Bill Klem was quoted in numerous sources to the effect
that Feller was the fastest pitcher he'd ever seen, and "has a chance
to be the greatest of them all." But only, Giants manager Bill Terry
added, if he improved his command. The New York writers, most
of whom had seen Feller struggle against the Yankees the previous

summer, were "bowled over" by how much the youngster had improved.

Still, he was wild more often than not, which was often to his
advantage. No one dared dig in against him. The control problem
had a serious consequence on April 4th, when the Giants and Indians met up again for a game in New Orleans. Feller and Hubbell
started the game, attracting a large spring crowd of more than
13,000 fans. Both pitched well, and Feller tossed five scoreless innings, fanning five. But an out-of-control curveball clobbered
Giants outfielder Hank Leiber in the head, damaging an optic
nerve and causing a concussion. He returned to action within two
weeks, but was bothered by dizziness for the rest of the season,
spending a considerable portion of the first half on the disabled
list.

Feller was shaken by the incident. Although he wasn't afraid to
throw inside, he was not a beanball artist. "It didn't break
enough," he tried to explain to everyone as he rushed toward
home plate. "It's all right, sonny," counseled Klem.[10] The incident
took away any desire Feller might have had to plunk hitters. "I
never hit a batter on purpose, and if any manager had ever ordered
me to do it—and no one ever did—I would have disobeyed. There
are some orders in life you simply don't have to obey because they
are so outrageously criminal or immoral."[11] Feller knew that his
fastball could be a lethal weapon, his curve only mildly less dangerous. He did not want to be involved in an incident like the one
that had killed Cleveland shortstop Ray Chapman in 1920. No one
blamed Feller publicly or privately for the Leiber incident, though
there was some press commentary about the advisability of adopting batting helmets. This wouldn't happen until the late 1950s.

Feller put the Leiber incident behind him, and continued to
pitch well on the exhibition tour. The Indians and Giants played
contests throughout the South, starting in Tyler, Texas, then gradually working their way east through Arkansas, Alabama, Georgia,
and the Carolinas, before finishing with a final exhibition game in
New York. This was a dynamic duel between Feller and Hubbell,
resulting in a 4–2 win for Cleveland, both starters pitching eight
innings. In 27 innings for the Indians against New York that spring,

Feller allowed seven runs, for a sharp 2.33 ERA. He fanned 37. He bore down especially hard on Bartell after the shortstop's comments regarding Feller's fastball came to light, fanning him 13 times.

Spring training ended with Feller confident that he was ready to thrive in the major leagues. He'd pitched extremely well against the Giants, and while his control still left much to be desired, it was better than it had been at the end of the '36 season, or so he thought. He'd made progress holding runners and reducing his leg kick. He was especially proud of the progress made in refining his curveball, the Leiber incident notwithstanding. Steve O'Neill decided that Feller would take the number two slot in the starting rotation, behind Mel Harder, who would start Opening Day in Detroit. Feller was honored; he wouldn't be "protected" by hurling mostly against the weaker clubs. He was a full-fledged, and critical, member of the staff. "We look for a lot of help from Feller," O'Neill told the press.[12] It was more than just the sporting pages who paid attention to Feller. *Time* Magazine ran a cover story featuring the young right-hander on April 19th, only the second time in history a baseball player had graced the front of the newsstand staple. The *Time* piece retold the basics of the Feller story for the casual fan, as well as reviewing the rookies expected to make an impact for '37. Feller was the big attraction, but Boston Bees outfielder Vince DiMaggio, Cardinals catcher Mickey Owen, and Giants pitcher John Hubbell (brother of superstar Carl Hubbell) were also mentioned.

Opening Day in Detroit was a disappointment, the Tigers nipping the Indians by a 4–3 score. Mel Harder pitched well, but was undone by several poor defensive plays, as well as a cycle from Tiger outfielder Gee Walker. Unfortunately, the next two games were rained out, delaying Feller's season debut. The club took the train back to Cleveland, for the opening series against the Browns. O'Neill tapped Johnny Allen to start the first game, pushing Feller back to the second game, April 24th.

Feller felt strong warming up, with better command than usual. Coach Schang and Indians catcher Frankie Pytlak suggested that Feller use his improved curve, rather than relying solely on his fastball. Feller readily agreed. The first hitter for the Browns was

Bill Knickerbocker, the former Indian traded during the winter. Feller's first pitch was a fastball for strike one. He followed with a poor curve for ball one. Frustrated, he decided to throw another bender for the third pitch, concentrating on getting the strongest break possible.

It almost ruined his career.

The pitch was wide, a ball. Of greater concern was the sharp pain that suddenly throbbed through his elbow. Terrified, Feller decided not to throw any more curves, but was too scared to admit he was hurt. Pytlak, unaware of his pitcher's distress, continued to call for curveballs. Feller kept shaking him off. He could throw his fastball without as much pain, but it was still uncomfortable, and the good control he'd had in the bullpen was gone. The Browns scored four runs off him, courtesy of two hits and four walks.

Returning to the dugout, Feller didn't admit to O'Neill that his arm was hurting, not wanting the other players to think he was making excuses for his poor performance.

Feller returned to the mound in the second inning, but again his control was off. He walked the bases loaded, before managing to strike out the next three hitters (including 41-year-old player manager Rogers Hornsby) with nothing but fastballs, albeit painful ones. He settled down in the third inning and pitched effectively. Although his arm was still tender, the sharp elbow pain had subsided. By the top of the sixth, he decided to throw another curveball. It was as agonizing as the first.

Returning to the dugout after the inning, Feller finally admitted to his manager that his arm hurt. "I think I better quit, Steve. I hurt my arm in the first inning and it isn't getting any better."

"You should have told me earlier," griped O'Neill. He sent Feller back to the clubhouse with trainer Weisman in tow, then got ex-Brown Ivy Andrews up in the bullpen.[13] In six innings, Feller had allowed just the four first inning runs, giving up only four hits, walking six, while fanning 11, a remarkable performance considering the game was pitched almost entirely with an injury. It was even more remarkable that his velocity was normal, by Feller's standards. No one suspected he was injured until he admitted it.

Feller was quickly examined by trainer Weisman and club physician Dr. Edward B. Castle. The diagnosis was a "pulled muscle in his arm," and the injury was not considered serious. Or so the Indians told the press.[14] The Indians put a brave front on the story at first, claiming that Feller would "be back on the job in days." The Cleveland papers were all over the story, of course, but it was national news as well, with frequent wire service updates on his condition. On April 26th, O'Neill told the Associated Press that Feller's injury was definitely not serious, and that he'd be back in action within a week.

Four days later, the story had changed, the *New York Times* reporting that Feller had torn "several fibers just below the elbow," and would be out at least two to three weeks, perhaps longer. It was only now that the Indians admitted that Feller had hurt himself in the first inning of that start against the Browns. Sportswriters across the nation speculated that Feller's career was over before it began, ended by his own stubbornness, or naïveté, in trying to pitch through the pain. Some attacked the alleged negligence of the Cleveland front office.

In the age before magnetic resonance imaging and arthroscopic surgery, treatment of pitching injuries was primitive. Trying to figure out which specific nerve or muscle was the source of the proverbial "sore arm" was often little more than guesswork. X-rays could diagnose broken or fractured bones and some muscle injuries, but there was no way to get at a specific muscle or nerve without surgery that would be radical by today's standards. Such surgeries were often more damaging than the original injury. Diagnosis of specific injuries often varied radically from doctor to doctor, specialist to specialist. Treatment beyond vibration therapy, massage, and simple rest was often more dangerous than the injuries themselves. The Indians were desperate to protect their investment in Feller. Cy Slapnicka took personal charge of the case, taking Feller personally to a variety of muscle and bone specialists. The arm was X-rayed, revealing little. Frequent rubbings and massage eased the soreness somewhat, but not to the point where the Indians felt comfortable sending Feller back to the mound. About the only thing the specialists agreed on was that rest would help. Eventually a consensus was reached that the problem was a "stretched muscle," and rest and heat treatments were the pre-scribed cure.

April turned to May and the spring wore on. Feller remained national news, though as much for his approaching high school graduation as for his arm problems. He returned to Iowa on May 10th, coming home in an aircraft provided by the *Des Moines Register-Tribune*.[15] The Indians had taken the precaution of acquiring a $100,000 life insurance policy on Feller, just in case the single-engine aircraft crashed.[16] The flight was without incident, and Feller returned home to a parade and two Des Moines radio interviews in which the condition of his arm was the main topic. Famous WHO broadcaster Ronald Reagan was the host in one interview.

Feller's graduation wasn't a done deal; he had to take final exams. This he did, posting passing grades in each topic (Physics 79, Psychology 79, English 74, History 70), below his usual academic standards, but not bad considering that, by his own admission, he hadn't cracked the books much recently. Named class president by the graduating body of 19 students, Feller's high school graduation ceremony was front-page news in most national papers, usually sharing space with the coronation of George VI in Great Britain, as well as the aftermath of the *Hindenberg* zeppelin disaster. The graduation ceremony itself was carried live by NBC on national radio. The president of NBC was an Iowan, and decided to air the ceremony against the advice of his subordinates, who said it would be too expensive. The broadcast ended up being a big success. Bob assured his anxious mother that he would go to college and get a diploma, should his arm fail to improve and his career end prematurely. Another worry for the Fellers was Bill Feller's health; he'd fallen ill the previous winter, and had just been diagnosed with a slow-growing brain tumor.

On May 16th, Feller returned to the Indians, joining his teammates in Chicago. But despite three weeks of rest, his arm still hurt. "It hurts to cut loose, fast ball or curve, but I can do it," he told the *New York Times*.[17] Fortunately, the Indians did not regard "cutting loose" with a sore arm as a test of manhood, unlike many managers and coaches through the ages. His arm was tested in a bullpen session with O'Neill on the 17th, at the end of which the Indians pronounced his arm "100 percent."[18] His velocity was normal, but the pain returned full force the next day; Feller would remain sidelined indefinitely.

Things were starting to get uncomfortable in Cleveland. The Indians were hovering above .500, but were (as usual) behind the Yankees and Tigers in the pennant chase. The Cleveland newspapers were increasingly critical of Slapnicka and O'Neill, the former for not doing enough to improve the roster, the latter for being "too nice" and too easy for the players to get along with. Hints that Feller's injury was from too much practice in the spring were also dropped. When rest and massage had no apparent effect on Feller's sore arm, Slapnicka decided that unusual measures needed to be taken.

On June 1st, the Associated Press reported that Feller was leaving Cleveland "for a rest." Two days later, the Indians announced that if Feller's arm did not improve quickly, he would "retire for the year" rather than try and pitch through the soreness. While these announcements were being made, Slapnicka had taken Feller to Milwaukee, for special treatment from one Dr. F. B. Ohm, a "bone specialist" who had a special vibration machine. Feller took two treatments in the machine, after which his arm felt better. He threw for 15 minutes after the second treatment, pronouncing himself fit for work. On June 8th, Ohm told the AP that Feller's arm was "virtually healed," and that he could return to pitching shortly.

The optimism proved short-lived. The symptoms returned within a few days; Ohm's machine cure was either a very short-term fix, or perhaps a case of "mental suggestion" as Feller himself admitted.[19] By June 15th, the word from Cleveland was that Feller was still out "indefinitely."

By late June, the uncomfortable situation in the standings had grown critical. The Indians had stood 22–15 and in second place in June 6th. But by late in the month the team had fallen under .500 and was out of contention, courtesy of a slump in hitting and a deterioration in the pitching staff. Mel Harder and Willis Hudlin were pitching well, but the rest of the staff was mediocre, or worse. Ace Johnny Allen was bothered with abdominal problems. Veteran

Earl Whitehill, one of Slapnicka's top off-season acquisitions, was getting hammered on a regular basis and looked washed up. There was no one in the farm system ready to help.

Not ready to give up on Feller's chances to help in '37 just yet, Slapnicka tried one last desperate measure. He took Bob to the office of A. L. Austin, a licensed practitioner of "mechano-therapy," known more commonly today as chiropractic, although he called himself a "bonesetter." Austin had a good reputation in the community, and "traditional" medicine had obviously failed to fix Feller's condition. "He may not help you, but he can't hurt you," Slap told Bob.[20] Trainer Weisman had apparently suggested similar treatment earlier during the injury ordeal, but had been overruled by a skeptical Slapnicka.

Austin's office was within walking distance of League Park: the solution had been right under their noses the whole time. Austin quickly diagnosed Feller's problem as a dislocated ulna bone. "He grasped my wrist with his right hand and my elbow with his left. He gave a sudden twist and there was a moment of blinding pain."[21]

The pain passed quickly, leaving only a mild tenderness. Austin assured the nervous Feller and Slapnicka that his arm would be fine now. "Rest 24 hours and then go right out and pitch." He further assured Feller that he could throw curveballs without trouble.

Feller took the mound again in a bullpen workout two days later. Austin was right: his arm was fine. His fastball was as good as ever, and he could throw his curve without pain. Best of all, his arm was without discomfort the next day. Everything was back to normal.

Getting Feller back into action was the next step, and the Indians didn't go for half-measures. Slapnicka and O'Neill selected a July 4th doubleheader at home against the Tigers as the target for Feller's return to the mound. The game was held in Cleveland Stadium, to handle the larger-than-expected crowd. Some 30,000 fans showed up, a good draw for a fifth-place club that had fallen out of the pennant chase. O'Neill was cautious with Feller, allowing him to work just the first four innings of game one. Working with only his fastball and rudimentary changeup, Feller gave up three runs, though allowing only one hit. His command was poor, but his velocity was as good as ever. Best of all, a postgame medical examination by Dr. Castle found no medical problems, the physician pronouncing Feller fit to resume regular work.[22] There was much rejoicing in the Indians family; their franchise player was saved.

Feller resumed regular work after the All-Star Break. At first, it was speculated that he would pitch only on Sundays, to make absolutely sure that his arm was healed. His next start was a week later, July 11th, in Detroit. Feller lost the game 3–2, but pitched creditably, allowing only two hits, but walking six and throwing a wild pitch. He fanned six, throwing all eight innings for the Indians. By modern standards, O'Neill and Slapnicka were fools for letting Feller pitch a complete game so closely removed from a potentially serious injury, but he showed no ill effects.

Feller's next game was back in Cleveland against the Yankees before a huge crowd of 59,000. Feller threw another complete game, in a losing effort, giving up four runs in the ninth inning to take the 5–1 loss. He allowed seven hits and seven walks, while fanning seven. His velocity was fine, and he was starting to use his curveball again, but his command was still weak. He'd lost the game on a home run by Joe DiMaggio in the ninth inning, prompting several Yankees to state outright that Feller belonged in the minor leagues.[23] This was ludicrous; as Indians partisans pointed out, Feller had handcuffed the World Champions for eight innings, but the insult still stung.

By late July, the Indians had decided to put Feller back in the rotation full time, O'Neill telling the AP on July 22d that Feller would pitch every fifth day. Regular work seemed to agree with Feller, and his command gradually improved as the season continued. Getting further away from the injury, he grew confident in his curveball again, no longer fearing that a sharp pain would follow a strong wrist snap.

Through his first four starts on the season, Feller was 0–4 with an ERA of 5.00. But as August began, Feller started to pitch better, becoming one of the very few bright spots for the Indians down the stretch run. "Flipper Feels Fine" was the suggested caption on an AP photo of Bob that ran in many papers the second week of August. It was about the only good news coming out of Cleveland. Johnny Allen was out with appendicitis, while the rest of the pitching staff was inconsistent. The hitting attack had tailed off as well, and rumors about O'Neill's job security (or lack thereof) were rampant. A disastrous 2–11 East Coast road trip in August put the seal on the season. Feller pitched a bizarre 12-strikeout, 10-walk game in Yankee Stadium during the road trip, a game the Tribe lost in 10 innings. A 16-strikeout performance against the Red Sox in late August, with just four walks and four hits, was a more promising sign that Feller was back.

The Indians played well in September, which was enough to keep O'Neill from getting fired immediately. In spite this rebound, the vultures were still circling. Despite strong pitching from Feller and a brilliant comeback by Johnny Allen from appendicitis (he won 15 in a row at one point), the Tribe was unable to make up ground on the Yankees, undone by another poor late-season road trip. Feller's final outing was a strong 4–1 win over the White Sox in Comiskey Park.

Despite his injury problems and poor 0–4 start, Feller finished the year with a 9–7 record and 3.38 ERA. The latter ranked ninth in the league, comparing very favorably with an Indians team mark of 4.39 and a league mark of 4.62. In 149 innings, he allowed just 116 hits, while fanning 150. Despite missing three months, he ranked third in the league in strikeouts, and his strikeout-per-nine-inning rate was the best in the circuit. Control was his Achilles heel: he had walked 106 men. But his low hit-per-inning rate and strong pitching with men on base kept his ERA low. No honest person could deny that this 18-year-old was one of the best pitchers in the league, and certainly the most overpowering.

Feller wasn't done pitching, however. After the season closed on September 27th, he departed on a barnstorming tour, playing games in Minneapolis, Cedar Rapids, Kansas City, Tulsa, Oklahoma City, and Los Angeles.[24] He earned $4,000 for the tour, 40 percent of his Cleveland salary for just two weeks of work. This was not unusual; most stars supplemented their major league salaries with fall barnstorming income, but Feller was quickly one of the most aggressive in tapping this market.

As Feller toured the Midwest, wheels were turning in Cleveland. Alva Bradley and Cy Slapnicka had decided that Steve O'Neill, for all his skills as a manager and coach, really was "too nice" for the job, and that someone with a harder attitude was needed to light a fire under their underachieving club. They settled on Oscar "Ossie" Vitt, manager of the Newark Bears in the International League, a top Yankees farm club. Vitt had a strong minor league managerial track record, being a successful manager in the Pacific Coast League for many years before joining the Yankees organization. His 1937 Newark Bears had won the International League pennant by 25.5 games. He'd played major league baseball from 1912 to 1921, earning a reputation for scrappy fearlessness. He was a knowledgeable baseball man, and very intense; no one could accuse him of being "too nice" or passive in the face of failure. He seemed an ideal candidate to replace the easygoing O'Neill, the perfect person to turn around a talented but sometimes listless ballclub.

It was not to be.

6

The Drill Sergeant

I don't know much about this team, but I can tell you one
thing. We'll have the damnedest fighting team you have
ever had here. There'll be no loafing. Ol' Os will see to
that.

—Ossie Vitt, October 1937

Bob Feller first became aware of the hiring of Vitt while on
his barnstorming tour. Everyone connected with Cleveland
knew that Steve O'Neill would likely be fired, so the hiring
of a new manager was not a surprise. Rumors that Bill Mc-
Kechnie or Bill Terry would get the job didn't pan out, but
Vitt seemed like a fine candidate. On the surface, there was no reason to expect Vitt *not* to be a good manager. His minor league managerial record was immaculate, and the former teammate of Ty
Cobb clearly knew what the major leagues were all about. For all
his fierceness, Vitt usually made a strong and positive first impression. Both Alva Bradley and Cy Slapnicka were "smitten" with
him at first, though Vitt quickly wore out their good graces, especially Slap's.[1] As for Feller, he had grown accustomed to O'Neill's
gentle touch, and was not happy to see his first professional manager go, feeling "sorrow" when he learned of O'Neill's fate while
barnstorming.

Expectations for Feller coming into 1938 were high. He had
been named as the American League's 1937 "Flop of the Year" by
the Associated Press. This was an unfair assessment, to be sure,
considering his elbow trouble, as well as the basic fact that he'd

actually pitched quite well when he did take the mound. Other observers were more charitable. Tris Speaker told the Associated
Press on December 26th that Feller reminded him of former major
league star Smokey Joe Wood, possibly the hardest thrower of the
1910s. Speaker predicted that Feller would pitch very well in 1938,
now that he'd shown some control, and had "possibilities of winning from twenty-five to thirty-five games."

The Indians didn't seem disappointed in Feller, and backed up
their faith with cash. The Fellers negotiated a 1938 contract for
$17,500 in early January without acrimony or controversy with the
club. This was right in line with what other young stars like Joe
DiMaggio were making, and brought Feller to the same level with
Allen and Averill as the highest-paid players on the Cleveland
team.

While leaving the foundation of the club intact, Slapnicka did
make two major transactions to infuse extra talent into the roster
and help give Vitt a fresh start. Catcher Rollie Hemsley, a fine defensive catcher, was acquired from the St. Louis Browns in exchange for Billy Sullivan and Roy Hughes. Feller had grown to
know Hemsley while barnstorming, and they had quickly become
friends, though Hemsley's infamous alcohol-induced rampages
were in sharp contrast to Feller's studied sobriety. The second
major change was the promotion of three players from the minor
leagues. Purchased from Milwaukee were third baseman Ken Keltner, outfielder Jeff Heath, and second baseman Oscar Grimes.
Grimes eventually proved to be a useful bench player, but both
Keltner and Heath quickly became regulars, demonstrating All-
Star talent at various points in their careers. The addition of Hemsley, Keltner, and Heath clearly improved the club's offensive and
defensive core, all without weakening the pitching staff. With this
influx of new everyday talent, a healthy Bob Feller, and a fiery new
manager, things were looking up in Cleveland.

Things were definitely *different* in Cleveland. Ossie Vitt made it
clear in spring training in New Orleans that lack of effort or sloppy
play would not be tolerated. O'Neill hadn't truly tolerated these
things either, of course, but his usual way of dealing with them
was through reason and gentle persuasion. Vitt had little patience

with such tactics: if he detected any lack of hustle on the part of a player, the player would hear about it loudly and abrasively, often in front of the other players, and sometimes even the press. The contrast with O'Neill was quickly apparent, and some players responded positively. Others did not, especially when Vitt mistook simple human mistakes for lack of effort. No one fields every ground ball cleanly, or throws strikes with every pitch, a fact of life that Ossie Vitt often failed to consider. Uneasiness with Vitt's style was an undercurrent in his first spring training, made stronger by the fact that some players in the Yankees system privately warned their friends on the Indians that Vitt was obnoxious. In public, the Tribe remained optimistic that the change would be for the best, but quietly many were concerned.

As O'Neill had done, Vitt took special charge of Feller, and the two got along well on the surface. Vitt decided that the time had finally come to cut back significantly on Feller's high leg kick, and reducing this was the main focus of Feller's work in spring training. Again, Wally Schang and Mel Harder were of assistance, although new coach Johnny Bassler (a friend and former teammate of Vitt's) was also helpful. Feller was uncomfortable with the mechanical change at first, although he knew that the Vitt and the veterans were right, and that something needed to be done about his inability to hold runners.

Vitt tinkered with the other players as well. He ordered Hal Trosky to hit more to the opposite field, rather than trying to pull for power. He prohibited the playing of clubhouse poker, banned "intemperate" drinking, and was far harder than O'Neill in the enforcement of curfew when on the road. Rollickin' Rollie Hemsley quickly drew Vitt's ire, especially after a drinking binge late in spring training that resulted in a week's suspension. Vitt went so far as to threaten any Indian caught carousing with Hemsley with a $500 fine.

Unlike O'Neill in '37, Vitt didn't use Feller much in spring training, concentrating on improving his delivery through bullpen work. When he did pitch, he wasn't as dominating as he'd been the previous spring. He threw three scoreless innings against the Giants on March 20th, fanning just two, and drawing commentary from both the press and the Giants to the effect that he wasn't throwing as hard as he used to. Feller himself agreed with this assessment, though he wasn't concentrating on impressing with his fastball at this point, as he was focused mostly on just trying to get comfortable with his new delivery.

The exhibition series with the Giants resulted in a 7–9 record for Cleveland, neither anything to get panicked over nor excited about. For all the roster changes and switch in managers, the Indians looked pretty much the same as they'd looked the previous spring: a decent team with some star talent. They could threaten the Yankees if everything went well, but were not a club that would run away with the league.

Feller pitched sparingly during the exhibition series, throwing only a handful of innings. His final effort was a horrendous 11–1 loss against the Giants in Cleveland, Feller giving up 12 hits in eight innings, with less-than-impressive zip on his fastball. Rumors that Feller's heater was gone continued to spread. He quickly put them to rest once the season began.

The Indians opened the season on April 19th in Cleveland, with Mel Harder opposing Buck Newsom and the St. Louis Browns on Opening Day. The Browns won the contest by a 6–2 score, disappointing the Cleveland Stadium crowd of some 32,000. Feller was tabbed to pitch the next game, April 20th in League Park.

Feller didn't feel that his fastball was especially strong in the bullpen that day, but his curveball was. Once on the mound in game conditions, the fastball came around, back to 1937 standards. To make things even harder on the Browns, Feller used his curveball frequently, even coming sidearm with the pitch at times to give the hitters a different look. He didn't use his changeup much, but had no real need to do so given how well his curve was working. Bob found Rollie Hemsley a joy to work with, the two almost always being on the same page about what to throw and when to throw it.

The Indians quickly took a 4–0 lead. Ex-Indian catcher Billy Sullivan got a bunt hit off Feller in the sixth inning, beating the play at first base on a close call. It was the only hit that Feller would give up, as he posted a 9–0 win, recording both his first career shutout and his first one-hitter. Feller fanned six and walked six, throwing an estimated 136 pitches.[2] The one-hitter eliminated any doubts about Feller's health: the spring rumors that he'd lost his stuff died down, though they did not cease entirely.

Feller defeated the Detroit Tigers by a 9–4 score in his next start. He then threw 11 shutout innings against the Washington Senators in a game eventually won by the Nats 1–0 in 13 innings. His fourth start, in Yankee Stadium, was another success, a 3–2 complete game win, with nine strikeouts. At each stop, press and players commented that Feller didn't seem to be throwing as hard as in '36 or '37, although his velocity was still rated as excellent. But his command was better and he was "a more polished pitcher," to quote Lou Gehrig. The Indians were playing well, hanging in second place through most of April, then pushing into first place by themselves on May 20th. The hitting was improved over previous campaigns, the pitching more consistent, the defense tighter. Vitt's hard driving seemed to be having a positive effect. Rookies Keltner and Heath were playing well. A healthy Feller was taking his turn every four days, while both Johnny Allen and Mel Harder were having good seasons. Even old-timer Earl Whitehill, who'd looked completely washed up in '37, was throwing effectively on occasion. A sore back in late May forced Feller from one start, but otherwise everything was fine. The Tribe was finally living up to expectations, with Bob emerging as the ace of the staff.

It didn't last long.

"The Indians will fold up . . . they always do," Yankees manager Joe McCarthy said in early June.[3] Ossie Vitt was supposed to keep that from happening, but his whip-cracking approach backfired when things began to go wrong. Things began to go sour for the Indians in late June. Johnny Allen was ejected from a game in Boston for pitching with a nonregulation shirt (it had extra ventilation holes) and refusing to change it. Instead of backing his player up, Vitt fined Allen $250 for leaving the game. The affair was quickly patched up, with a Cleveland department store purchasing the shirt for the exact amount of the fine. Allen and Vitt made up publicly, but it was a sign of increasing tension in the clubhouse.

A July 4th doubleheader loss to the Tigers in Detroit (Feller lost

the first game by a 7–3 score) put the Yankees and Indians in a tie
for first place at the All-Star Break. Feller, along with teammates
Allen and Averill, was named to the All-Star game. Feller didn't
pitch. In those days, winning the All-Star game was much more of
a point of pride than it is today. Starters usually pitched three or
four innings. Lefty Gomez of the Yankees started this game, throwing three innings before being relieved by Johnny Allen. The fiery
right-hander threw three effective innings for his leaguemates, in a
game eventually won by the Nationals, 4–1. But Allen's performance turned out to be a disaster for the Indians. He'd slipped in his
bathtub the night before the game and hurt his elbow, but had
tried to pitch through the pain the next day. He did so, but at the
cost of his career: he was never the same pitcher afterward, bothered by bone chips that took the zip off his fastball and that eventually required surgery.

The Indians fell into a slump after the All-Star Break. Following
a particularly tough 9–8 loss to the Senators, Vitt lambasted his
club in a clubhouse tirade. Moose Solters was Vitt's main target.
Solters was pulled from the lineup, and Vitt publicly declared that
the outfielder would never play for him again. Solters, struggling
to keep his batting average over .200, was demoted to pinch-hitting
duty. Feller lost a tough game against Philadelphia on the same
road trip, only to be blasted by Vitt. By August 1st, the Yankees
had sole possession of first place, with the Indians falling further
and further behind. The clubhouse atmosphere was poisonous.
Vitt's attempts to motivate his charges with sarcasm and insult
only made the team play tighter.

Feller was not immune to this pressure; after several rough
starts in late July, he began to lose confidence in his stuff. Knocked
out of an early August start in the third inning by the Red Sox,
Feller had a long conversation with *Cleveland News* reporter Ed
McAuley.

> "I'm not sure what it is. . . . All I know is that I don't seem to be
> able to throw the ball fast any more."
>   He looked at me for a moment.
>   "Do you mind if I print that?" he asked.
>   "No. Why not? It's true."[4]

McAuley's story caused a firestorm in Cleveland. Not everyone agreed that Feller had actually lost anything. *Cleveland Press* sports editor Stuart Bell thought that the kid was just "excited," and resisted pressure from his bosses to rewrite the *Press* game-day story to include Feller's comments. Bell finally gave in to pressure from his superiors, but not before predicting that Feller would pitch well in his next start, and that he (Bell) would resign his position if made to look bad.[5] "You may know more about your business than I do," Bell told his superiors, "but I know more about young baseball pitchers." Another skeptic was Bill Feller, who took the train out to Cleveland to console his son after the disastrous road trip. "Look here son . . . It's like driving a fast racing car. After you ride in it for a while, it doesn't seem to be going as fast as it was in the first place." Bob proved both his father and Stuart Bell correct in his next start, fanning 10 Philadelphia Athletics in a complete game 4–2 victory. Stuart Bell made good on his threat and resigned.

Just as they had done during the O'Neill years, the Indians faded as the dog days wore on. Feller pitched well through August and September, but the hitting attack tailed off, Johnny Allen's elbow injury forced him out of action, and Mel Harder lost time to a broken finger. The Indians drifted into third place, in danger of falling into the second division at times. Boston pushed into second, and a summer hot streak by the Yankees propelled them into first place and another relatively easy pennant. Vitt constantly juggled his lineup and pitching rotations, trying to find the magic formula to revive Cleveland's pennant chances. Nothing worked, and by the first of September, the Indians had given up hope.

The main tension in the American League at the end of the season was centered on Detroit slugger Hank Greenberg, who was making a run at Babe Ruth's single-season home run record. The season wound down with a Sunday doubleheader between the Tigers and Indians on October 2d, Greenberg needing two homers to tie and three to surpass Ruth's record. Feller started the first game of the set, opposing Detroit curveball artist Harry Eisenstat. Feller's stuff was excellent that day, his fastball having great life and his curve "whipping."[6] He fanned one in the first, then struck out the side in the second inning . . . and then again in the third inning, and the fourth. Two more whiffs followed in the fifth. But the game was still a 0–0 contest, Eisenstat keeping the Cleveland hitters off-balance with his curveball, changeup, and mediocre fastball.

Feller fanned two more in the sixth inning, but gave up two runs on a single-double-double sequence by Roy Cullenbine, Greenberg, and Birdie Tebbetts. He punched out Eisenstat in the seventh inning, then posted another K in the eighth, but three walks and a double by Mark Christman plated two more runs for the Tigers. Feller followed up with two more strikeouts in the ninth inning, giving him 18 total, and setting a new American League record. Chet Laabs struck out five times; only Cullenbine and Tebbetts were spared striking out. Greenberg didn't homer, and settled for hitting 58 on the season, two short of Ruth's record. But for all Feller's heroics, he didn't win the game, losing by a 4–1 score to the crafty Eisenstat. Bob walked seven.

The season complete, Feller went on another lucrative barnstorming adventure. While the Indians had not quite lived up to preseason expectations, the club finished at 86–66, finishing in third place and improving their winning percentage over the previous campaign. Feller had laid all doubts to rest about the health of his arm or his ability to harness his talent. He matched Mel Harder for the Cleveland lead with 17 wins. He led the American League with 240 strikeouts, and bested the circuit in strikeouts per inning. He also led the league in fewest hits given up per inning. His 277.2 innings ranked third in the circuit; he also ranked third in games started and complete games. Despite all this, his earned run average of 4.08 was only 14 percent better than the league average (when adjusted for park effects), a good mark but not spectacular. The flaw that inflated his ERA was his control, or lack thereof: Feller walked an incredible 208 men. Clearly, Bob still needed to improve his command.

The Indians braintrust, meanwhile, was busy once again trying to find ways to improve the team. The process was complicated by a rift between Cy Slapnicka and Ossie Vitt. Slap, originally a strong Vitt supporter, had soured on him, especially after the manager criticized the GM in front of reporters. By the end of the season, the tension between the two veteran baseball men had boiled over into outright hatred. But firing Vitt wasn't wise politically, at least not just yet: the team *had* played better for him than they had under O'Neill, even if the clubhouse atmosphere was much less congenial. From Vitt's perspective, he'd been hired because he was a tough guy, not in spite of it. The fact that he was willing to speak his mind without regard to the feelings of others was a key personality trait. No one should have been shocked, especially an old baseball hound like Cy Slapnicka. Cy was perhaps surprised that some of Vitt's bile ended up directed at him, but he should have expected this, or at least not been taken aback by it.

With a managerial change for 1939 not feasible, further roster shuffling was in order. Both Cy Slapnicka and Alva Bradley called for a general roster purge. But again, as in previous seasons, Cleveland's ability to make big moves in the trade market was rather restricted. Despite all the talk of housecleaning, they still didn't want to trade core players. Most of the players available on the trade market weren't appreciably better than the ones they were willing to let go. Slapnicka did pull off one good trade, an exchange with Boston. The Tribe sent pitcher Denny Galehouse, an average talent who'd started 12 games for Cleveland with mediocre overall numbers, to the Red Sox for outfielder Ben Chapman, who'd hit .340 the previous season. The acquisition of Chapman improved the hitting attack, which already looked to be on the upswing with projected improvements from youngsters Ken Keltner and Jeff Heath. No big moves were planned for the pitching staff. Oldster Earl Whitehill drew his release, but the Tribe expected good things from youngsters Joe Dobson and Bill Zuber. Lefthander Al Milnar was also penciled in for a larger role. With Feller, Harder, and Allen anchoring the staff, the Indians had good reason to expect they would contend again in 1939.

Spring training in New Orleans was even more tense than it had been in '38. Coach Wally Schang, a critical influence on Feller's early development, had been let go by the club. There were rumors of discontent in the clubhouse, players once again chafing under Vitt's iron hand. Earl Averill held out again, carrying on another public war of words with Alva Bradley over his bonus. Catcher Frankie Pytlak was disgruntled about both his salary and his playing time. Jeff Heath was benched by Vitt for not hustling. The health of the pitching staff became a concern: both Harder and Allen came down with arm problems and were unable to pitch effectively. Feller was used sparingly during the spring exhibition tour against the Giants, Vitt wanting him to work instead on his mechanics and physical conditioning, saving his strength for the regular season. This seemed wise, given the fact that Feller would be relied upon to carry an even greater pitching burden with both Harder and Allen ailing.

Feller was given his first Opening Day assignment against the Browns in St. Louis, but this was rained out. He instead started the first game of the season in Cleveland, against Detroit, fanning 10 and allowing only three hits and two walks, winning the game 5–1. Although a 10-walk, 10-hit start against the Yankees ten days later was something of a disaster, Feller was in fine form for most of the first half. His control was improved again, and he won six of his first seven starts. His sixth victory occurred on Mother's Day in Chicago, May 14th. Bill, Lena, and Marguerite had traveled from Van Meter to watch the game. But the family excursion was marred by a foul ball off the bat of White Sox third baseman Marv Owen; the ball sliced into the stands and hit Lena in the face, knocking her unconscious. Though revived a moment later, she had to be helped from the park and taken to a local hospital. Distraught and sick to his stomach, Feller considered coming out of the game. But informed that his mother was bruised but not seriously injured, Feller kept pitching, leading his club to a 9–4 win, though he was distracted enough that three runs scored due to his wildness. Lena required a few stitches and had a nasty bruise, but was otherwise unharmed.

Feller lost his next start, May 20th, against the Senators, by a 6–3 score in Washington. But he regained his form five days later on May 25th in Boston, a park in which he frequently struggled. Feller threw an 11–0 shutout against the Red Sox, allowing only a second inning single by Bobby Doerr. It was his second career one-hitter, the contest made even sweeter for Cleveland fans by three homers off the bat of Ken Keltner.

The team, however, was struggling, hovering around .500 with considerable unrest in the clubhouse. Averill and Heath were sulk-ing. The middle infield situation was unsettled, with Vitt shuffling Skeeter Webb, Oscar Grimes, and Odell Hale in and out of the lineup. The hitting was inconsistent, the pitching not much better. Feller was throwing very well, keeping the Indians in almost every start and ranking among the league ERA leaders. Mel Harder was pitching adequately despite a sore arm, and Al Milnar was adjust-ing well to his larger role. But Johnny Allen's sore elbow had taken the zip from his arm, and he was pitching only average baseball. Willis Hudlin was struggling, and the rest of the staff wasn't pick-ing up the slack.

The Indians finally found a taker for the aging (and unhappy) Earl Averill, trading the 37-year-old star to Detroit in mid-June for, of all people, Harry Eisenstat. The move made sense on purely baseball grounds: Averill was expensive, old, disgruntled, and be-coming a clubhouse distraction. The Indians had younger players who could use the playing time. Eisenstat was no great pitcher, but he was a lefty with some experience, and a useful complement to a heavily right-handed pitching staff. Despite the baseball logic in the trade, the press ripped the move, reacting in concert with angry fans, unhappy to see the longtime Cleveland star go, especially to the rival Tigers. The trade did nothing to improve the clubhouse atmosphere, which remained sour.

The club's failure to move beyond the .500 level, plus the obvi-ous clubhouse discontent with Vitt, put the manager under addi-tional pressure, much of which was self-imposed. A perfectionist of high order, Vitt could not stand mistakes, even honest ones, and he grew increasingly irritable. Vitt's lineup tinkering grew more pronounced. Nothing worked.

Looking for a way to boost attendance and shift the focus of publicity away from the acidic clubhouse, the Indians installed lights at Cleveland Stadium. The first night game in American League history took place on June 27th, with Bob Feller facing off against the Detroit Tigers in front of a crowd in excess of 50,000. Feller's fastball was blazing that night; the Detroit players, unac-customed to the lighting conditions, were virtually helpless against it. He fanned 13, throwing a 5–0 shutout. Best of all, he allowed only one hit: an ironic single to center field by Earl Averill in the sixth inning.

Feller was selected to his second All-Star game, and this time he pitched. Relieving Tommy Bridges in the sixth inning, Feller pitched three and two-thirds innings, allowing no runs, and impressing observers with his fastball and poise on the mound. The fact that the game was played in Yankee Stadium, site of previous Feller nervousness, adding icing to the cake.

Unfortunately, the Vitt situation was spinning out of control. Rumors that Vitt would be fired began to spread, with coach Luke Sewell the rumored replacement. Nothing came of this, but the rumors did nothing to improve Vitt's mood. His feuding with Jeff Heath came to a head when he fined the outfielder $50 for failing to run out a ground ball. At one point, Heath and pitcher Johnny Broaca fought in the dugout, though the confrontation turned out to be staged for Vitt's benefit. The pair hoped Vitt would intervene, with Heath planning on landing a punch on his manager.[7]

The club was still looking for a solution to the middle infield muddle. Trying to shake the team out of its torpor, Slapnicka promoted a pair of hot prospects from the minor leagues on August 2nd. Shortstop Lou Boudreau and second baseman Ray Mack moved up from Buffalo. To clear roster space, Moose Solters, buried deeply in Vitt's generally expansive doghouse, was sold to the Browns, while Skeeter Webb was sent to Buffalo. The arrival of Boudreau and Mack helped generate some enthusiasm. Boudreau took over the daily shortstop duties, solidifying the middle defense, while Mack shared playing time with Oscar Grimes and Odell Hale at the keystone. The team began to play better, but the dissension continued.

The clubhouse was filled with "gossip and petty jealousy."[8] Both Gordon Cobbledick in the *Plain Dealer* and Ed McAuley in the *News* wrote early August stories about troubles in the clubhouse, Cobbledick going so far as to predict a player rebellion. When Vitt got wind of this, he directly challenged his players to speak up. No one had the courage (or foolhardiness) to do so, and the rumors of insurrection subsided.

Despite all the troubles, the Indians' record was gradually improving. A doubleheader sweep of the Yankees in New York on August 4th improved the mood, Feller winning his 16th game. Boudreau quickly showed the look of a future star, at least defensively. The Indians went 36–20 after Boudreau and Mack were promoted, pushing into third place. On August 11th, Alva Bradley announced that Vitt would definitely return to manage the club in 1940; this relaxed the situation even further. Most of the team still didn't like Vitt, but the improved situation on the field, and the certainty that he would return next season, put a lid on the situation. Vitt himself seemed a bit more relaxed. The season ended on a positive note. A September road trip to the East saw the Tribe go 9–2. Feller won his 20th game on September 8th, beating the Browns by a 12–1 score in St. Louis. He then won his last four starts.

Overall, despite all the clubhouse trouble, the 1939 season was counted a success, the Tribe finishing in third place with an 87–67 record. Hal Trosky led the offense with a .335 average and 25 homers. Ken Keltner hit .325 with 13 homers, while newcomer Ben Chapman hit .290 with 18 steals. Jeff Heath, though he constantly battled with Vitt, hit .292 with 14 homers and 31 doubles. Mel Harder threw 208 innings with a fine 3.50 ERA, while Al Milnar won 14 games and contributed a 3.79 mark. Harry Eisenstat had pitched very well after coming over from Detroit, but both Johnny Allen (plagued with elbow problems) and Willis Hudlin struggled.

The 1939 season established Feller as the undisputed ace of the Cleveland staff. He pitched in 39 games, starting 35. He led the American League with 24 wins, led with 296.2 innings pitched, led with 24 complete games. He also topped the circuit with 246 strikeouts, in strikeouts per nine innings, in fewest hits allowed per nine innings, and in walks allowed. His ERA of 2.85 ranked third, and was 54 percent better than league average when park-adjusted. And he did all this while being the youngest regular pitcher in the league at age 20. Finishing third in the MVP voting, Feller drew universal acclaim as the best pitcher in the league, and would have won the Cy Young Award had it existed at that stage in history. He was chosen "Star of the Season" by the Associated Press, edging out fellow 20-year-old sensation Ted Williams. He was the youngest pitcher to win 20 games to that point in history.

Although Feller's control still needed to improve, it was much better than it had been in '38. There was mixed opinion about whether his velocity had dropped from when he'd first appeared in the majors. "Some observers believe Feller has sacrificed speed for accuracy," noted *The Sporting News*, "but not many rival batters will indorse [*sic*] that opinion."[9] Everyone agreed that Feller had greatly improved his ability to hold runners, and that his poise on the field under pressure had become that of a veteran. For all the bile he was willing to direct at other players, manager Vitt was full of praise for his young ace. "The kid never forgets anything you tell him," Vitt said, possibly wondering why the same wasn't true for the rest of his team.[10] The relationship between the young fire-baller and the tart manager seemed to be positive.

Not everyone on the Cleveland roster, and on other teams, felt the same way about Bob. It was an open secret that many of his teammates were jealous of Feller's success. He was a great draw on the road. Veteran sportswriter Jimmy Powers in the *New York Daily News* wrote that "wherever the Indians went, fans bellowed from the stands, 'We want Feller!' How the established stars, Averill, Allen, Lary, and Trosky burned!"[11] Feller was aware of this feeling against him. "There's a whole dugout full of players on the other side of the field trying to pin my ears back . . . what difference do a few more make, even though they wear 'Indians' on their chests and sit on the same bench with me!"[12]

"There is no more sincere person in baseball," commented Powers, "no pitcher works harder or studies his job more."[13] This sincerity cut both ways. It endeared him to many sportswriters. As Feller's natural shyness gave way to confidence, he gained a reputation for honesty and straight-talking. But he sometimes spoke his mind without considering the repercussions of what he said. This had first been apparent in the "loss of fastball" controversy in '38, and it would get Feller into other controversies as his career advanced, sometimes with the press, sometimes with the fans, and sometimes with his teammates.

The undercurrent of resentment about Feller's success was there, but it was a minor factor at this point, and would pale in comparison to the chaos that disrupted the Indians clubhouse in 1940.

A posed re-enactment of a young Bob Feller signing his first professional contract with the actual bargaining partners, Cy Slapnicka (left) and his father (right), 1937. (The Sporting News)

Feller greets his sister and his parents in Cleveland before a 4-2 win over the Athletics, July 26, 1938. (National Baseball Hall of Fame Library, Cooperstown, NY)

An ace in his prime.
(National Baseball Hall
of Fame Library,
Cooperstown, NY)

Feller with manager Ossie Vitt (left) in a rare friendly moment, 1939.
(Transcendental Graphics)

A star volunteers: Feller being sworn in, December 8, 1941. (National Baseball Hall of Fame Library, Cooperstown, NY)

Chief Specialist Feller, 1943. (National Baseball Hall of Fame Library, Cooperstown, NY)

The USS Alabama, one of Feller's homes away from home during the war.

Back at home and waiting to resume his career: Feller warms up as player/coach at the Great Lakes Naval Training Center, 1945. (National Baseball Hall of Fame Library, Cooperstown, NY)

Feller deals to Joe DiMaggio during his no-hitter against the Yankees, April 30, 1946. (Transcendental Graphics)

Feller poses with his barnstorming acquaintance turned teammate, the great Satchel Paige, 1948. (Transcendental Graphics)

Laying it down: Feller at the plate against the Yankees, 1951. (National Baseball Hall of Fame Library, Cooperstown, NY)

Bob Feller and Larry Doby, 1954 (Transcendental Graphics)

The Tribe's four aces in 1956, with their manager (left to right): Bob Lemon, Feller, Mike Garcia, Herb Score, and manager Al Lopez. (Transcendental Graphics)

Feller surveys the crowd that turned out in Van Meter for Bob Feller Day. (The Sporting News.)

Calling it quits: Feller hangs up his number 19 just days after Christmas, 1956. (National Baseball Hall of Fame Library, Cooperstown, NY)

Bob with his first wife, Virginia, and their three sons, pondering his induction into the Baseball Hall of Fame, 1962. (Transcendental Graphics)

7

The Crybabies

What happened here, I think, is something that any schoolteacher can relate to. Sometimes a class just gets away from you.

—Bill James, on Ossie Vitt, in *The Bill James Guide to Baseball Managers*, p. 106

The Indians were again consensus contenders for the 1940 American League pennant. Many observers felt the Yankees were due for a slump, with the Red Sox, Tigers, and Indians all looking to knock them off their pedestal. The main off-season change was the acquisition of outfielder Beau Bell from Detroit, traded for Bruce Campbell. Bob Feller, of course, would be awesome if he merely maintained his current level of performance, and unbeatable if he actually managed to improve. Mel Harder's arm seemed sound, and anything that Johnny Allen could contribute could only be a plus. Big things were expected from Al Smith, a new left-hander promoted from the minor leagues.

On the offensive side of the roster, Hal Trosky was still in his prime, and both Ken Keltner and Jeff Heath were expected to continue improving. Lou Boudreau and Ray Mack promised defensive stability in the middle infield, something the Tribe lacked in previous seasons, and both were expected to improve offensively with experience. Catcher Rollie Hemsley announced that he hadn't had a drink for the entire 1939 season, thanks to the blessings of Alcoholics Anonymous.

The Indians had moved their spring training from New Orleans to Ft. Myers, Florida, a better facility and symbolic of a fresh start. The season began with great optimism; even Ossie Vitt seemed in a better mood, spring holdouts from Frankie Pytlak and Allen notwithstanding. The general consensus was that the Tribe didn't have the huge offensive firepower of past teams, but was greatly improved defensively and by the pitching staff. In a preseason preview, the Associated Press called Feller the best pitcher in baseball and the key to Cleveland's season.

Bob's dreams had come true. He was now a clearly established star player, not merely a boy wonder. His 1940 contract was for $40,000, superstar money. He set aside about half the money to build his family a new house back on the farm in Van Meter. A strong brick structure, it was equipped with all the amenities. Running water and electricity, still not terribly common in rural areas of Iowa, were installed, though they weren't considered huge luxuries by the Fellers. On the other hand, the air-conditioning system *was* a luxury, and the basement recreation room, equipped with a pool table, was a rare delight designed especially for Bill Feller. The handsome house was built on the Feller farmstead right up close to the gravel road running by their property. Some local townsfolk felt that the location had been picked deliberately so that no one could miss the house, a form of braggadocio and a final "we told you so" to the doubters who'd told Bill Feller he was crazy during Bob's formative years. The Fellers simply said that the location had been picked because it was the most convenient place to lay a new foundation. Indeed, the house was actually farther away from the road than the main barn was.

As usual in the Vitt years, Feller was used sparingly in the spring of 1940, seeing only limited action in the traditional exhibition series against the Giants; the series had been kept despite the shift in spring training venue. Feller was named Opening Day starter once again, and the season was to begin April 16th in Chicago. To say that the season got off to a promising start would be an understatement.

The weather was cold in Comiskey Park, even cooler than typical for a mid-April day, hovering around 40 degrees. The wind was blowing in from center field, adding to the discomfort, and the crowd was on the sparse side for Opening Day, rated at just over 14,000. Bill, Lena, and Marguerite had traveled from Van Meter to take in the first game of the season, and they saw Bob pitch a historic game. The combination of the cold weather and Feller's blistering heat was more than the White Sox hitters could handle. Although the Indians managed themselves to score just one run, it was enough, as Feller shut down the White Sox without a hit. It was the first, and so far only, Opening Day no-hitter in the history of Major League baseball.

The cold weather made it hard to grip the curve that day, so Feller used his fastball "almost exclusively."[1] He felt it wasn't one of his best games in terms of pure stuff. He'd had trouble getting loose in the frigid conditions and never felt that comfortable on the mound. He struck out "just" eight men. He walked five, including the bases loaded in the second inning. "I've seen Bob better," said Rollie Hemsley, "but he was plenty good enough."[2]

Feller wouldn't have gotten the no-hitter were it not for strong defensive support. Ben Chapman made a difficult running catch on a long outfield drive by Taffy Wright in the fourth inning. A terrific play by second baseman Ray Mack saved a hit in the eighth inning. Feller attributed his first no-hitter to a combination of luck, cold weather, and the strong assistance of his fielders. Tribe fans felt the Opening Day masterpiece was a good omen for the rest of the season: it was certainly the prototype of how Vitt and Slapnicka wanted to win games with pitching, defense, and timely hitting. The game took on a special meaning for one Cleveland fan, eight-year-old Paul Hauschulz, Jr., of Canton, Ohio. Hospitalized with a mastoid infection and spiral meningitis, young Paul improved greatly while listening to the contest via radio. Feller dropped in to visit the youngster on April 18th.[3] Hospital visits with ailing children were a baseball tradition, one Feller participated in frequently, though usually without much publicity.

Things went fairly well early in the season. The Tribe was welcomed home the evening of April 18th by a cheering train station crowd, Cleveland mayor Harold Burton personally present to congratulate Feller on his achievement.[4] Although Feller was knocked out of the box in the third inning by the Tigers in his second start, he won his third start on April 25th, a reprise against the White Sox, by a 3–1 score. A 4–0 shutout against the Yankees on May 9th in New York was especially sweet. By this time, the struggling New Yorkers were in the second division, while the Red Sox, Indians and Tigers battled at the top, no team able to gain much traction at the expense of the other.

Feller was in fine form as the spring progressed. Milnar, newcomer Smith, Harder, and Allen were all pitching well. Youngsters Boudreau and Mack were living up to expectations. But Jeff Heath was struggling, and fellow outfielders Beau Bell and Ben Chapman were showing signs of age. Although Cleveland was contending, the Indians failed to run away with the league, and Ossie Vitt quickly returned to his old habits. If anything, he was worse than in the past two seasons, cursing in the dugout, sarcastically insulting players in front of the entire team, fiddling with lineups constantly (after pledging not to do so in spring training), and, in the opinion of some Tribesmen, making poor in-game decisions.

On May 24th, Feller beat the St. Louis Browns for his sixth victory, outdueling Elden Auker in the first night game ever played in that city. He hit his first career home run in that contest, clearing the right field fence in Sportsman's Park by a tiny margin. His next start, May 29th against the Tigers, was another victory, putting him at 7–2 on the season. By June 1st, the Indians were 23–14 and in second place.

The Indians were winning. But the tension in the clubhouse was almost unbearable.

On a road trip to Boston, the situation spun out of control. Feller had a rough day on June 11th, losing to the Red Sox 9–2. While Feller was struggling on the mound, Vitt complained to the rest of the team in the dugout. "There's my star out there, the great Feller," he groused. "How can I win a pennant with him? Look at him. He's supposed to be my ace."[5] Feller's no-hitter and strong pitching throughout the spring were apparently forgotten. Vitt had a bad habit of magnifying a player's failures and ignoring his successes; one bad day from a good player was enough to trigger a torrent of insults. Feller apparently heard Vitt's tirade from the mound. He said nothing, but Steve O'Neill had never acted that way.

On June 12th, Vitt asked Mel Harder, a fine human being and probably the most popular player in the clubhouse, "When are you going to start earning your salary? It's about time you won one, the money you're getting."[6] Picking on Mel Harder was a great way to get the rest of the players to hate you, but Vitt didn't need the help. They already despised him.

By the end of the road trip, most of the players had had enough. Meeting in the smoking lounge on the train back to Cleveland, they came up with a plan of action. The ringleader was possibly Hal Trosky, but Allen, Harder, Hemsley, and Milnar were also involved . . . as was Bob Feller. Boudreau and Mack weren't involved, being deliberately excluded from the plot because they were rookies, and the veterans didn't want to hurt their careers should the plot go sour. Roy Weatherly knew about the conspiracy, but didn't get directly involved. On June 13th, arriving home from the road trip, Mel Harder asked for a meeting with Alva Bradley, and got one.

Harder, Feller, and ten other players appeared in Bradley's office and listed their grievances against Vitt's tyranny, with Harder and Allen the main spokesmen. Trosky wasn't present; he'd gone back home to Iowa to attend the funeral of his mother, who'd died suddenly. Harder, as the clubhouse leader, took the point, explaining the general gist of the situation, then turning to the other players for supporting evidence. The group told Bradley that they thought they could win a pennant, but that a new manager was needed. They complained that Vitt was sarcastic, unstable, and unpredictable. He flew into rages at the slightest pretext, often in the middle of a game. He held grudges. He insulted players in front of other players. He badmouthed his own men to the press. "He tears us down to other teams," complained one Tribesman.[7] It was this last complaint that, according to Feller, was the final blow that set off the revolt.[8]

Alva Bradley was not a dumb man; he had to know the truth of the situation. His own GM and trusted baseball aide, Cy Slapnicka, had grown to hate Vitt. But Bradley also knew that, if word ever got out about this clubhouse rebellion, all hell would break loose. Bradley told his men to be patient, and not to speak a word of the situation to anyone. "You're only 1¹/₂ games behind Boston in first place. Worse tangles than this have been straightened out," he told them. "If this story ever gets out, you'll be ridiculed the rest of your life."⁹

The Indians returned to the clubhouse with some feeling of relief, but Bradley's prediction came true. Gordon Cobbledick of the *Plain Dealer* had been tipped off by someone. Cobbledick never revealed his source; some speculated that it was Rollie Hemsley, but this was never proven, and those who know, including Feller, won't say. An accurate account of the meeting appeared in the next day's paper. All the Cleveland beat writers, Cobbledick, Lewis, Gibbons, and McAuley, were aware of trouble in the clubhouse and had been dropping hints in their columns, but this revolt went beyond standard player carping. It was the biggest news in Cleveland that day, spread across the *Plain Dealer*'s front page, and receiving equal treatment in the other papers the next day. It shared space with the fall of Paris and the conquest of France by the armies of Adolf Hitler.

Firestorm would be too mild a term to describe what happened next. Associated Press and UPI stories describing the fiasco spread the news across the country. The situation in the clubhouse, if it was tense and nearly unbearable before, became impossible. It was clear that Vitt had lost all authority over his men, but firing him, now that the story was public, was politically unwise. The decision to hire and fire managers belonged to the front office, not the players; to dump Vitt under these circumstances would make the situation even worse, at least from Bradley and Slapnicka's perspective. On June 16th, the complaining players (at Bradley's insistence) issued a statement rescinding their criticisms of Vitt: "We the undersigned publicly desire to withdraw all statements referring to the resignation of Oscar Vitt. We feel this action is for the betterment of the Cleveland Baseball Club."¹⁰ But it was too late.

It was hard to feel sorry for a grouch like Ossie Vitt, but his situation was untenable. He met with Alva Bradley and had his authority as manager confirmed. "Mr. Bradley told me I'm still the manager of this team," he told his rebellious retinue. "I still am."[11] Vitt attempted to joke with reporters about the problems, but admitted that he was emotionally bruised by the rebellion. The fact that young stars like Feller and Keltner, whom Vitt had worked with closely and whose success he felt partially responsible for, were involved was very hurtful. "The greatest kid in the world," Vitt had said of Feller. "Like a son to me. That's what he is."[12]

By this point, Feller did not reciprocate Vitt's alleged warm feeling. Feller still had a reputation for being reserved, but his growing self-confidence manifested itself as an increased willingness to speak his mind, in succinct and not always diplomatic terms, when asked for his opinion. *Cleveland News* writer Ed McAuley asked Feller point blank if he truly disliked Vitt, or if he was just going along with the older players. "I hate his guts," Feller replied directly, "and I don't care who knows it."[13] Feller told other reporters that "Oscar makes us nervous. I wouldn't want to play for him next year."[14] The most intriguing thing about the latter comment was that it occurred *after* the rest of the team had gone silent on the matter. The clubhouse situation settled into what Feller called "an armed truce," neither side willing to give in on the particulars, but aware that the situation could not be resolved immediately.

The fans were unmerciful; taunts of "Crybabies" were but the mildest of insults hurled at the Indians, both at home and on the road. Vitt was cheered, the rest of the team jeered. Sportswriters in opposing cities were no more humane than the fans. Shirley Povich of the *Washington Post* wrote that the Indians were a club of "prima-donnas," and ridiculed Bradley's business acumen. More than one writer pointed out that Vitt had a better record than Cleveland's previous "nice guy" managers like Steve O'Neill and Walter Johnson, and implied that the club simply lacked the guts to succeed.

If the revolution accomplished one thing, it did limit Vitt's sarcasm. He became silent much of the time, talking with his players only when necessary. The insults and putdowns no longer flowed like a flash flood down a mountain. But he also became something of an automaton in the dugout, to the point where the veteran players eventually developed their own sets of signs, running the game without input from Vitt, ignoring his orders when they didn't jibe with what they felt were appropriate. Amazingly, despite all the insults and catcalls and clubhouse tension, the Indians actually played better baseball after the aborted revolution than before. On June 20th, Feller defeated the Senators by a 12–1 score, winning his tenth game of the season and pushing the Indians into first place past the Red Sox. The club won 19 of 27 games after the revolt. Alva Bradley publicly predicted the club would win the pennant.

Feller won his 12th game of the year on June 29th in Chicago, beating the White Sox 7–2 with 11 strikeouts to his credit, pitching in front of an extremely hostile Comiskey Park crowd. Feller, along with teammates Keltner, Milnar, Hemsley, Mack, and Boudreau, was named to the American League All-Star team the next day, making the third consecutive year that Feller was so honored. His 13th victory came at the expense of the St. Louis Browns on July 3d.

The Indians were one game ahead of the Tigers when they met for a July 4th doubleheader. Feller didn't pitch, but the game was notable for the abuse the crowd in excess of 50,000 sent the way of the Tribe, diapers and baby bottles being thrown onto the field at various times. It also showed the extent to which Ossie Vitt had lost control of his club. At one point in the first contest, Vitt called in Johnny Allen for a relief appearance, only to be talked out of the move by Hal Trosky, who suggested that Allen be saved for the second game. Trosky's strategy made sense. The trouble was, Allen had already arrived on the mound after warming up in the bullpen. He walked jauntily back to the dugout, embarrassing the Cleveland manager.

Feller lost a 3–1 duel to Chicago's Ted Lyons on July 7th, Lyons at age 39 being almost twice as old as Bob. This put Feller's record at 13–5 going into the All-Star Break, the Indians themselves holding first place with a 45–29 record. Feller appeared in the Midsummer Classic two days later in St. Louis, pitching two innings and allowing one run in a 4–0 National League victory. His next regular start, on July 12th against the Athletics, nearly resulted in another no-hitter. He fanned 13 in outdueling Philadelphia rookie

Johnny Babich in a 1–0 contest, but a single off a fastball in the eighth inning by Dick Seibert made the game a one-hitter. Catcher Hemsley attributed Seibert's hit to the fact that a blister on Feller's pitching hand made it hard for him to throw his curveball late in the game. By the eighth inning, Hemsley was calling for nothing but fastballs, and Seibert hit one.[15] This fourth one-hitter was the 71st victory of Feller's professional life.

Although Feller was pitching well, things started to go badly for the club as a whole in the second half. Ossie Vitt was forced to give variations on the "I won't quit" and "I'm still in charge" speeches to the press at each stop on road trips. The club was swept in Washington by the woeful Senators in mid-July; at one point in the series, Vitt appeared "panicked" when trying to decide on a pitching change.[16] Feller threw 13 innings against the Yankees in New York on July 17th, only to lose by a 4–3 score. The Tribe was swept in three games by the Yankees, but managed to win three in Boston to finish the road trip. Their record was now 51–35.

On July 29th, Vitt named Hal Trosky team captain, granting official recognition of his leadership role in the clubhouse, though Vitt was apparently unaware of the extent to which Trosky and the other team veterans were ignoring him. Feller beat the Red Sox the next day with a strong eight-strikeout performance.

The Indians and Tigers continued their battle over first place into early August. The Yankees came to Cleveland in a key series to begin the month, and Feller defeated them by a 3–1 score on August 4th, winning his 18th game. It was an unusual contest, as Feller's curve was very weak that day. Relying entirely on his fastball, Bob held the Yanks to one run on five hits, but struck out only one batter, the lowest strikeout starting appearance of his career to this point. Vitt told the assembled press after the game that he was confident that the Tribe would win the pennant, provided they made a final move to improve the offense. "Give us one dependable hitter and we'll walk in from here," he said.[17]

With the Tigers and Indians slated to meet 11 times in August and September, the race looked like a classic. And it was. The Indians swept the Tigers in a brief two-game set on August 12–13, pushing back into sole possession of first place. The rebellion against Vitt was still an issue. At one point, Tigers pitcher Bobo (Buck) Newsom teased Feller about the situation, taunting him with a "Why, ain't you fired Vitt recently?" Feller's reply was "He's acting alright for a change. But he'll probably be worse than ever someday."[18] Although most people expected the clubhouse problems would hurt the Indians' chances, it actually seemed to have a galvanizing effect on the morale of the club by pitting the players against two different enemies. Although Vitt's sarcasm was greatly reduced (he still argued with Jeff Heath on occasion), the team was still united against their manager. They were also united against the taunters, in Cleveland and on the road. Baseball author Bill James theorizes that the rebellion and the public reaction against it "almost certainly" worked to Cleveland's advantage. "If any team had something to play for, this team had."[19] Feller confirms this theory. "The revolt helped us in the pennant race," he told me. "We were united against Ossie."[20]

Although many of Vitt's in-game signals were being ignored by the club, he still made the lineup and starting pitching decisions. One controversy erupted in late August, when Senators owner Clark Griffith requested that Feller be held out of a scheduled start in New York in order to pitch a Sunday game in Washington. Griffith wanted the extra gate receipts that a Feller start would bring. This wouldn't be the only time he tried to manipulate an extra appearance out of the Cleveland ace. Vitt refused to alter his pitching rotation, and Feller took his regular turn that Saturday, losing to the Yankees by a 3–2 score.

By August 22d, the Indians had pushed their lead over the Tigers to five games. The Tigers got hot at this point, while the Indians lost several games to the surging Yankees and the annoyingly competitive Senators. Vitt was still concerned about the need for another bat, but Slapnicka was either unable or unwilling to make a trade acquisition, and wouldn't purchase a player from the minor leagues. Some believed that Slap was intentionally refusing to find another hitter in order to sabotage Vitt. This seems unlikely, as Slapnicka wanted a pennant as much as anyone. He wasn't the type to consciously undermine the team he himself had put together, though his subconscious motivations were possibly another matter.

On August 30th, Feller defeated the White Sox by a 4–2 margin, struggling with his curveball, but using his heater to fan 11 Chicagoans. It was his 23d victory of the season, and pushed the Tribe to a 73–50 record, 2.5 games ahead of the Tigers. A double-header sweep by the Browns on Labor Day could have been a disaster, but Detroit lost their own double-dip to the White Sox. On September 4th, the Tribe and the Tigers met for a critical set in Detroit. Feller was blasted in game one, losing to the Tigers by a 7–2 score. More Tiger victories on the 5th and 6th moved Detroit to within one game of the leaders. The Yankees were now in third place, one game behind. Feller pitched again on the 8th against the White Sox, winning a 5–4 contest. The Tigers, meanwhile, won their fourth game in a row, and were now one half game behind the Indians.

On September 9th, the Indians lost to the White Sox, putting the Tigers in first place. With the hitting attack in a funk and the starting pitching struggling, Vitt decided to use Feller on short rest for the rest of the season.

His next start was on September 11th, as part of a doubleheader in Cleveland against the Yankees. Feller pitched well, but was undone by lack of hitting support, losing the game 3–1 and dropping his record to 24–9. The Tribe regained first place with a double-header sweep of the Athletics on September 15th, Feller triumphing in the first game with a 5–0 shutout. This was another near-perfect contest. Not only were Bob's curveball and fastball working that day, but his command was excellent as well. He gave up just two hits, one a bloop outfield shot and one an infield single, while striking out seven and walking none. He started again three days later in the 18th, holding the Senators to a single run on five hits in a 2–1 win. After the game, Feller told both reporters and Vitt that he was physically tired, but was willing to start and relieve for the rest of the season if it were in the best interests of the team.

Vitt took Feller up on the offer on September 20th, in a critical game in Detroit. Mel Harder had things well in hand, taking a 4–1 lead into the eighth inning. But a walk and a bloop single apparently convinced Vitt that Harder was fading. He called in Feller to relieve him. It was a controversial decision. On the one hand, Feller had offered to pitch relief. On the other hand, his arm was tired, and he'd told Vitt that before the game. The move backfired, as Feller gave up the tying run. The contest was eventually lost 6–5, Feller taking the loss. The game put the Tigers in first place.

Vitt was blasted in the press, and in the clubhouse, for his decision to pull Harder. A 6–0 loss to Detroit the next day didn't help matters, as it put the Tigers two games ahead. Desperately, the Indians turned to Feller again on the 22d, sending him out to start the Sunday game against the Tigers and try to stem the tide. Exhausted, Feller pitched his heart out without his best stuff, getting knocked for five runs in nine innings, but winning the game by a 10–5 score, and putting the Tribe back to within a game of the lead. He had thrown 27 innings in eight days.

On the 24th, the Indians lost to the Browns 7–2, putting them 1.5 games behind the idle Tigers. A victory against St. Louis on the 25th kept them in the race, but the Tigers swept a doubleheader against the White Sox, pushing their lead to two games over the Indians with three to play. The pennant would be decided in the last three games of the season, all between the Tigers and the Tribe in Cleveland.

Feller took the mound on September 27th, the biggest game of his life to that point. He'd had four days of rest and felt much better physically. Expecting to lose the game, the Tigers decided to use a rookie, Floyd Giebell, and preserve their best pitchers for the final two contests. The game was almost a debacle from the start, as riotous Indians fans pelted the Tigers with fruit and other miscellaneous debris, nearly resulting in a forfeit. Vitt himself had to get on the public address system to convince the fans to stop tossing objects on the field. Feller had good stuff that day, though his control was off and he had to pitch his way out of several jams after eight walks. Yielding just three hits, Feller held the Tigers to only two runs, on a short home run by Rudy York.

But it was the unknown Floyd Giebell, not superstar Bob Feller, who had his career day. Giebell threw a shutout, mixing his curveball and mediocre fastball like a master, winning the game by a 2–0 score and clinching the pennant for the Tigers. Giebell would never win another Major League game, but his place in history was secure. No one blamed Feller for the loss; it was Cleveland's poor hitting that had finally done them in. The Indians won the last two games of the season to finish 89–65, one game behind the Tigers.

The year 1940 was another statistical triumph for Bob Feller. He led the league with a 2.61 ERA, with 27 wins, with 320.1 innings pitched, and with 261 strikeouts. He led in most strikeouts per nine innings, and with fewest hits allowed per nine innings. He led in games started, complete games, and shutouts. He'd walked 118 men, but this was 24 fewer than in 1939, despite the fact that he threw more innings. Feller finished second in league MVP voting, and would certainly have won the Cy Young Award for the second straight year had it existed. The only regular starting pitcher in the American League younger than Feller was Detroit's 19-year-old Hal Newhouser, with whom Feller would eventually form an intense rivalry.

Feller was named "1940 Player of the Year" by the Baseball Writer's Association of America. A UPI article given national distribution that October credited his development into the game's best pitcher to the addition of poise and control to his blazing fastball. As in '39, direct comparisons were drawn between Feller and the great pitchers of the past, Johnson, Alexander, and Mathewson. But despite these personal honors, Feller still felt that the season was a bitter disappointment. Winning the pennant was the goal, but the Indians had finished a single game short.

No one was more disappointed, though, than Ossie Vitt. At the end of the last game, he went around the clubhouse and silently shook each player's hand. It was open knowledge that Vitt would be fired at the end of the season, even if the Indians had won the pennant and the World Series. Alva Bradley had spent much of the summer "interviewing" players about the clubhouse troubles, and was convinced that their complaints against Vitt were, for the most part, valid. At one point in later years, Bradley admitted to a reporter that he should have fired Vitt before the situation had gotten so out of hand.

In his three years at the Tribe helm, Ossie Vitt posted a 462–262 record, a .570 winning percentage. He never managed in the Major Leagues again.

8

Another Nice Guy

Diplomats are only useful in fair weather. As soon as it
rains, they drown in every drop.

—Charles de Gaulle

Bob Feller was physically and emotionally exhausted by the
end of the 1940 season. He decided to pass up a fall barnstorming tour, returning home to Iowa instead in order to
relax and spend time with his family. For the fifth consecutive season, Van Meter held a homecoming celebration for
its (only) famous son. Governor Wilson and Cy Slapnicka gave
speeches to the estimated crowd of 10,000, many of whom then
went to the Feller farm to take a glance at the new house. The house
itself was becoming a huge tourist attraction, drawing interest na-
tionally. The bible of baseball, *The Sporting News*, included a large
article with several pictures describing the home and its many
amenities in the December 19th issue.

Spending time with the family was becoming a major priority,
since there might not be much time left for Bill Feller, who was very
ill. The brain tumor originally diagnosed back in 1938 was slowly
growing, and there was little that could be done to remedy the situation. Bill was gradually losing his hearing and was frequently as-
saulted by horrendous headaches. The patriarch took some
comfort in his son's success. The beautiful new English brick home
gracing the Feller farmstead was the outward manifestation of the
faith he'd shown in Bob's abilities. His son was an established superstar, now supremely confident in his own talent. The boy

who'd been a self-described bumpkin four years previous was now a man, mature emotionally and professionally, and increasingly sophisticated as a businessman. Bob could take care of himself now, and the family, once Bill passed on.

The winter of 1940 was spent hunting, shooting, and playing billiards in the basement of the new house. The biggest interruption was an October trip back to Cleveland: Bob needed to register for the military draft. Europe was embroiled in war. France had collapsed, and much of the country was occupied by the Nazis; the rest was controlled by the collaborationist Vichy government. Great Britain held fast against the onslaught of Hitler's Luftwaffe and U-boats, but obviously could not defeat Germany by herself. Stalin's Soviet Union was an enigma. Tensions between the United States and Japan over control of the Pacific and the resources of East Asia were growing. The United States was gradually coming to the realization that it would eventually be drawn into the war, one way or another. The draft had been reinstituted, and military production was ramping up. Franklin Roosevelt stood for reelection that November, winning an unprecedented third term to office.

Bob was classified 3-C by the Cleveland draft board, physically able to serve, but deferred from military service because he was the sole support of his family, his father being terminally ill and unable to work. Feller didn't expect war to break out immediately, but vowed to himself that he would enlist right away if it did, draft deferment or not. A joke that made the rounds among journalists at this time was that Feller should have been declared 4-F rather than 3-C, since he was the sole support of the Cleveland Indians.[1]

In mid-November, Alva Bradley announced what everyone already knew: Ossie Vitt would not return as the manager in 1941. The new field general was to be Roger Peckinpaugh, a long-time coach and former Major League manager . . . with the Indians. Peck had managed the Tribe from 1928 to midway through the 1933 season. He'd been fired in '33 because of concerns that the club was underachieving, and that his laid-back manner didn't do enough to motivate the team. He was too nice, in other words.

Peckinpaugh was a curious choice to replace Vitt. The expectation, among both players and press, was that coach Luke Sewell would be named as the new manager. But Bradley was apparently concerned that Sewell would be unfairly tarred with the events of 1940; he didn't want rumors spread that his new manager had campaigned for the job or worked to undermine his predecessor. It was unfair to Sewell, who had stayed out of the Vitt controversy as much as possible, but Bradley needed to make it clear that the choice of manager belonged to him and Slapnicka, not the players. Sewell was retained as a coach under Peckinpaugh, but would be hired to manage the St. Louis Browns later in '41. Although Bradley denied it publicly, it was clear that Peckinpaugh had been chosen because his personality was radically different than Vitt's. Bringing in a strict disciplinarian had failed, so Bradley went back to the softer approach. The decision would prove unfortunate. In retrospect, the problem with Vitt was not so much that he was a disciplinarian, but rather that he was temperamentally incapable of managing a Major League club without belittling his players. In swinging from O'Neill to Vitt to Peckinpaugh, Indians management went from one extreme, to another, then back to the previous extreme. They needed to find a middle ground, someone that could be focused and strict when needed, but without being unnecessarily nasty. Roger Peckinpaugh was a good baseball man, but he was not this middle ground.

There were other changes as well. Slapnicka traded Frankie Pytlak, disgruntled for several years over his lack of playing time, Sammy Hale, and Joe Dobson to the Boston Red Sox, receiving outfielder Gee (Gerald) Walker, catcher Gene Desautels, and pitcher Jim Bagby in return. Slapnicka also brought in several new and promising players from the farm system, including catcher Jim Hegan, outfielder Soup Campbell, and infielder Bob Lemon.

Spring training began with great optimism. The Indians had fallen only a game short in 1940, and looked stronger going into the season on paper than when they'd finished it. Of the regular infielders, Hal Trosky was at his peak at age 28, while Ray Mack (24), Lou Boudreau (23), and Ken Keltner (24) were all young and improving. The Tribe had the best defensive infield in the American League, and all four members were dangerous with the bat. In the outfield, Jeff Heath and Roy Weatherly were both 26. Both were inconsistent, but had hit well in past seasons. Newly acquired Gee Walker would take over in left field; at 33, he was on the downside of his career, but had hit .294 in 1940. Rollie Hemsley, now dry for two seasons, would handle catching duties once again.

The pitching staff looked little different. Feller, of course, was the ace. Lefties Al Smith and Al Milnar had combined for 33 wins in '40. On the other hand, Slapnicka had given up on the sore-armed and aging Johnny Allen, selling him to St. Louis for the waiver price. Mel Harder had won 12 games in '40, but his arm was wearing down, and counting on him for 200 innings was risky. The sale of Allen and the decline of Harder changed the complexion of the staff, but the Indians were prepared for this. Jim Bagby would provide a solid replacement for Allen, and promising rookies like Mike Naymick and Steve Gromek could supplement Harder. Former Tribesman Earl Whitehill was brought in as a new pitching coach. The Indians were confident that they would be in the thick of things again, and most experts agreed, predicting a hard-fought race between the Tribe, the Tigers, the Red Sox, and, as always, the Yankees.

While at spring training in Fort Myers, Feller began a romance with Virginia Winther, a student at nearby Rollins College. An art student with a taste for books, Winther knew nothing about baseball, a fact which Bob found "a relief."[2] It meant that she was free to be herself, and honest in her interest in him. She also came from a wealthy Chicago family; her father was an engineer, and had invented the form of air conditioning used on Pullman railroad cars. She wasn't looking for a ballplayer for the excitement, fame, or fortune. Bob and Virginia managed to keep their romance a secret from the press for some time, which was no easy feat considering that gossip about Bob's love life was rampant. Said love life was actually very tame, to the point that newspapers greatly exaggerated, or in some cases outright created, all-American romances for Feller. In reality, for all his fame, Feller tried to keep his family life as private as possible. The extent to which he succeeded in this endeavor would only be revealed several decades later.

Spring training went very well. The poisonous clubhouse atmosphere under Vitt was a thing of the past, Peckinpaugh putting his team at ease with his patient, teaching-style manner. With Ossie Vitt off his back, Jeff Heath "pledged himself to a year of unceasing effort."[3] Mack and Bourdeau were playing well defensively, and Ken Keltner showed signs of breaking out of the hitting doldrums that had limited his production in '40. The Tribe made quick work of the New York Giants in their exhibition series, posting a 9–3 record as the teams moved north on tour. Everything looked in order for a pennant along the Cuyahoga.

Feller opened the season against the White Sox in Cleveland, but lost the contest by a 4–3 score. After the game, a rumor started that Feller had been tipping his pitches. White Sox third base coach Mule Haas allegedly held the secret about whether Feller was going to throw a fastball or curve, then would pass this information along to his hitters. It was further rumored that the Tigers had picked up the secret last year, manager Del Baker being especially skilled at this. It was supposedly the reason they'd hit Feller well in several games. Feller and Peckinpaugh looked over his delivery, and traced the problem to an unconscious curling of his free fingers "farther under the ball when he threw his curve than was the case when he threw the fast ball."[4] This was corrected easily enough, but the incident did not pass without controversy.

Asked by an AP reporter after the Chicago game about whether he was tipping his pitches, Feller replied, "If it's true it's pretty dangerous for the hitter. Somebody might get hurt if the coach guesses wrong and the batter gets an inside fast ball instead of the curve he is expecting. They'll be picking baseballs out of their ears." The press picked up the latter part of the statement, interpreting it as a threat from Feller that he would brush back anyone he suspected of being tipped off. Needless to say, this did not go over well in Detroit. Feller was wild enough as is. He could kill someone if he deliberately threw at him. Tigers star Hank Greenberg, for one, refused to take signs from Baker about what Feller was going to throw. "If Baker told me a curve was coming up and he was wrong—if it was really a fastball—I could be in big trouble . . . if I hung in there expecting it to break, but it was really a fastball and didn't break, I could get killed."[5]

Although Tigers manager Baker understood the context of Feller's quote and assured reporters that he knew no harm was meant, there was still some grumbling. Feller seemed annoyed by the episode, especially when someone asked if he should apologize. "Why should I explain or apologize to anyone about a matter in which I'm entirely innocent?" he asked.[6] The controversy passed quickly, *The Sporting News* taking the lead in defending Feller. The entire incident was another example of Feller's tendency to speak honestly, but without considering the way his words could be interpreted.

The Indians got off to a good start, holding first place through part of April, all of May, and early June. Feller was pitching well, at one point throwing 30 consecutive scoreless innings. The club was relaxed. Jeff Heath was red hot, hitting well over .300 with outstanding power production. Weatherly and Walker's bats heated up as the weather warmed. One trouble sign was the infield, where Ray Mack and Lou Boudreau were playing well defensively, but not hitting much. Smith and Bagby were pitching well in rotation behind Feller, but Mel Harder was struggling with a sore arm, and Al Milnar was erratic.

Bob Feller was now enjoying some of the more unusual trappings of superstardom. On June 2d, one Joseph C. Motto, a Cleveland sculptor, made a cast of Feller's right arm, in order to preserve it in bust form "for the ages" at the Hall of Fame. An AP wire photo and caption of the casting ran in many papers across the nation the next day. Feller also made a somewhat awkward radio appearance, a romantic skit with Dinah Shore on her national show. The skit involved a tryst between Bob and Dinah. "We were supposed to be sparking on the farm," recalled Feller. "'Oh, Bobby,' cooed Dinah, 'it's so nice to have your arms around me. But why don't you take off your pitcher's glove?'" This was the punchline in the love scene.[7]

A more baseball-oriented stunt took place in Chicago. A lot of people wanted to know exactly how fast Feller threw the ball, though there was no easy or convenient way to test this given the technology of the time. The general consensus was that Feller didn't throw quite as hard as he did when he first reached the Majors, though his fastball was still regarded as the best in baseball. Veteran baseball man and Feller friend Lew Fonseca devised a method to estimate Feller's velocity. Feller would throw a ball through a target, while at the same time a man on a motorcycle would drive by, thus giving a basis for comparison. The test was clever, although flawed; Feller wound up and released the pitch a split-second too late, giving the motorcycle a jump on the ball. The ball still beat the cycle, going 86 mph, to the target. Calculations showed the ball traveling at 104 mph.[8]

Did Bob Feller really throw 104 mph, in street clothes, on a flat surface, without warming up? It seems hard to believe; even in game conditions, very few pitchers have exceeded 100 mph on modern radar guns. If one accepts the 104 mph figure under these conditions, how hard must Feller have thrown at his best in an actual game? 105? 107? The technology in the motorcycle test was too primitive for us to draw any accurate conclusions, though more advanced, and accurate, tests of Feller's velocity would be devised later. The important point is that Feller's velocity was so good that, when the 104 mph figure was released, no one doubted that it *could* be accurate. He clearly had the best fastball of his era, and possibly the best of all time, although some who'd seen Walter Johnson in his prime disputed that.

While the Tribe had entered June in the thick of the pennant chase, by the end of the month things were going sour. Roy Weatherly had been knocked in the head by a pitch and was out of action. Mel Harder's sore arm finally forced him to the sidelines. More seriously, Hal Trosky, the most consistent hitter on the team and the clubhouse leader, was bothered by severe migraine headaches, which kept him on the bench much of the time and eventually forced his retirement. From May 26th through June 6th, Cleveland won just three games, all of them started by Feller. Bob had 15 victories by the end of June, but the rest of the team was fading. Their pennant hopes went with them.

On June 25th, the surging Yankees, led by the amazing Joe DiMaggio in the midst of his historic 56-game hitting streak, moved into first place.

Bob Feller had 16 victories to his credit, and was once again named to the All-Star Game, despite a late June/early July slump that saw him lose three games in a row. For the first time, Feller was the starting pitcher, and he put on a great show, throwing three strong innings, fanning four, and allowing only one hit. But the star of the game was Ted Williams, who hit a three-run homer off Claude Passeau to win the game for the American Leaguers in the ninth inning.

The second half was miserable in Cleveland. The team dropped to second place, then third, then fourth, as the Yankees ran away from the league. One exciting moment occurred on July 17th, when Joe DiMaggio was finally held hitless by a combination of Al Smith's screwball and Ken Keltner's defensive prowess at third base. This stopped his streak at 56, a record unbroken to this day. By the end of July, the Indians were clearly out of the race, the only drama revolving around whether they could finish over .500. Feller won his 20th game on August 3d, and there was hope that he could win 30 games. But the collapse of Cleveland's offense in the second half soon dashed that prospect.

The Indians stumbled lifelessly down the stretch, finishing with a disappointing 75–79, tied for fourth place with the equally disappointing Tigers. The Yankees had dominated the league, winning 101 games, a full 17 games ahead of the second place Red Sox and 26 ahead of the Tribe. Indians fans were gloomy. Hal Trosky's career looked over, done in by the migraines; he would come back during the war in 1944, but was not the same hitter. The Indians retained a decent core of talent, but new blood was clearly needed to boost the offense and rebuild the pitching staff beyond Feller. Although Alva Bradley retained trust in his staff, Cy Slapnicka was emotionally drained. Not up to another rebuilding job, Slap re-signed his position as general manager at the end of the season, though he remained on the payroll as a scout and adviser to Bradley. Peckinpaugh replaced Slap in the GM post, so a new manager would be needed as well.

Feller's 1941 season was not quite as successful as his previous two campaigns, although they set the bar extremely high. His earned run average, adjusted for park effect, was "only" 25 percent better than league average, as opposed to the 61 percent mark he'd posted in 1940. His raw 3.15 ERA still ranked fifth in the circuit, however, and his other statistics were still extraordinarily impressive. Although Feller fell short in his quest for 30 wins, he still led the American League with 25. As was becoming traditional, Feller also led the circuit in games, games started, innings pitched, batters faced, strikeouts, and strikeouts per nine innings. Feller bore the heaviest workload of any pitcher in baseball with 343 innings. Only Bucky Walters of Cincinnati, with 302 innings, and Thornton Lee of the Chicago White Sox, with 300, came close to bearing the same workload. And both Walters and Lee were control pitchers; Feller was still wild enough to walk 194 on the season. His pitch counts would have been regarded as murderous in modern times.

Feller passed up barnstorming again that fall, concentrating instead on his family, as well as his burgeoning romance with Virginia. Bill Feller's condition was continuing to worsen, and Bob wanted to spend as much time as possible in Van Meter. This was only prudent; the world in the fall of 1941 was a highly uncertain place. Hitler had launched an invasion of Russia that spring, and while the attack on the Soviet Union later proved to be an ill-conceived gamble that doomed the Third Reich, this was not apparent at the time. As far as anyone west of Berlin knew, the Red Army was just barely hanging on against the Nazis. Meanwhile, tensions in the Pacific were growing critical. FDR's oil embargo, trigged by Japanese aggression in China, had pushed Japan into an economic and strategic corner. War in the vast expanse of the Pacific was imminent, though many failed to realize the gravity of the situation at that point. The draft was starting to take more and more ballplayers into the military, Detroit's Hank Greenberg being the most famous catch in '41.

Baseball went on. On November 25th, Alva Bradley announced that he'd hired a new manager. The thought was that he'd bring in a veteran baseball man to replace the promoted Peckinpaugh, possibly Bucky Harris, Bill Dickey, recently fired Tigers manager Del Baker, or veteran coach and manager Burt Shotton. Speculation centered on the personality style of the new manager. Would it be a hard-nosed boss in the Vitt mode, primed to whip the team into shape? Or would Bradley bring in another nice guy teacher-type to keep the clubhouse calm and perhaps oversee an extensive rebuilding effort? The new manager turned out to be Lou Boudreau, the 23-year-old shortstop. Although Boudreau had only been in the major leagues for two years, he had a magnetic personality, great baseball knowledge, and was already a clubhouse leader despite his youth. Bradley had initially been opposed to the idea of Boudreau as manager. But he had been impressed by Boudreau's own confidence in his abilities when the subject of his becoming manager was broached, and allowed himself to be talked into it by other club officials. It was a risky gamble, but after the Vitt Disaster and the club's mediocre 1941 performance, trying something new to shake the team out of its leadership torpor made sense. Shotton and Baker were hired as coaches, available to lend experienced hands to Boudreau on matters of strategy if needed.

About the only thing that was certain in the minds of Cleveland fans and front office personnel was the fact that Bob Feller would be the centerpiece of the team in 1942. In a review of Bob Feller's achievements in this period, the first thing that comes to a mind with a sabermetric bent is the sheer size of his workload. From the time he entered the starting rotation full time in 1938 to the end of the 1941 season, Feller made 148 starts, completing 103 of them, averaging 310 innings per season. He led the league in both strikeouts and walks during this period, both of which are usually pitch-intensive outcomes. Although estimating exact pitch counts with the available data is nearly impossible, Feller certainly threw more pitches in this period than any other hurler in the major leagues. His power style was not especially conducive to "easing up," although Feller says that he tried as hard as possible to "pace himself" during games, going for maximum velocity only when runners were on base. Still, even "easing up" for Feller resulted in much better velocity than most pitchers could muster when making maximal effort. Consider also that Feller's mechanics were considered less than ideal, especially early in his career. Many baseball men felt he would burn out quickly because of the stress of his delivery on his shoulder.

Despite his extreme workload, Feller seldom demonstrated any physical weakness. His back was occasionally sore, but it usually wasn't a problem for more than a few days, and seldom cost him time on the mound. He was clearly tired down the stretch in 1940, but had no lasting ill effects from the experience. Somehow, Feller's shoulder and elbow held up under the strain, a testament, no doubt, to his general physical condition. There must have been something of a genetic freakiness to Feller's success. Some arms bounce back faster than others, and Feller was clearly blessed with a resilient arm, made even more so by the muscle memory built up over years of playing catch with his father back in Iowa. That, as well as his own impressive devotion to strength training, flexibility exercises, good nutrition, and clean living, kept his arm healthy. Still, whatever his organic advantages, Feller's performance in the 1938–41 time frame was a remarkable achievement, a testament to his physical and emotional endurance. At age 22, Bob Feller was on top of the world. He was the best pitcher in baseball. His future, professional and financial, couldn't be brighter. He had an attractive, intelligent girlfriend in Virginia Winther. The only negatives on his mind were his father's ebbing health, and nagging concern over the deteriorating world political situation.

Driving his brand-new 1941 Buick Century, Bob set off from Van Meter on December 7th, driving east toward Chicago on Route 6 for a meeting with Peckinpaugh and Slapnicka. They would negotiate a contract for 1942. As he reached the Illinois side after crossing the Mississippi River, Feller heard on his car radio (an expensive option in those days) about the Japanese attack on Pearl Harbor. He decided immediately to join the Navy, and drove on to Chicago to inform the Tribe braintrust of his decision. Bob Feller would exchange the uniform of the Cleveland Indians for the uniform of the United States.

9

War

I'm no hero. Get this straight. The heroes didn't come back. Only the survivors did.

—Bob Feller, interview with John Sickels, October 18, 2002

Despite his father's terminal illness, Bob Feller had considered enlisting at the end of the 1941 season. He wrestled with the issue, weighing the financial and emotional needs of his family against what he felt was his patriotic duty to serve. There would be no dishonor in *not* enlisting; Feller had a clear draft exemption, and at this point those exempt weren't rushing in droves to sign up for the military. If war did break out, Feller's 3-C farmer status would keep him out of the armed forces, but would probably have forced him into staying on the farm in an "essential war occupation" as the only support of a family. He probably would have had to give up baseball, by 1943 at least.

The bombing of Pearl Harbor galvanized the nation in support of the war effort. Tens of thousands of draft-exempt men volunteered; hundreds of thousands more who were eligible for the draft but hadn't been called joined up on their own volition. In that sense, Feller was far from alone in setting aside his civilian job to serve his country without being forced into it. But few of these workers were already famous and wealthy. Some thought Feller crazy for leaving his lucrative baseball job when he didn't have to right away, but in Bob's mind, his duty was clear. He would enlist in the Navy, the branch of service most critical in carrying the war to Japan and avenging the attack on the Pacific Fleet.

Arriving in Chicago on the afternoon of the 7th, Feller immediately informed Cy Slapnicka and Roger Peckinpaugh of his decision. He then phoned Gene Tunney, a friend and the head of the Navy's physical fitness program, who flew out to Chicago immediately to swear in Feller. On the 9th, Feller went down to the Navy recruiting office in Chicago, and along with thousands of other young men, joined the armed forces of the United States of America.

After enlisting, Feller returned to Van Meter for a couple weeks before driving out to Norfolk, Virginia, for basic training and his introduction to Navy life. This focused on physical workouts and fitness exercises: marching, running, calisthenics, and military education. Feller's status as a professional athlete and self-trained fitness nut made basic a tolerable experience for him physically. He was used to hard work, and while the environment of military life was something new to him, he'd already had plenty of practice surviving in pressure situations. Working in a team environment was not new to him either.

Feller's fame made him an attractive recruit for Gene Tunney, a former heavyweight boxer and world champion from 1926 to 1928. Tunney held the rank of commander in the Navy, and was in charge of the service's physical training program. He'd been trying to talk Feller into joining the Navy before December 7th, attempting to recruit the young pitcher for his program. Along with many other professional athletes, including baseball players Fred Hutchinson and Sam Chapman, Feller became a Navy physical training drill instructor under Tunney's direction.

It made for good publicity for the military. A photo of Feller being sworn in on his arrival in Virginia graced the January 15th, 1942, edition of *The Sporting News*, under the caption "Now Pitching for Uncle Sam at Norfolk." Another wire service photo, this one of Feller and Sam Chapman in uniform, received wide national distribution in newspapers on January 28th and 29th. Using well-known athletes in this way made a great deal of sense from the Navy perspective. Aside from the patriotic publicity that Feller and other famous recruits could generate, what better person could there be to whip a bunch of soft enlistees into shape than a notable professional athlete?

On completion of basic, Feller was given the rank of chief petty officer. He was assigned as a physical drill instructor under Lt. Commander J. N. Schofner at the Norfolk base. Feller and the other athletes worked with recruits, giving fitness tests. It was important work, though tedious and dull. More interesting from Bob's perspective was the baseball team he quickly became a part of. The armed services formed clubs at many bases and training stations, for purposes of troop entertainment, morale building, and publicity. These clubs would play other clubs from nearby military bases, or in some cases local college or minor league teams, in exhibition contests. Feller, along with Fred Hutchinson, Sam Chapman, and minor league pitcher Maxie Wilson, became the stars for the Norfolk Training Station club.

The season began in March, with Feller, Hutchinson, and Wilson forming a knockout pitching trio that Norfolk's inexperienced opposition could seldom match. The club won 20 of its first 22 games, Feller turning in strong performances nearly every time out. He fanned 21 in a game against Wilson of the Bi-State League on April 26th, then followed that with 11 more strikeouts against the Army's Camp Lee team on May 1st.[1] The contests were given national exposure in baseball's weekly bible, *The Sporting News.* They ran an amusing publicity photo on May 7th of Feller throwing a pitch while dressed in khaki uniform, complete with regulation tie and CPO hat. This was not the usual in-game attire; the Navy club was fully outfitted with baseball uniforms and equipment, but it looked good in the papers.

The exhibition series was extremely popular with both players and fans. Feller himself enjoyed the experience greatly. "Baseball in the Navy was always much more fun than it had been in the major leagues . . . it was the best kind of recreation and I believe it furnished a great amount of pleasure for thousands of sailors who often found little else to do in a town as crowded as Norfolk."[2] His Navy baseball exploits continued to draw national attention as the spring progressed. In early June, he splintered the bat of an Army player in a contest in Rhode Island, the incident making enough of an impression on observers to merit a mention in *The Sporting News*. Former minor leaguer Joe Kwanslewiski, playing for the Army, had his bat shattered by a Feller fastball. Kwanslewiski found himself "standing in the batter's box with little more than a foot-long stub of his favorite bat" in hand, as the crowd roared in appreciation.[3]

Feller spent the spring and summer months playing baseball and drilling recruits. Although the games were mostly played for fun and Feller himself commented on the lack of pressure, Bob was still looking toward the future, and used the contests to hone his professional skills. He developed a new pitch, adding a slider to his repertoire. Feller claimed this wasn't intentional ("I just threw one one day, the ball slid, so I've been throwing 'em ever since"), but he continued working on the pitch, which could hardly have been necessary given the level of competition he was facing.[4] One can imagine the trauma of college and minor league players going up against Feller's bat-shattering fastball and knee-buckling curve, only to face a new devil in the arsenal.

Although exact records have not survived, the Norfolk team played approximately 100 games that spring and summer, Bob estimating that they won 92.[5] He started about 35 of these contests, splitting the starts with Hutchinson and Wilson, likely throwing well more than 200 innings. The competition wasn't major league, of course, but it was still baseball, and Feller pitched to win. The bottom line is that, despite being in the military, Feller threw a lot of baseball in 1942, not quite a complete workload to match what he'd borne in Cleveland, but enough to take away the idea that the season was particularly "easy" on his arm.

Between playing baseball and exercising recruits, Feller had other issues on his mind. His father's health continued to deteriorate; there was absolutely nothing he could do about it. Also, Bob's connection with Virginia Winther was growing more and more serious. Although the couple communicated mostly through letters and the occasional telephone call, they were growing closer, to the point where marriage became the obvious destination of their relationship. Bob proposed to Virginia while walking with her along a beach while on leave; they decided they would marry in January 1943.

The nature of his service also troubled him. Playing baseball and drilling recruits were "easy" gigs as military duty went, though honorable ones. But for Bob, this wasn't enough. He decided to volunteer for combat duty. His first choice was pilot training. Feller had learned to fly in 1940, but he was rejected for naval aviator training after failing a high-frequency hearing test. He then selected naval gunnery school, choosing that branch due to a lifelong interest in firearms. It was also a position in which one was likely to see action. The gunnery course involved some four months of instruction in every gun used by the Navy. Feller trained as an antiaircraft gun crew chief. Once graduated from the course, Feller would be assigned to a combat post, which would take him away from the United States, his family, Virginia, and the baseball diamond.

He requested assignment to the battleship USS *Iowa*, under construction since June 1940 at the New York Navy yard. The 56,000-ton vessel would be the most heavily armed ship in the Navy when finished, as well as being the fastest battleship ever built by the United States. A fine tribute to her namesake state, she would be a prime posting. But when Bob's orders came down, he found himself assigned not to the *Iowa* but to the USS *Alabama*. It seemed that every Navy man from the Hawkeye state had requested a posting aboard the *Iowa*, and there wasn't room for everyone.

The *Alabama* was also a battleship, of the *South Dakota* class, built at the Navy yard right there in Norfolk. She'd been launched in February of '42, and was fitting out that summer while Feller played baseball and began his gunnery training. The *South Dakota* class was smaller and slower than the later *Iowa* class, but the *Alabama* and her three sisters (the *South Dakota*, *Massachusetts*, and *Indiana*) were still formidable opponents, outclassing every comparable Japanese battleship except the gigantic *Yamato* and *Musashi*. During the war, the battleships would be used mostly for shore bombardment and as escorts for the fast, hard-hitting, far-reaching aircraft carrier fleets that made the big-gun battleship obsolete. But the armored behemoths were still the pride of the Navy in 1942, and service aboard the *Alabama* quickly became a matter of pride for Bob Feller and the rest of her crew.

The ship was commissioned on August 16th, and Feller joined her crew in September. At 44,000 tons, *Alabama* was a floating fortress, manned by a crew of more than 2,000 sailors, armed with 9 16-inch main guns, 20 5-inch dual-purpose secondary guns, and 6 (later upgraded to 12) quadruple .40 millimeter Bofors antiaircraft mounts. Feller was assigned as chief for one of the .40 millimeter mounts, supervising a crew of 24, manning the port-side mount just aft of the superstructure. His duty was not as glamorous as operating one of the giant gun turrets, but it was one of the "hottest" and most important posts on the ship, for the *Alabama*'s role as a carrier escort would make her antiaircraft (AA) crews vital. The AA crews were also the personnel on the ship most exposed to enemy fire. Most *Alabama* sailors would be protected below decks when the ship was at battle stations, but not the AA crews, who would be unprotected by the battlewagon's thick armor.

The *Alabama* and her crew, including Feller, left for their shakedown cruise on November 11th.[6] This involved running the ship through trials, testing the engines and equipment, further training, and building a sense of community and camaraderie among the crew. Such instruction and experience were crucial. The blast effect from the *Alabama*'s huge 16-inch main batteries was especially tough on novices. "I staggered all over the place from the concussion when they first were fired," said Bob, "and it knocked the cotton out of my ears, but I'm okay now. I know where to stand now."[7] Feller adapted quickly to the realities of shipboard life, finding himself (despite his landlubber background) immune to seasickness and comfortable on the ocean swells.

The vessel sailed up and down the coast of the northeastern United States in November and December, and was based for a time at Casco Bay, Maine. In early January, the ship was headed back to Norfolk to prepare for permanent assignment with the fleet. Bob planned on taking a few days leave after the ship arrived, in order to meet Virginia in Chicago, where the couple would be married. But the plans changed when Feller was called into the chaplain's office.

Bill Feller had died. The cancer had finally claimed him.

Bob was granted a 10-day emergency leave, and was taken off the ship and carried back to harbor by a Coast Guard cutter. He arrived back in Iowa in time for his father's burial on January 14th. Bob was numb at first, in mourning, but intellectually "agreed with the sentiment that death was a release from suffering" for his father.[8] Buried in a Des Moines cemetery, Bill Feller was eulogized in both Iowa and Cleveland. The Cleveland city council passed a formal resolution of condolence for the Fellers, citing William Feller as an excellent father who "demonstrated the best tradition in raising the youth of our land."[9] The story of how Bill Feller built his son into a pitcher was told and retold again, with extra emphasis on the soft but firm touch that Bill showed in dealing with his son. The fact that Bob was now the personification of the all-American athlete/patriot/soldier reflected well on his upbringing and the values inculcated by Bill and Lena Feller.

Bill Feller's passing had an additional complication: Bob and Virginia had planned to marry during his scheduled January leave. At first, Virginia had decided to call off the wedding, but after consulting with Bob and Lena, the plans were put back into place. "He wanted us to be married," Bob told Virginia. Lena confirmed to her soon-to-be daughter-in-law that Bill had wanted the marriage to go forward.

The ceremony took place in Waukeegan, Illinois, on January 16th, just two days after Bill's death. Ex-Indians outfielder and current Army lieutenant Soup Campbell was the best man, and Lou Boudreau and Rollie Hemsley also attended. The ceremony took place at the First Methodist Church. Virginia wore a long ivory satin gown. Feller wore his Navy uniform. The wedding was front-page news in *The Sporting News* of January 28th, 1943, the paper spending a considerable amount of space discussing Virginia's inability to cook anything but fudge. "I can't cook anything else," Virginia admitted. "That's all right, honey," replied Bob, "by the time I come out of the Navy, I'll be able to digest anything."

The couple took an airplane to New York after the wedding,

where they spent a brief three-day honeymoon before Bob returned to Norfolk to rejoin his ship. While in New York, Feller gave an interview to Bob Considine of the *New York Daily Mirror*. Feller predicted that the war would end in the spring of 1945, leaving him enough time to get back into an Indians uniform by June of that year. "They won't keep us heavy ship men in uniform very long after the war ends," he said. "There won't be any need to protect any more convoys. I'll be 26 then. That will give me ten more good years." Although Feller missed his end-of-war target by a few months, it was a remarkably prescient estimate of his future.

But baseball was still at least two years away, and fighting a war was foremost on Feller's mind when he returned to Norfolk and his shipmates.

The *Alabama* left Norfolk again on February 13th, 1943, heading back to Casco Bay for further tactical training. In early March, the British Royal Navy asked for American capital ship reinforcements to help escort convoys along the North Atlantic corridor. The main threat to Allied shipping at this time came from Germany's U-boats, against which a battleship was no use. But there was still the possibility that German surface raiders, particularly the dangerous battleship *Tirpitz*, could sortie from their bases in Norway to destroy convoys headed for Great Britain or Russia. The *Alabama* and her sister ship the *South Dakota* were chosen to reinforce the British Home Fleet, arriving at its main base at Scapa Flow on May 19th. During May and June, the two battlewagons and their escorts covered convoys heading to and from the British Isles. At one point, they covered a reinforcement of the island of Spitzbergen, an operation that took the *Alabama* into the frigid waters of the Arctic Circle.

Although these missions in European waters did not result in contact with German forces, being at sea itself was a dangerous occupation. In his first memoir, Feller recalled an incident when a sailor stopped by his quarters (located over the ship's propellers) for an autograph, a frequent occurrence. They talked baseball for a while, then the sailor went topside to dump some garbage overboard. It was night; the weather was cold and rough. The sailor apparently fell overboard, never to be found, either drowning or succumbing to exposure in the frigid waters of the North Atlantic. Feller had likely been the last man to see the lost sailor alive, and the tragedy stuck with him. "Of all the memories I retain from that tour of the Atlantic," wrote Feller, "the one I remember most vividly" was this incident.[10]

In early August, the *Alabama* and *South Dakota* were detached from the British Fleet and recalled to Norfolk. The danger in the Atlantic was lessening, but the Navy needed ships in the Pacific to escort the growing number of aircraft carriers that were leading the "island hopping" invasion counterattacks against the Japanese Empire. After a ten-day overhaul in Norfolk, during which Bob was able to spend some quality time in the evenings with his new wife in a local hotel, the two battleships were reassigned as reinforcements for the Pacific Theater of Operations. They left Norfolk on the 20th of August, heading for the Panama Canal. It would be nearly 18 months before Bob Feller and the rest of the *Alabama* crew saw the United States again.

Their next anchor didn't come until September 14th, when they arrived at the naval base at Efate, in the New Hebrides Islands. Efate was being developed as a forward base for the fleet. It already boasted a repair yard and relatively good shore leave accommodations for the sailors and Marines. For the first time since September of 1942, Bob had a chance to play some baseball at Efate, pitching for the *Alabama*'s baseball team, while also playing first base for the softball squad. The diamond was primitive, rough, and dangerous, so Feller took the lead in laying out and constructing a proper baseball facility that would be safer to play on. Teams were organized, and the *Alabama*'s baseball squad, led by Feller's pitching, eventually won the Third Fleet championship. September and October were spent in additional training during the day, with baseball, food, and movies in the evenings and nights. But the realities of war returned soon enough.

In early November, the *Alabama* was assigned to Operation Galvanic, the invasion of the Gilbert Islands. She initially escorted aircraft carriers, then helped cover the bloody landing at Tarawa on November 20th. The *Alabama* also took part in attacks on other islands in the Gilberts. On November 26th, Japanese aircraft approached the portion of the fleet the *Alabama* was guarding, but were driven off by her antiaircraft fire, including that from Feller's mount. On December 8th, the *Alabama* used her huge 16-inch gun batteries to bombard the Japanese-held island of Nauru.

As Operation Galvanic wound down, *Alabama* was sent back to Efate for resupply, then went to Pearl Harbor to replace a defective propeller. She rejoined the fleet on January 21st, 1944, acting as escort for the aircraft carrier *Essex*. Her next assignment was Operation Flintlock, the invasion of the Marshall Islands. The *Alabama* conducted two more shore bombardments against Japanese shore positions, along with the battleships *South Dakota* and *North Carolina* on January 29th and January 30th. By this time, Feller was well used to the concussion effects from the huge main batteries, but had only limited experience firing his own .40-millimeter guns in action against enemy aircraft. That would change.

Throughout early February, the *Alabama* roamed the Central Pacific, taking part in carrier and shore bombardment attacks on islands such as Truk, Tinian, Saipan, and Guam. This was part of the "softening up" operations intended to prepare these targets for direct amphibious assault. The Japanese forces in these areas were isolated and low on supplies, but were still fierce fighters and dangerous when cornered. A Japanese air strike on February 21st saw Feller's gun crew in action once again. Although the ship wasn't damaged by the attack itself, five *Alabama* crewmen were killed in an unusual friendly fire accident. One of the ship's 5-inch gun batteries went past its stops and accidentally fired into another mount, blowing it apart. Such are the dangers of combat: even when the enemy misses, soldiers and sailors can die.

The fast pace of operations continued. On March 29th, while she was escorting the aircraft carrier *Yorktown*, six Japanese aircraft moved in to attack the force, four of them very near the *Alabama*. Two of these aircraft were shot down. Assessing which gun crew was directly responsible was impossible, of course, what with thousands of rounds of ammunition being expended each second. All the gunners on the ship took satisfaction in their accomplishment, and the crew fire directors like Feller took special pride, for it was they who decided *where* the guns would aim. Without accurate firing solutions, the guns were useless. While the monstrous 16-inch guns were the sexy part of the *Alabama*'s weapons array, it was the antiaircraft guns and the crews manning them that proved especially valuable during the war.

In April, the *Alabama* provided escort for the carrier *Enterprise*, participating in strikes along the Japanese-held coastline of New Guinea. Most of late April and May was spent in refit and training at the island of Majuro, where Feller got another opportunity to play some baseball. Feller led the *Alabama*'s baseball team to a series of victories against teams from other ships, throwing 47 consecutive scoreless innings at one point.[11] He took the contests seriously, and continued working on the slider he'd developed back at the Norfolk base.

In early June, the *Alabama* left harbor again, this time to participate in Operation Forager, the invasion of the island of Saipan. She conducted shore bombardment operations from June 13th through June 15th, before moving off to screen a group of American aircraft carriers. On June 19th, the Japanese navy attempted a counterattack, but the resulting Battle of the Phillipine Sea was one of the most lopsided contests in the history of naval warfare. Of the estimated 430 aircraft launched by Japanese carriers and air bases in the battle, only 35 survived. Three of Japan's dwindling number of valuable aircraft carriers were sunk. The battle was nicknamed the "Marianas Turkey Shoot" by naval aviators and antiaircraft gun crews, as the poorly trained, badly equipped, but nonetheless brave Japanese pilots launched wave after wave of attacks into the teeth of thick antiair defenses and swarms of American fighters. The *Alabama* emerged unscathed from the battle, although her sister, the *South Dakota*, took a bomb hit, and two bombs nearly hit the *Alabama* herself. Again, it was impossible to determine which gun crew downed which specific aircraft, but the entire fleet took great pride in the stunning victory. Feller referred to it as "the most exciting 13 hours of my life. After that, the dangers of Yankee Stadium seemed trivial."[12] During the Saipan battle, Feller helped save the life of one sailor. Spotting someone adrift in the water, Feller quickly got the word to Sky Control, which dispatched a destroyer to pick the man up. The sailor later personally thanked Feller, who'd been the only person on the *Alabama* to see him afloat in the water.

After a brief respite for repairs and resupply, the *Alabama* set out again after the Japanese in July and August, this time escorting the carriers *Bunker Hill* and *Essex* for a series of air strikes in support of landings on Guam, Palau, Ulithi, and Yap. The pace of operations quickened even further as the forces of Admiral Chester Nimitz in the Central Pacific and the forces under General Douglas MacArthur in the South Pacific pressed inexorably into the heart of the Japanese Empire. In October, the *Alabama* was sent to support the liberation of the Philippine Islands from Japanese occupation. Again, her main task was as an antiaircraft escort for the carrier groups. On October 14th, the *Alabama* helped drive off a Japanese air attack, downing three aircraft and damaging a fourth.

The desperate Japanese tried one last gamble to save their hold on the Phillipines and stem the American onslaught, launching an ambitious, if overly complex, counterattack in late October. The resulting Battle of Leyte Gulf was the largest naval battle in history. The *Alabama* served as an escort for the *Enterprise*, but did not make contact with the enemy in that battle. Although Leyte Gulf was an American victory and the outcome of the war seemed assured, the danger for gunners like Feller was actually growing.

The despairing Japanese were adopting new kamikaze tactics, using the aircraft themselves as weapons. These suicidal methods were utterly foreign to Westerners, but to the Japanese, they made sense. Japanese aircraft were outclassed by new American models. This made traditional dive-bombing and torpedo attack very difficult. The shortage of fuel and ammunition was becoming acute, making it difficult to train pilots. On the other hand, there was no shortage of young men willing to die for the emperor. A kamikaze attack was unlikely to sink a heavily armored battleship. But it could badly damage or cripple the less-protected cruisers, and could easily sink small ships like destroyers. An aircraft carrier, loaded with bombs, torpedoes, and aviation fuel, could become a funeral pyre for thousands of sailors if struck by a kamikaze. And even on a battleship, the kamikaze inspired fear, especially for the vulnerable antiaircraft gun crews. Feller compared the kamikaze pilots to "blind, maddened bulls," and felt they presented the gravest danger for sailors in his profession.[13]

The *Alabama* took part in operations around the Phillipine Islands throughout October, November, and December, escorting various carriers while air strikes were constantly launched against the still-formidable Japanese garrisons in the Phillipines. A new enemy presented itself on December 18th, when the *Alabama* and many other ships of the fleet were caught in a savage typhoon. Wind gusts of over 80 knots damaged her superstructure, but she was in no danger of sinking. She did lose one man, washed overboard by a giant wave, but many other ships were worse off, including three destroyers that ran out of fuel and sank in the tempest.

The *Alabama* had seen more than a year of hard Pacific fighting and was due for overhaul in any event, typhoon damage or not. She was sent back to the Puget Sound naval base in Seattle for repairs, refit, and crew rotation. She would go out to the Pacific again in April, but not with Bob Feller. His combat tour was over; the Navy had other plans for him. Bob went ashore in Seattle on January 12th and immediately called Virginia, who was living in a Norfolk hotel. She flew out to meet him. Bob Feller had been married for almost two years, but had spent just five nights alone with his wife since the end of their honeymoon.

Later, Feller would look back on his *Alabama* service with tremendous pride; his museum in Van Meter has a large display on her exploits and his time aboard. He was part of the crew that earned eight battle stars for the *Alabama* and speaks with depth and conviction about his war experiences even today. As for the ship that was his home for almost three years, the *Alabama* served out her days as a carrier escort in the Pacific, but was considered obsolete in the Cold War environment. Decommissioned in 1947, she was stricken from the Navy list in 1962, and is now berthed in Mobile, serving as a floating museum.

Although Feller's combat tour had ended in January, he was still in the Navy. His return to the States produced the publicity you would expect; he'd been out of circulation for two years, and had a lot to say. Feller had kept in touch with baseball happenings and events in Cleveland through armed services reports, as well as newspaper clippings sent to him by the hundreds from fans. He wrote a letter to Ed McAuley of the *Cleveland News* early in January, complaining about rumors that baseball would be shut down for the 1945 season, making the point that such rumors were having a negative impact on morale in the military. "The most obvious and biggest peeve among servicemen," Feller wrote, "is directed against those who are attempting to scuttle competitive athletics."[14] Feller continued this theme in an interview with reporter Royal Brougham after his arrival in Seattle. "Baseball and malted milks and a duck hunting trip are the things that fellows want to come back to when this thing is over. The vast majority want baseball continued as long as possible."[15] Asked about how he felt about resuming his career when he finally received a discharge, Feller was confident. "I try to keep in condition, but it's no cinch about ship, although I play catch occasionally, box, wrestle, and jog around in heavy sweaters. I'm not worried about my arm—it's my legs."

Feller received a leave in early February, and returned to Van Meter with Virginia to visit his mother. From there, he received orders to head to the Great Lakes Naval Training Station, officially to take the same position he'd held back in Norfolk: physical fitness instructor. The Navy had also decided to return Feller to baseball duty: he would take over as the manager of the Great Lakes baseball team, replacing Mickey Cochrane, who'd been sent to the Pacific for active duty. Cochrane was a lieutenant commander, Feller an enlisted man, so the assignment raised a few eyebrows, but the Navy was apparently impressed with his leadership skills. He'd successfully led a 24-man gun crew; he could certainly lead a 25-man baseball team. And besides, he was Bob Feller; the publicity would be excellent.

Arriving in Great Lakes, Feller found his club stocked with several professional players, including Indians teammate Ken Keltner and major leaguers Dick Wakefield and Clyde Shoun. At first, Feller was just the manager, not the pitcher, but the lure of the mound proved too strong, and he eventually took his turns in the box, probably looking on it as a prelude to a return to professional action. He threw an estimated 100 innings for Great Lakes, the high-light coming on July 21st, when, before an estimated crowd of 10,000 sailors, Feller threw a 10-strikeout no-hitter.[16]

On August 6th, the United States dropped an atomic bomb on Hiroshima, Japan. On August 8th, the Soviet Union attacked Japan. On August 9th, a second nuclear weapon was dropped, this time on Nagasaki. Despite the use of these unholy devices, the Russian intervention, and the horrific destruction rained on Japanese cities by American B-29 conventional firebombings that summer, most Japanese military leaders stubbornly resisted the idea of surrender. Their economy was destroyed; the navy was either sunk or immo-bilized for lack of fuel. The war was clearly unwinnable, and a hu-manitarian catastrophe threatened the Japanese people, yet many in the delusional leadership wanted to continue to the bitter end. But on August 14th, the government was finally prodded into sur-rendering by Emperor Hirohito. The Second World War was at last at an end.

On August 21st, Bob Feller was discharged from the U.S. Navy. He had survived.

10

Return to Glory

Experience is not what happens to a man. It is what a
man does with what happens to him.

—Aldous Huxley

At 2:20 A.M. on August 22d, 1945, Bob and Virginia Feller arrived at the airport in Cleveland and were greeted by a crowd of reporters. The following afternoon, Feller signed a contract for the duration of the 1945 season. Terms were not disclosed, but it was assumed by the press that he was paid at the same rate he'd earned in 1941, prorated for August and September.

The Bob Feller who returned from the Navy in 1945 was not quite the same man who had enlisted. Physically, he was nearly identical, weighing in at 183 pounds when he was discharged, the same weight he'd been when inducted. But there were faint physical differences, discernable if you examine pre- and postwar photographs. The prewar Feller, even as late as 1942, still presented a rather boyish face, masculine but still very youthful. The postwar Feller, even right at discharge, was visibly more mature. He was still just 26, but there was an aura of experience about him. His face had a few more lines than before, especially around the jaw. This change became more pronounced over the next three years.

The other change was psychological. Feller had always been somewhat reserved, though he'd tell you exactly what he was thinking if you asked him. He had already gained a reputation for straight-talking, something that had gotten him in trouble a few times. The postwar Feller was similar but subtly different, more willing to engage and direct conversation himself. Reporters noticed this immediately. Ed McAuley of the *Cleveland News* observed this when talking with Feller before his discharge, noticing that the pitcher had developed a "disarming conversational gadget" since joining the Navy.[1] This "gadget" was a newly developed habit of Feller's to ask probing questions of those questioning him, in order to steer the conversation on his own terms. He was also much more vocal than before in giving out his opinions on various topics. A frequent theme for him in the summer of 1945 was the necessity for physical fitness training programs in the public schools. His experience in the Navy, particularly as a fitness instructor, had apparently shown him the necessity of physical training at a young age. Feller told McAuley that sports should be both compulsory and competitive for all physically able children, for physical as well as mental reasons. "Except for those who are sick or crippled, there is at least one sport in which everyone can become experienced enough to have a lot of fun as well as stay in good condition," he opined.

There is a big difference between a 21-year-old and a 26-year-old, so simple emotional maturity probably had a great deal to do with these changes in Feller. But it was impossible for his war experience not to have had an impact on his psychology. Feller had faced kamikazes. He'd seen shipmates and friends drown, and get killed in friendly-fire accidents. Feller's war experiences might not have been as traumatic as those of a foot soldier storming the beach at Normandy, or a Marine facing a fanatically suicidal foe among the rocks of Iwo Jima. But he had seen the brutality of war, as well as the sheer randomness with which its cruelty struck. Yankee Stadium, hostile fans, and snooping reporters were no longer frightening things in comparison. As he would reflect in 2002, "After coming out of war, you realize that sports are insignificant. Sports are only a game. A lot of people don't understand that. It's only a damn game."[2]

Feller worked out in League Park after signing his contract on the afternoon of the 23d, patiently posing for local photographers and reporters. The Indians wasted no time in getting their star back into action, scheduling him to start the next day, a Friday night game against the first-place Tigers. The Indians were out of contention, hovering around the .500 level, but they wanted to get a good look at Feller, to see if he'd lost anything while in the service.

Like most clubs, the Tribe had scraped the bottom of the barrel for personnel during the war years, relying on the few draft-exempt holdovers from the prewar club, mixed liberally with other draft-exempt players brought up from the minor leagues. Lou Boudreau had managed the team throughout the war to mixed reviews, but no one thought it fair to criticize managers considering the circumstances. The club had finished 75–79 in 1942, 82–71 in 1943, and 72–82 in 1944. Boudreau's basketball-damaged ankles kept him out of the service, but the 1945 team to which Feller returned bore little resemblance otherwise to the club he had left. Jeff Heath, Jim Bagby, Mel Harder, and Al Smith were still around, but the rest of the old Indians were either in the military or working in war industries.

Feller was given a hero's welcome in pregame ceremonies. The crowd in excess of 45,000 saw Cleveland great Tris Speaker present Feller with a complimentary jeep for use on his farm. *Cleveland Press* writer Franklin Lewis received a $1,000 check from Feller for the Press Memorial Fountain Fund. The ceremony was national news, given strong coverage by the wire services, as well as a full-page spread in the August 30th edition of *The Sporting News*. Feller gave a brief statement to the crowd, then proceeded to show everyone that he had lost nothing on the mound.

The crowd hadn't come to see the ceremony; they'd come to see him pitch, and they were not disappointed. Feller was in top form. His fastball was quickly up to prewar standards. Although he used his old-fashioned curveball at times, he mixed in his new slider more frequently, giving the Tigers fits. Feller threw a complete game, allowing just four hits and two runs, walking four, while fanning 12. Feller's return was capped off the next day at a downtown luncheon that drew 1,000 guests, including Detroit's manager, the redoubtable ex-Indians chief Steve O'Neill. O'Neill joked to the crowd that he'd wished he'd "given Bob's wrist a firm twist" when shaking hands before the event.

Feller made eight more starts for Cleveland in September, finishing with a 5–3 record but a solid 2.50 ERA. In 72 innings, he fanned 59 and walked 35. His velocity and movement were at prewar standards immediately, though he needed some time to get his command back in order. His best game came on September 19th, when he held the Tigers to a single hit, a bloop third inning single by Jimmy Outlaw. It was the sixth one-hitter of his career, and proved beyond any doubt (as if there were any) that Feller was back.

But let's pause for a moment and think what might have been.

So far, this book has followed a chronological approach, while keeping certain themes alive, because it's been the best way to show Feller's impact during the times he lived. As the book progresses, the approach will gradually become more thematic. When dealing with the "missing years" in Feller's statistical record, one must by necessity do so with an awareness of "how the story ended," how Feller's career ended up statistically. Thus we have to skip forward a bit, before we return to the chronological narrative. It is important to discuss the missing seasons soon after the actual narrative description of those years, to keep it from becoming too abstract, to address this issue while the reality of Feller's war record is still fresh in our minds.

What would Bob Feller have done professionally if he had not joined the Navy?[3] First, consider the context. If he had taken advantage of his draft exemption and kept playing baseball while the war raged, he would have pitched in a period of diluted talent. Feller was already the most dominating pitcher in baseball before the war. If Feller had pitched against wartime competition, with the less-lively baseball used in the 1942–45 period, he would quite probably have been even more dominant than he was before the war. If the Second World War had been avoided entirely and there had been no draft, then one could predict Feller continuing to pitch as well in the 1942–45 period as he had before.

In the four seasons before the war, Feller averaged 252 strikeouts, 23 wins, and 310 innings per season. Just those numbers, assuming he continued pitching on approximately the same level for the 1942–45 seasons, would add 1,008 strikeouts, 92 wins, and

1,240 innings to Feller's career totals. This would give him 358 wins, 3,589 strikeouts, and 5,067 innings, vaulting him into eighth place on the all-time win list, sixth place in strikeouts, and 13th place in innings. He would have held the career strikeout record from his retirement until being passed by moderns Nolan Ryan, Steve Carlton, Roger Clemens, Bert Blyleven, and Don Sutton. More sophisticated metrics exist to measure Feller's achievements, but those will be saved for later. The purpose of this exercise is to show in general terms what the war cost Feller. He would undoubtedly have ranked much higher in the raw "counting stats" that get players noticed by the casual fans.

There is, however, another complication that must be dealt with. If the war had not intervened, would Feller have gotten hurt? He'd shown remarkable durability in the 1938–41 period, but there's no guarantee he would have stayed healthy, or at least able to throw 300 strong innings every season. Evidence from later in his career suggests that Feller wasn't especially vulnerable to the catastrophic injury—the blown elbow or shredded rotator cuff—but that his arm would wear down gradually from use. On the other hand, there are all sorts of injuries suffered by pitchers that aren't related directly to pitching. Johnny Allen's slip in the bathtub that ruined his elbow comes to mind. Feller could certainly have suffered something like that. But if he avoided that sort of trouble, it is very possible he could have continued working at the 300-inning pace throughout the war years, perhaps with some decline in performance.

All of this is theorizing, of course. But one thing that should be remembered is that Feller *did* pitch during the war years, more than 200 innings in 1942 and more than 100 in 1945. Shipboard service in 1943 and 1944 kept him off the Navy's primitive South Pacific diamonds most of the time, but he did pitch in recreation contests when given the opportunity. We know he threw at least 50 innings in 1944. That's not the same as throwing 300 innings in professional ball, but it does eliminate the concept that the war years represent a complete four-year rest for Feller's arm.

Ultimately, any conclusions that could be drawn about the missing years are entirely speculative. One thing that is not, however, is the financial cost of the war for Feller. While in the military, he earned between $80 and $100 a month, missing out on his five-digit baseball salary, as well as income from barnstorming. Feller knew that, as a baseball player, his livelihood was entirely dependent on his health. If he hurt his arm and lost effectiveness, the money would quickly disappear. The war had robbed him of four years of earning power, possibly as much as $300,000 in lost income. With a wife and mother to provide for, making as much money as possible while he remained healthy and effective became paramount in Feller's mind.

The imminent expansion of the Feller family made this even more imperative. On December 10th, Virginia gave birth to a baby boy, whom the Fellers named Stephan. He closely resembled his father physically, especially in the structure of his legs and chest. Bob decided to adopt his own father's attitude in regards to baseball. "We'll certainly find out if he likes baseball," he told Virginia. "If he doesn't, he will do his pitching in some other line."[4]

Shortly after his son was born, Feller signed his 1946 contract with the Indians. His September performance had removed any doubt in the minds of the Indians braintrust about Feller's ability to come back from the war, so they came up with a healthy contract for their ace: $50,000, plus a bonus clause based on attendance. The details of the contract were not released immediately, but at this point Feller clearly rated as the best-paid player in the game.[5] His immediate financial concerns abated, Feller bought a boat and prepared plans for a Florida vacation with his wife and new son. Soon, however, an additional offer came to his attention: Jorge Pasquel, a Mexican millionaire, offered Feller $100,000 to come to Mexico and join his new league. Feller did not respond. At one point, it was rumored that Pasquel had offered Feller a three-year guaranteed deal at a hundred grand per season. With the tax man taking a large bite out of Feller's early salary, speculated Ed McAuley in the *Cleveland News*, would Feller take the money and run south of the border?[6]

The answer was no; Feller turned the offer down. "No chili con carne baseball for me," he told the press. He'd spent two years away from the United States, and wasn't going to leave again. The new family arrival, and the chaos that moving to a new country would cause, also made the offer less tempting. Other major leaguers did take Pasqual up on his offer, including established players like Sal Maglie, Max Lanier, Lou Klein, and Mickey Owen. Commissioner Chandler decreed that any player jumping to Mexico would be banned from organized baseball for five years, which kept the number of defections to a minimum.

There were other changes brewing in baseball, and American society in general. The influx of discharged servicemen was placing a great strain on the economy, and many feared a return to prewar Depression conditions. Race relations were becoming a spur for social conflict. The blatant hypocrisy of America fighting a war for freedom while millions of American citizens were denied basic rights on the basis of race was starting to bite. The unspoken agreement between owners that kept African Americans out of the ranks of organized baseball was becoming more and more difficult to justify. If a Negro boy could fight and die for his country as well as any white boy, asked many citizens, why couldn't he play in the major leagues? Jim Crow was becoming impossible for anyone of good conscience to defend, at the lunch counter as well as the baseball diamond, or at least it should have been. The signing of Jackie Robinson by the Brooklyn Dodgers brought this question to the forefront of debate in the sports world, a debate that would eventually involve Bob Feller.

Feller got his season started early and creatively. He decided to set up a "Free School" for baseball's returning war veterans, organizing and finding financing for the endeavor. Held in Tampa in late January, the school was originally designed as a refresher baseball course for recently discharged major and minor league players, but was broadened to include any player age 17 to 21, provided they had a recommendation from a coach or mentor. The application form was printed in the January 3d edition of *The Sporting News*, in order to reach the widest possible audience of baseball fans. The form asked for name, address, age, height, weight, parental signature (if the person was a minor), and a recommendation from a scout, coach, sportswriter or broadcaster. It also included a disclaimer: "Coaches, editors, and sportscasters are asked to make sure applicant has necessary qualifications, especially in running and throwing, thus avoiding undue expense for applicant and saving time of instructors."

The school was a class affair. Feller recruited several major league stars to act as staff and faculty, including Joe DiMaggio, Spud Chandler, Tommy Bridges, Eddie Miller, and teammate/ manager Lou Boudreau. Retired major leaguers Lew Fonseca, Bill Dickey, and Dizzy Dean were also tapped to serve. The school charged no tuition, although attendees had to bring their own uniforms and gloves, and were responsible for transportation and boarding. Tampa's Chamber of Commerce advised early applications, and assured that lodging would be available at "economical rates" for those who signed up quickly. Feller himself handled most of the business tasks for the school, convincing *The Sporting News* to act as publicity agent and information clearinghouse for the event. He also arranged donation of bats and balls by their respective manufacturers. Feller and the staff were unpaid volunteers; the benefits of participation were not financial, but rather social and educational. Feller's main motivation was compassion for his fellow vets. He knew that, despite his combat service in the Pacific, he was more prepared for a return to baseball than many soldiers.

> I was lucky, being on a battleship big enough to allow me a regular chance to throw and catch, skip rope, swim and take systemic exercise. I was lucky to be stationed at Great Lakes where I could work back gradually into the job of testing my arm. I was ready for the big leagues mentally, as well as physically.[7]

But the same would not be true for many returning players, especially those who'd spent the war in foxholes. "He envisioned a raft of disappointed and disillusioned ex-players," noted *Baseball Magazine*, "struggling with overweight or lack of weight, pampering swollen ankles . . . and balky muscles unused to the special demands of baseball competition." Feller acted as the head coach and coordinator, setting firm behavior guidelines (no drinking, midnight curfew), though he found few problems enforcing them.

Most of the attendees were former servicemen, anxious to get back into professional baseball. The school was an unqualified success. The three-week course drew 186 players, and 66 eventually signed professional contracts.[8] Feller found the one-third-success rate particularly gratifying, as few such camps ever produced a large number of professional players.

Following the success of the baseball school, Feller transitioned into spring training for the Indians. The '46 edition of the Tribe was very different from the one Feller had left in 1941. Boudreau was still there, manning shortstop as well as the managerial post. Ken Keltner was still at third base, Ray Mack was present at second. Thirty-six-year-old Mel Harder was still around, unable to throw in regular rotation, but still useful as a spot starter. The rest of the club bore little resemblance to the prewar Tribe, and was clearly not as talented. Jeff Heath had been traded. New left fielder George Case was fast, but lacked power. First baseman Les Fleming also lacked power; outfielder Pat Seerey had that in droves, but couldn't hit for average and struck out too much. Wartime acquisitions Allie Reynolds and Red Embree were the main pitchers behind Feller; both were talented, but it was unclear how they would do against the "real" major leaguers returning from the war. While in the past Feller had had to share some of the spotlight with players like Trosky and Heath, he was clearly going to be the heart and soul of the Tribe's fortunes in '46. If the Indians were to make noises in the pennant chase, most of them would have to come from Bob.

It didn't look good in spring training. The Indians played poorly in their exhibition series against the Giants, and Feller wasn't throwing with his usual authority. He was not concerned: Bob's main focus in the spring was conditioning, not throwing as hard as possible. But skeptics, ignoring his good pitching in September of '45 as well as his history of mediocre spring performances, said that Feller had left his fastball back in the Navy. An Opening Day 1–0 shutout against the White Sox quelled the doubters temporarily, but a 3–2 loss to Detroit and a 4–0 loss to Chicago in his next two starts brought the doubters back.

On April 30th, Feller put any doubts about his ability to rest, and started rolling through one of the greatest seasons of pitching in major league history.

A crowd in excess of 37,000 filed into Yankee Stadium on a Tuesday afternoon to watch Bob Feller go up against pinstripe hurler Floyd Bevens. Feller was aware of the rumors circulating that he'd lost his fastball, and was determined to prove the doubters wrong. "It maddened me as nothing ever written about me had before," he said about one wire service article in particular.[9] Feller's fastball was good that day, though not in peak form. His slider was working well. A tremendous defensive play by Lou Boudreau in the first inning saved a hit. Feller's control was not outstanding. He walked five, and was frequently behind in the count. But his pitches had movement, and the Yankees were unable to get a good read on his delivery. By the end of the fifth inning, it was apparent that this was going to be a special day for Feller.

There was just one problem. Feller was throwing a no-hitter, but Floyd Bevens was throwing a shutout.

The game came into the ninth inning still as a scoreless tie. Bevens' shutout was broken with a home run by Indians catcher Frankie Hayes, giving Feller a run to work with in the bottom of the frame. Yankees third baseman Snuffy Stirnweiss led off with a bouncer down the first base line. The ball was muffed by Les Fleming for a clear error, preserving the no-hitter, but putting the shutout, and the game, at risk. Tommy Henrich, the number-three hitter in the Yankees order and one of the few players in the American League who hit Feller well, laid down a sacrifice bunt on the orders of manager Joe McCarthy to move Stirnweiss to second base. Joe DiMaggio was up next. The count went to 3–2, with DiMaggio fouling off several pitches. Finally, he broke the tension by hitting a ground ball to shortstop, which moved Stirnweiss to third base, but with two out.

The next man was Charlie Keller, an extremely dangerous hitter. A mistake, even a passed ball or wild pitch, would tie the game. Feller reached back for his best stuff, firing two fastballs past Keller. On the 0–2 pitch, Keller tapped a weak ground ball to second base, finishing the game and giving Feller his second no-hitter. He fanned 11. It was a sweet victory, coming against Feller's greatest rivals, and ending the rumors that he was on the decline. Feller threw 133 pitches in the game, which he regarded as "light work."[10]

Feller continued to pitch well, but the rest of the team was struggling. The hitting attack was weak, and the pitching staff after Bob was inconsistent. The Tribe played under-.500 ball through April and May, falling behind the surging Red Sox, who even outpaced the Yankees. While the postwar baseball business was booming in most of the country, Indians fans were restless. Attendance was mediocre. The local economy was sluggish, dragged down by the transition from wartime to peacetime production, and this seemed to be reflected in the lethargy of both the fans and players. There were rumors of financial trouble in the Cleveland front office. In June, rumors spread that the club was for sale, rumors that Alva Bradley vigorously denied, but that quickly proved to be true.

On June 21st, the *Cleveland Press* reported that the Indians were about to be sold. Bradley denied it, his denial published in the *News* and the *Plain Dealer*.

On June 22d, the club was sold to a new consortium of investors headed by the flamboyant Bill Veeck. The Alva Bradley Years were over.

If there was anyone who could revive baseball in Cleveland, it was Bill Veeck. Aggressive, imaginative, and creative, Veeck breathed new life into a franchise that had grown stale under the well-meaning but depleted Bradley. Famous for his bizarre promotional stunts while owner of the minor league Milwaukee Brewers, Veeck was regarded as something of a rogue and clown by the other baseball owners. He didn't wear a tie. He would sit in the bleachers and talk baseball with the fans. He had attempted to purchase the Philadelphia Phillies during the war, but had been outmaneuvered by Commissioner Landis, probably, it was rumored, because Veeck had expressed a willingness to stock the club with talent from the Negro Leagues. But despite his eccentricities in the eyes of the baseball lords, Veeck was a smart baseball man with a good eye for talent. He loved both sides of the game, business and baseball.

Attendance picked up, although the Indians weren't playing

any better than they were before the switch. The hitting remained weak and the pitching inconsistent, though the atmosphere in the stadium was much livelier, thanks to Veeck's promotion skills. Feller was doing his part to keep the Tribe afloat, holding 15 wins at the All-Star Break, putting him on pace for another shot at the coveted 30-win mark. He also had 190 strikeouts, meaning the single season strikeout record was within reach as well. He was selected to start for the American League team in the Midsummer Classic in Fenway Park, and pitched effectively, holding the National Leaguers to no runs and two hits in three innings, fanning three.

On August 14th, Feller fanned seven Detroit Tiger hitters, though he lost the game in a tough 1–0 defeat to Dizzy Trout. This gave him 262 strikeouts on the season, besting his personal record, but with six weeks still left in the campaign. Feller realized at this point that he had a chance to break the all-time strikeout record of 343 held by Rube Waddell. Wheaties breakfast cereal offered him a $5,000 bonus should he break the record. With the support of Veeck and Boudreau, it became his goal.

Everything was working for Feller in mid-season. His fastball was back to prewar standards. His curveball was working well, and the new slider was dominant at times. He mixed in very few straight changeups, having little need for the pitch. The combination of the fastball, slider, and curve was devastating enough. On July 31st, Feller threw another one-hitter, this time against the Red Sox in League Park. Bobby Doerr ripped a sharp single to left field in the second inning, a clean hit, but Feller shut down the Sox for the rest of the game. A 4–1 victory, it was the seventh one-hitter of his career. Nine days later, on August 8th, Feller threw *another* one-hitter, this time against the White Sox in Comiskey Park. Sox catcher Frankie Hayes, who had been traded from Cleveland earlier in the year and had caught Feller's no-hitter in Yankee Stadium, broke this one up with a single in the seventh inning. The hit was a near affair, an outfield bloop that fell between shortstop Boudreau and center fielder Seerey. The ball was not well struck, and of all Feller's one-hitters, this one came closest to being a no-hitter. Still, it was the eighth one-hitter of his career, breaking the major league record held by Addie Joss. It was the 133d victory of Feller's career.

In late August, another attempt was made to measure Feller's velocity. On August 20th, Washington owner Clark Griffith approached Feller in the Indians clubhouse before the scheduled game against the Senators. Looking for a gate boost, Griffith had set up a way to test Feller's speed. The U.S. Army had a device called a "lumiline chronograph," used to measure the speed of artillery shells. It was claimed to be accurate to one ten-thousandth of a second. The device was an awkward contraption, a large wooden frame around a generator that created electric beams five feet apart, then measured the speed of the ball as it passed between the two points. Placed at home plate, it would measure the speed of any ball as it crossed the plate. It had previously been used in a 1939 test, clocking Atley Donald of the New York Yankees, owner of a hot fastball, at 94 mph. Griffith hyped the event for a week in advance, and a large crowd turned out to watch Feller throw through the device.

Griffith had neglected to ask if Feller would participate.

Feller had read about the promotion in the newspaper, and was offended at Griffith's lack of grace in failing to ask his permission. Feller had all the leverage. The crowd was waiting, and Griffith's apparent rudeness put the veteran baseball man on the defensive. Feller asked for $1,000.

Griffith balked. "Bob, this kind of promotion is good for baseball. The fans really appreciate this sort of thing." "That's all well and good," responded Feller, "but you've got thousands and thousands of people out there who've come to watch it. You're not losing anything on it, are you?"[11] Feller also pointed out that, after the event, he'd have to go out and pitch a game against Griffith's team, having of course expended at least some energy during the test. Eventually they settled on a compromise at $700.

The incident became public knowledge that fall, and has, over the years, been used as evidence of venality on Feller's part. This is unfair. The experience was a factor in Feller's hardening attitude toward ownership's exploitation of players. Feller accepted that promotional appearances, speaking gigs, and the like were a part of acting as an ambassador for the team, an activity he felt was part of his salary. But to take the field and work for free for the benefit of an owner, to whom he was not under contract, even just to toss some pitches through a machine, was different. In Feller's view, anytime a player acted as a performer, exposing himself to risk of injury, he deserved to be compensated. In the case of Clark Griffith and the speed machine, "it was like telling Fred Astaire he'd be doing his dance routines before the game . . . and the owner was going to make a lot of money, but he wasn't going to give Astaire anything. You can imagine what Fred Astaire would have said about that. Well, I was saying the same thing."[12] Feller later admitted that he would probably have done the test for free, if Griffith had simply had the courtesy to *ask* first before promoting it.

Feller warmed up for ten minutes in the bullpen and proceeded to the mound. He fired a strike on the first pitch, then threw three more. His fifth pitch hit one of the wooden supports, shattering it, to the consternation of the Army observers, and ending the test. Calculations showed that the fastest pitch was the first one, clocked at 98.6 mph. The speed test was national news, earning full-page treatment in *The Sporting News* on August 28th, and drawing mention in AP and UPI wire service reports. It was the fastest pitch ever accurately recorded to that point in history.

How accurate was the test? The Army was confident in the precision of their device, since it was used in critical artillery shell tests and calibrations. It was the best measurement possible with the technology of the time. The intriguing thing to consider is this: modern radar guns measure the velocity of a pitch when it leaves the pitcher's hand. This velocity is usually 3 to 4 mph faster than when the pitch actually reaches the plate. Thus, Feller's 98.6 reading in 1946, recorded when the pitch reached the plate, would likely measure 101–102 mph on a modern gun. Most experts, Feller included, believed that he threw harder when he first signed with the Indians than he did in 1946. One wonders what sort of bonus a high school pitcher with a 104 mph fastball would garner in the 21st century.

The Indians were clearly out of the race by August, well under .500 and mired in the second division. With the permission of

Veeck and Boudreau, Feller decided to make breaking the strikeout record his goal for the year. He would work on short rest, and even make the occasional relief outing if the situation called for it. Feller entered September with 291 strikeouts, needing 52 strikeouts to match Waddell's record. He was blasted by the Tigers on September 5th, losing 10–0 and fanning only two. He rebounded in his next two games, fanning eight against the Browns on September 9th and seven against the White Sox on September 12th. On September 15th, he fanned seven in a victory over the Athletics. This gave him 315 with fewer than two weeks left in the season. His next start, September 19th, resulted in just five strikeouts against the Senators.

With eight games left in the season, of which Feller could conceivably start three, he had 320 strikeouts.

On September 22d, Feller lost to the Tigers by a 3–0 score, fanning seven. He complained after the game that the Detroit hitters, with the exception of Dick Wakefield, weren't taking their full cuts, going instead for swinging bunts in an attempt to just make contact and avoid strikeouts.[13] On September 25th, Feller took the mound in Cleveland against the White Sox. He lost 4–1, but fanned ten men in the process, putting him on target for the record. Lou Boudreau announced that Feller would pitch in relief on September 27th, the first game of the Detroit series. Entering in the fifth inning, Feller threw five innings, fanning six. This gave him 343, tying Waddell's record, and with one start to go.

The final game of the season was September 30th, and it was a classic matchup, Feller against Detroit ace Hal Newhouser, himself owner of a 26–8 record. The weather was cool and cloudy, but there was no rain, and a crowd in excess of 47,000 came to watch the two fireballers pitch. Newhouser was throwing hard, although the Indians got to him for three runs in the fourth inning. Feller, though, was tired, and lacked velocity. He didn't strike out anyone until the fifth inning, when he fanned his fellow mound opponent for the 344th strikeout. Five Tigers fanned altogether, giving Feller 348 strikeouts, his 26th win, and the 138th victory of his career.

It was a disappointing overall season for Cleveland, the club finishing in sixth place with a 68–86 record. But Feller's achievements were remarkable, even overshadowing his prewar iron man performances. He appeared in 48 games, making 42 starts. He won 26 while losing 15. He completed 36 games, threw ten shutouts, and fired an incredible total of 371.3 innings. He allowed only 277 hits in those 371 innings, while fanning 348 and walking 153. His ERA of 2.18 ranked third in the American League. It was his huge volume of pitching that was incredible; his numbers on a per-inning basis were not the best in the league. He actually ranked second in strikeouts per nine innings, and second in hits allowed per nine innings, finishing a notch behind Newhouser in both categories.

His season was one for the ages, no doubt. But there was a bittersweet tinge to 1946. Amazingly, Feller finished just sixth in the MVP award voting, the honor going to Ted Williams. Despite Feller's tremendous pitching, he would probably have lost to Newhouser if there'd been a Cy Young Award. The Detroit ace had finished second in the MVP hunt. Both Williams and Newhouser had excellent seasons; losing out to them was no dishonor. But Feller was also bested in the MVP voting by Bobby Doerr and Johnny Pesky of Boston, and Mickey Vernon of the Washington Senators.

The other disappointment was the strikeout record itself, for additional research eventually revealed that Waddell had fanned 349 hitters in 1904, not the 343 previously recorded. This meant Feller fell one strikeout short of the record. Both Waddell and Feller were eventually passed by other pitchers, making the issue moot. Still, missing the record by just one strikeout had to hurt after all he'd accomplished. It was especially unfortunate since, if he'd known what the real record was, he could possibly have picked up two additional strikeouts with an extra relief appearance somewhere along the line.

Although Cleveland's '46 campaign ended on September 30th, Feller's did not. Sportswriters had remarked several times during the season that Feller seemed to have boundless energy. He was pitching more than anyone in the game; he also followed his ruthless conditioning program to the letter. But somehow he also had time for business affairs, and not just the normal sort that any player had to deal with from time to time. "Telegrams and letters follow him to the Tribe's locker rooms in all cities," noted *The Sporting News*.[14]

Feller had always been busy, handling endorsement deals and managing his growing network of finances. But the events of the summer of '46 were different, for Feller wasn't just managing his money. He was organizing the barnstorming tour to end all barnstorming tours. And, noted Ed McAuley in the *Baseball Digest*, "he did this . . . while doing more pitching than anyone else in the business."[15]

11

Storming into a New Era

Barnstorming was baseball at its best, innocent and fun, in towns big and small. But it was a business, too. . . .

—Bob Feller, *Now Pitching: Bob Feller*, p. 136

ob Feller had been intrigued with barnstorming since the day he saw Babe Ruth and Lou Gehrig come through Des Moines as a child. He'd taken advantage of barnstorming opportunities in previous seasons, though he curtailed the practice in the years just before the war. Feller had taken a brief barnstorming tour following the 1945 season, the highlight of which was a well-publicized, and very well-attended, game against the Kansas City Monarchs on October 5th in St. Louis. More than 20,000 fans saw this contest, which was historic because the crowd was an integrated one. Seating in Sportsman's Park was normally segregated, but the interest in the game from both white and black fans was so great that management had no choice but to open the "reserved for whites only" sections to black fans.[1] It was a taste of things to come.

Major league regulations limited barnstorming by major league players to a 10-day window after the World Series, the idea being to keep players from wearing themselves out or getting hurt. At least that was the official explanation. Many players, Feller included, believed that the real reason for the 10-day limit was to restrict the earning power of the individual player, for barnstorming could be very lucrative. The biggest stars often earned almost as much from a brief barnstorming tour as they did during the regular season. By limiting independent barnstorming, the owners kept players dependent on organized baseball for their income. A player without a large barnstorming check in his pocket was less likely to hold out in the spring, or complain loudly about having his salary reduced or frozen.

Feller first considered the idea of a huge tour while still serving in the Navy. His plan for 1946 was for the ultimate barnstorming production, involving as many star players as he could recruit, playing in as many cities as possible. But 10 days wasn't long enough for what he had in mind. Feller negotiated an extension of the barnstorming deadline with the new commissioner, Happy Chandler. Chandler agreed to increase the postseason barnstorming window from 10 days to 30, in appreciation of Feller's efforts in setting up the spring training camp for returning vets.

The organizational task was immense: hotels had to be reserved, travel plans arranged, press releases issued, ballparks booked. Feller handled most of the preliminary work himself, with assistance from a publicity man and a lawyer. Teams had to be recruited. Feller's club would consist of fellow major league players, and Bob corralled some of the best to participate. The pitching staff was himself, Bobo Newsom and Dutch Leonard of the Washington Senators, Johnny Sain of the Braves, and Spud Chandler of the New York Yankees. First base would be handled by Senator Mickey Vernon. Browns second baseman (and future soap opera star) Johnny Berardino and Yankees star shortstop Phil Rizzuto handled the middle infield. Bob's teammate Ken Keltner took the hot corner. The outfield was outstanding: Yankee Charlie Keller, St. Louis Brown Jeff Heath, and St. Louis Cardinal Stan Musial. Frankie Hayes of the White Sox, Jim Hegan of the Indians, and Feller's old friend Rollie Hemsley, now of the Phillies, handled the catching chores. Bob Lemon of the Indians, who could play the field or pitch, was brought on board as a utility player. Indians trainer Lefty Weisman would provide any needed medical attention and keep everyone in shape. All of these players, as well as secretaries, the team lawyer, and travel aides, were paid salaries out of the gate receipts and provided free transportation and board. One innovation was the mode of travel: Feller charted two DC-3 airliners to carry the team from city to city. Before this time, clubs traveled exclusively by train, since airplanes were still regarded with suspicion by many. Feller had tried to recruit Ted Williams and Hal Newhouser for the team, but their owners balked. Each were eventually paid a reported $10,000 by their owners *not* to participate, for fear of injury (or plane crash).[2] Feller estimated that financing the tour cost some $50,000, all of it out of his own pocket. He was forced to incorporate in order to handle the liability insurance he carried in case either team died in a plane crash.

Even without Williams and Newhouser, Feller's club was very impressive. Chandler had gone 20–8 with a 2.10 ERA. Sain had finished second in the National League with 20 wins, posting a 2.21 ERA. Newsom had won 14 games, splitting the season between the woeful Athletics and the mediocre Senators. Leonard was 37 and had seen better days, but was still an effective pitcher when kept within his limits. Keller had hit 30 homers, Heath had knocked 17, Vernon had hit .353 to lead the American League, and Musial .365 to lead the National. Berardino, Rizzuto, Keltner, and the catching staff were all sharp with the glove, if mediocre with the bat. The club had good pitching, strong defense, some power, and two batting champions on its roster. It would have been a very competitive club in a "real" major league season; a starting rotation of Feller/Sain/Chandler/Newsom/Leonard would probably have been the best in baseball.

This aggregation of talent, "Bob Feller's All-Stars," was slated to play 34 games in 27 days, covering some 13,000 miles of travel. Local opposition would be provided in some cities, but for the most part the opponents would be "Satchel Paige's Negro All-Stars," which would travel alongside the Feller group. Feller had a long-standing relationship with the legendary Negro League ace and barnstormer dating back to 1936. Although Feller consistently refers to their relationship as a "friendship," a better term might be "mutually beneficial business association." Paige's flamboyance was in sharp contrast with Feller's deliberate staidness, but both men were interested in making money. The two men were radically different in background and temperament, but both were bound by the color green, with the racial difference being, in Feller's mind, just an extra spark for the fans. Said Feller, "We were in this thing to give a lot of good entertainment and to give the fans a chance to see the whites against the blacks—it was a racial rivalry thing. We made a lot of money . . . everybody smiled all the way to the bank. And that was all there was to it. Nothing more, nothing less."[3]

The racial rivalry aspect was one of the best selling points, according to Feller, who says the thought of having a white vs. black tour first occurred to him when he was serving on the *Alabama*. Paige and the management of the Kansas City Monarchs put together a strong club. The choice of a Negro team to oppose Feller's stars, rather than just another team of major leaguers, was made in an increasingly charged baseball racial environment. It was well known that Commissioner Chandler, unlike his predecessor Landis, would not stand in the way of integration. Jackie Robinson had played the 1946 season in the minors for Montreal, and was considered a good bet to make the Dodgers roster in '47, if he were given a fair opportunity. There were rumors that a few other teams were thinking about signing Negro League players, but there was extremely strong resistance to the idea in many quarters, inside and outside baseball. Feller would eventually be drawn into this controversy.

The press release issued by Feller in announcing the tour was a straightforward accounting of the talent and accomplishments of the players on the Negro team.

> Satchel Paige, the old wizard of colored baseball, virtually is overshadowed by outstanding players on the aggregation of "All-Stars" he has organized to oppose Bob Feller's All-Stars on a nationwide tour.
> Paige's roster reads like a "Who's Who in Negro Baseball." From the veteran right-hand pitching marvel, whose name is legendary on two continents, to Manager Frank Duncan, who is in his 27th season with the famed Kansas City Monarchs, the club represents the best in Negro baseball.
> Four other members of the Monarchs, champions of the Negro American League, will barnstorm with Paige. They are Hilton Smith, clever right-hand pitcher; Henry Thompson, speedy second baseman; Williard (Home Run) Brown, center

fielder, and Johnny (Buck) O'Neil, flashy, dependable, hard-hitting first baseman.

O'Neil captured the Negro American League batting title with a .350 average, topping Brown by two points.

Three members of the Newark Eagles, champions of the Negro National League, are with Paige's All-Stars. The trio includes Monte Irvin, 27-year-old former Lincoln University football, basket ball, and baseball star; Leonard Pearson, 6-foot 2-inch, 210-pound first baseman, and Max Manning, also a former Lincoln U. luminary. Manning is a bespectacled right-hand pitcher who won the NNL championship with an 11–1 record. Irvin, incidentally, won the most valuable player award in the Puerto Rican Winter League last season.

The Philadelphia Stars have sent two crack players in pitcher Barney Brown, a southpaw, and Frank Austin, Panama-born shortstop. Brown, a sandlot product of Hartsville, S.C.—home town of Bobo Newsom of the Feller All-Stars—has only 155 pounds in his 5-foot 11-inch frame but has a respected fast ball. Austin hit .313 this year after compiling .354 and .390 averages the two previous seasons. Austin's .390 hitting in 1944 won the NNL batting championship, the only time a rookie ever captured the crown.

Sammy Jethroe, Cleveland center fielder, is a two-time NAL batting champion, hitting .350 in 1944 and .393 in 1945. Howard Easterling, Homestead Gray's third baseman, returned to baseball in midseason after three years of military service in the Pacific and batted .321 in 42 games.

Quincy Trouppe, catcher-manager of the Cleveland club, has toured with Paige previously. He was fifth among NAL batters this season with a .313 average.[4]

This was a strong conglomeration of talent, though some of the best black players were absent. Legendary slugger Josh Gibson was aging and had not been invited. Jackie Robinson, unwilling to accept the payment arrangement offered by Paige and Feller, was playing with a barnstorming club in California, teaming with Buck Leonard and Roy Campanella. Many experts felt that Paige's team was not the best the Negro Leagues had to offer, though to be fair Feller's club, as strong as it was, also lacked some of the best major league players, like Williams and Newhouser.

Like Feller's All-Stars, the players on Paige's club were motivated by the desire for a paycheck. "I was excited to be chosen for the Satchel Paige All-Stars," remembered Buck O'Neil, "because I knew I'd be making more money in one month than I had made in the last six."[5] But the idea of proving themselves against the white players was also present, made even more prominent by the Robinson situation, according to O'Neil. "I also felt that, even though it was black against white, this tour was an event that could be a real effect on big-league integration, because it took place after Jackie had proven himself, and if a lot of us weren't that lucky, we could at least prove ourselves against big-leaguers in these games."[6]

Accounts of the barnstorming tour are incomplete. A schedule issued by the Feller All-Stars was used by the *Sporting News* staff to record the game scores and attendance figures. The series began on September 30th, Feller having received special permission from Chandler to start the tour during the World Series. The first game was in Pittsburgh before a crowd of 4,592, Paige's All-Stars winning by a 3–1 score. Although box scores and statistics for all the games have not been found, archival material from the Feller files does give attendance and won-loss records for most games; we also have anecdotal accounts and statistics for some contests. The pace was brutal—more than one game was played on many days, and both Paige and Feller pitched in most games. The games in table 11.1 list do not include contests the Feller team played against local competition; there were 11 such games according to the *Sporting News* list.

According to the table, Feller's team beat Paige's 17 games to 5. But this differs from the accounts given in other sources. John Holway, building on the newspaper accounts available in 1991, finds clear evidence of the outcome of 13 games that has Feller's team holding a slight advantage at 7–6.[7] Glenn Stout and Dick Johnson, writing in 1997, give the Feller team's record as 13–5 in the series.[8] All sources agree that the exhibitions drew an estimated 250,000 fans in total, which the figures in the table, prorated for the missing attendance games and the contests against the non-Paige clubs, confirm.

As the schedule shows, the series was grueling, if fun. Feller was kept extremely busy, not just pitching but managing the club, both on the field and on the business side. On one occasion, his extensive business interests almost got the best of him. He had

TABLE 11.1.
Bob Feller's All-Stars: 1946 Barnstorming Tour

Date	Town	Score	Attendance	Start Time
9/30	Pittsburgh, Pa.	1–3	4,592	8:30 P.M.
10/01	Youngstown, Ohio	11–2	5,000 est.	3:00 P.M.
10/01	Cleveland, Ohio	5–0	9,700	8:30 P.M.
10/02	Chicago, Ill.	6–5	21,131	8:30 P.M.
10/03	Cincinnati, Ohio	3–0	11,000 est.	8:30 P.M.
10/04	New York, N.Y.	4–2	21,291	8:30 P.M.
10/05	Newark, N.J.	13–10	13,000 est.	8:45 P.M.
10/06	New York, N.Y.	0–4	27,462	2:30 P.M.
10/06	Baltimore, Md.	4–7	5,000 est.	8:45 P.M.
10/07	Columbus, Ohio	3–4	9,044	8:30 P.M.
10/08	Dayton, Ohio	7–6	4,000 est.	8:30 P.M.
10/10	Richmond, Ind.	7–2	unknown	unknown
10/12	Omaha, Neb.	3–2	4,100	2:30 P.M.
10/12	Wichita, Kan.	5–3	7,000 est.	8:30 P.M.
10/13	Kansas City, Mo.	2–3	2,800	8:30 P.M.
10/14	Kansas City, Mo.	4–1	5,300	8:30 P.M.
10/16	Los Angeles, Calif.	4–3	22,577	8:30 P.M.
10/17	San Diego, Calif.	2–0	10,600	8:30 P.M.
10/18	San Francisco, Calif.	6–0	9,813	8:30 P.M.
10/24	San Diego, Calif.	W	?????	
10/25	Los Angeles, Calif.	W	?????	
10/26	Long Beach, Calif.	W	?????	

agreed to appear at a milk convention in Atlantic City during the tour, earning some $2,000 for the event. But the convention was scheduled at the same time that the tour was playing on the West Coast, October 21st specifically, a date scheduled for one of the non-Paige exhibitions. Feller had everything worked out: he would pitch, take a plane to the East Coast for the convention, then get back to California in time for the next day's game. A pilot's strike almost derailed this plan. Feller had reservations on a TWA Constellation red-eye flight out of San Francisco, giving him plenty of time to start the game and get to the airport. But the flight was cancelled by the strike, forcing Feller to take an earlier United Airlines flight. The trouble was, the United flight was scheduled to leave at

8:40, and game time was 8:00. Rather than disappoint the fans in Sacramento, Feller took the mound early, at 7:50, pitched two innings, then left the stadium barely in time to catch the United flight. He made it to Atlantic City in time for the convention, then flew back to California in time for the next day's game.[9]

A second, and more frightening, bit of air travel drama occurred at the end of the tour. Flying from San Diego to Long Beach, the DC-3 chartered by Flying Tiger Airlines and filled with Feller and his teammates encountered mechanical difficulty on takeoff. The aircraft had flown some 13,000 miles in less than a month and was apparently as weary as her cargo. On takeoff from San Diego, one of the Pratt and Whitney engines began sputtering when the plane was about 200 feet off the ground. The pilot managed to bring the wheezing airliner back in for an emergency landing. Everyone emerged safely, and Feller quickly arranged a bus charter to carry everyone to their destination. But it was a close call, and what would have been the biggest disaster in baseball history was narrowly averted.

Financially, the tour was a huge success. Each player received $100 plus expenses per game, bringing the total haul for most players over $3,500. This was nearly equal to what each St. Louis Cardinal received for a full World Series share that year ($3,742), and greater than what member of the American League champion Red Sox received ($2,060). Feller himself netted some $80,000 after expenses. Combined with his salary from the Indians that year and endorsements, Feller earned an estimated total income of $175,000. This made him the highest-paid player in history to that point, beating Babe Ruth's record of an estimated $130,000.[10] The financial success of the tour, for both Feller and the major league players, caused some grumbling among ownership ranks, though this would not come out in the open until later.

The tour's first goal, to make money, was an obvious success. The second goal, to provide good baseball for the fans and to showcase the "racial rivalry," was also met. Feller and Paige started almost every game for their respective clubs, usually turning it over to the bullpen after two or three innings. We have reliable records of 23 innings for Feller and 26 for Paige; the data are interesting for anyone curious about the relative level of competition between the white team and the black team. In 23 innings, Feller allowed 20 hits, and seven runs, for a run average of 2.73. He walked six and struck out 19. In his 26 innings, Paige allowed 15 hits and five runs, for a run average of 1.73. He walked nine while striking out 23. From the available data, Paige outpitched Feller, although Bob was far from ineffective, posting numbers that were very similar to what he did in the major leagues. But by the end of the tour, Feller was tired and showing a noticeable drop in velocity. At least one writer warned Feller that he risked hurting himself by trying to match the rubber-armed Satchel, especially given the huge workload he'd already borne for the Indians that year. All told, Feller pitched over 450 innings in 1946.

As for Paige, anyone who knew anything about baseball and wasn't a horrendous bigot knew he had major league talent and was one of the best pitchers in the world. Even some people who *were* horrendous bigots admitted this. He'd demonstrated it for years in barnstorming events, although this series proved it beyond any doubt. It was also clear that at least some of the Negro players were of major league caliber, especially speedster Sam Jethroe and slugger Hank Thompson, who hit at least two long home runs off Feller in the series.

At least it should have been clear. By late autumn, it seemed possible that Jackie Robinson would get his shot in 1947 and that others would eventually follow, although who they would be and when they would get the chance remained to be seen. There were plenty of Negro League veterans waiting for the opportunity. But it seemed every team except Branch Rickey's Dodgers was unable or unwilling to take the leap, the majority because of outright racism, some because of social pressures, clubhouse concerns, or pure fear. On the other hand, a few teams had sent scouts to the Negro Leagues World Series that fall, an acknowledgment from at least some front offices that allowing black players into the majors was inevitable. But even the few major league organizations potentially interested in Negro talent seemed leery of the more experienced players. This might have been because of the desire to sign younger players with a "future," which was the excuse that Bill Veeck would eventually give. More probably, the reason was that signing veteran players like Paige or Gibson would be a tacit admission that they had been major league caliber all along, and had been barred only because of the color of their skin.

As curiosity mounted about black players in the major leagues, it was only logical that someone would ask Bob Feller what he thought. Feller had played black players for years on the barnstorming circuit, and was regarded as being a reasonably objective observer. *Sporting News* correspondent Steve George asked Feller if any of the "colored" players could "make the big league grade." "Haven't seen one—not one," Feller replied. "Maybe Paige when he was young. When you name him you're done. Some are good hitters. Some can field pretty good. Most of them are fast. But I have seen none who combine the qualities of a big league ball player."

"Not even Jackie Robinson?" George asked?

"Not even Jackie Robinson," Feller replied.[11]

Feller said more about Robinson in an interview with a *Los Angeles Times* reporter that was quoted nationwide. He admitted this time that Paige and Josh Gibson qualified for the major leagues in their youth, but that they were probably the only ones. As for Jackie, Feller "could not foresee any future" for him in the major league game. He was a fine athlete, but was built for football and "couldn't hit an inside pitch to save his neck." His bat was too slow to hit major league fastballs. "If he were a white man, I doubt if they would consider him big league material." Perhaps sensing his comments would bring offense, Feller then stated, "I hope he makes good. But I don't think he will."

Robinson was incensed. He'd only played Feller twice, in two of the southern California barnstorming games in late October; how could Feller make such an evaluation? "If you lined up ten of us [Negroes], I'll bet he couldn't pick me out of the bunch," Robinson told a New York reporter.[12] This was the beginning of a long dispute between Robinson and Feller, which boiled up now and again, but was frequently an undercurrent in discussions of race and baseball, especially during the Civil Rights movement in the 1960s. Robinson was certain that Feller's criticism of him was motivated by racism on Feller's part. Robinson's feelings, as well as later statements by Feller, did much to tarnish Feller's image in later decades.

But before Robinson broke in, Feller was not alone in questioning his qualifications. *The Sporting News* was highly skeptical, insultingly so in some editorials, contending that Robinson's abilities were more akin to "Class C" baseball than the major leagues. While the *Sporting News* editorial seems to have been motivated by racism, even journalists and others who supported integration were unsure that Robinson was the right player to make the jump. Many Negro Leaguers felt that Paige, Gibson, Monte Irvin, or Buck Leonard were more deserving candidates. Robinson would prove everyone, including Feller, wrong.

Was Feller's skepticism about Robinson racially motivated? Only Feller knows what went on in his mind at the time, and even memories can be self-edited. He resolutely denies any racial factors, maintaining to this day that he was honestly skeptical about Robinson's ability to hit major league pitching, particularly the high fastball. As noted, others shared this skepticism at the time, including some black players. In at least one interview, Feller tried to pass off the incident as a "tongue in cheek" thing, an attempt to spur publicity.[13] This seems unlikely; no one at the time picked up any such hint of humor in the statements. Another possibility, mentioned by many commentators over the years and hinted at in Feller's own words, is money. Robinson was angry at the financial arrangements for the black players, which is part of the reason he'd refused to join Paige's team from the beginning of the tour, preferring his own barnstorming arrangement in California. According to Feller, Robinson confronted him in the clubhouse before the second of the two games he did play against Feller's squad, demanding more money. "This is the major leagues, and you don't pull that stuff up here, not right before a game," Bob allegedly told Jackie.[14] There are two points worth noting about this incident. First, it possibly slanted Feller's view of Robinson, consciously or unconsciously. Second, Robinson's tactic of confronting Feller before the game was similar to the strategy employed by Feller before the speed-measuring event in Washington earlier that year, using the expectant crowd as leverage. The situations aren't quite the same, as Clark Griffith was attempting to take advantage of Feller, while Robinson was at least getting paid and was aware of the payment arrangements before the game. On the other hand, it obviously *wasn't* fair that the black players weren't paid on the same scale as the white players, or that they had to stay in segregated accommodations in many cities on the road trip. From Robinson's perspective, Feller was taking advantage of black players to line his pockets just as surely as Clark Griffith had taken advantage of Feller with his speedball stunt. And the fact that, in Robinson's view, Feller apparently didn't appreciate the talent of his black opponents made it even more galling. Even worse for those who wish to exculpate Feller from charges of racism is a statement he made in 1949 that was quoted in *Ebony*, that there were few black players who could "make the grade" in major league baseball—this, despite the fact that, by this time, Feller had played with Paige and Larry Doby in Cleveland, and that several other blacks had reached the majors and done well.[15]

Was Bob Feller a racist? This becomes a matter of retroactive psychology. By the social standards of the time, the mid-to-late-1940s, he clearly was not. Feller spent his formative years in a state that had a strong civil rights law on the books and actually enforced it on occasion. Iowa schools were integrated. Overt, Ku Klux Klan–style bigotry was not as widespread in Iowa as it was in the South or other areas of the Midwest. Bill Feller had black players on the Oakview team, and Feller says that his parents always taught him to judge people as individuals, not by the color of their skin. Yet Feller's early social environment was also one in which minor crimes committed by blacks were front-page news. Even the most talented black person in Iowa in the 1920s and 1930s had only limited options in terms of professional advancement. And even some of the most open-minded and liberal whites were condescendingly aware that blacks had "a peculiar sense of rhythm." The assumption that a talented young violinist like Bernard Mason *must* attend a Negro college gave no one pause.

Feller's attitude toward race was fairly typical of an Iowan of his period: liberal in comparison with much of the country, and not so liberal by today's standards. He was certainly more open to playing with blacks than many major league players at the time; he expressed none of the resentment or outright hatred of African Americans that many of his white major league counterparts did. In recruiting for his barnstorming tour, Feller refused to have players on his club who were openly racist or who insulted black players. "I wouldn't have them on my team," he says indignantly about white players who harassed their black counterparts.[16] While some of the Negro barnstormers he faced felt he was taking advantage of them for financial gain, others were happy to get the opportunity to showcase their abilities, and gave Feller credit for making it possible. In 1987, Feller was invited to a Negro League Old-Timers' Reunion in Kentucky, in recognition for his historic help in giving black players the chance to shine against their white counterparts. He was the only white player so honored, and was justifiably proud of that fact.

By the standards of 2002, the issue is more clouded. Feller played against blacks and gave them a platform, but it was not an equal partnership. When asked about segregation, Feller flatly stated, "It was wrong," and that he knew this at the time. But Feller was not a social crusader demanding that his black opponents be treated equally in restaurants and hotels. By today's standards, his unwillingness to challenge social inequality for the black players was racist. But condemning him for this ignores the sad news that American society in 1946 almost universally accepted this inequality, in most places to a much greater extent than Feller did. It was "the way things had always been." Recognition of this fact hardly excuses the racism of that era, but to judge Feller or anyone else in a historical vacuum is pointless. Within the context of his time, Feller's attitude on race was on the progressive side. That said, the events of the Civil Rights era would pass Feller by, doing much to harm his reputation with later generations.

12

The Uneasy Crown

Feller now owns everything to the left of first base.
—Indians owner Bill Veeck, January 1947

"Feller to Cop $80,000-Plus as New Pay King," triumphed the front page of *The Sporting News* on January 15, 1947. Feller had actually yet to sign a '47 contract, still negotiating the matter with Bill Veeck. But speculation in Cleveland was that his '47 contract would exceed the $50,000-plus-attendance bonus contract he'd signed in '46, an agreement that eventually netted him some $70,000. By way of comparison, Tigers ace Hal Newhouser, who'd been more effective than Feller on a per-inning basis in '46, worked his innings for $45,000.

Feller appeared in Cleveland for negotiations on January 21st. They'd had two previous discussions about the matter, and negotiations were cordial and reasonably quick. A 40-minute conference at League Park settled the matter; Feller and Veeck agreed on a base $70,000 salary, plus attendance bonus clauses that Veeck expected the club to meet easily. The Indians had drawn in excess of one million fans in '46, despite the mediocre performance of the club on the field, thanks to a combination of Feller's heroics and Veeck's creative promotions. He expected the same to hold true for '47. "It's the biggest [contract] ever signed by me, by Bob, and to my knowledge, the largest signed by anybody," Veeck told the gathered reporters. "I understand Babe Ruth's biggest salary was $80,000. Well, this will be more."[1] Wire service photographs of the signing ceremony ran in many newspapers, a smiling Feller, dressed in dark business suit and tie, putting his name on the contract, as a sweater-clad Veeck smiled next to him.

Feller claimed that too much emphasis was being placed on his financial concerns. "It's the best contract I ever signed and I'm happy about it. I think there's too much emphasis on it. Let's talk about the ball club. I'm sure we're going to be a much better ball club this year."

Veeck overhauled the roster that winter, looking especially for middle infield help. He found a willing trading partner in Yankees president Larry MacPhail, who was trying to improve his pitching staff. The Yankees had had a disappointing '46 campaign, and MacPhail was looking for a strong starting pitcher, since the incumbent ace, Spud Chandler, was 38 years old. Veeck and Mac-Phail swung a major trade, the Indians sending right-hander Allie Reynolds to New York in exchange for second baseman Joe Gordon. Gordon had hit just .210 in '46, but Veeck thought he was poised for a rebound, and would be a significant upgrade over Ray Mack and Drew Meyer. He boasted that the Boudreau/Gordon middle-infield combination would be the best in the league. Veeck and MacPhail swung another, less noticed, deal during the winter meetings. Ray Mack, who'd lost his job with the acquisition of Gordon, was packaged with catching prospect Sherman Lollar and sent east in exchange for outfielder Hal Peck, pitcher Al Gettel, and minor league pitching prospect Gene Bearden. A late winter transaction sent outfielder Gene Woodling to Pittsburgh, in exchange for veteran catcher Al Lopez. These two minor trades would have major consequences down the road.

Veeck loved Lou Boudreau's playing ability, but remained uneasy about his abilities as manager. Still, canning Lou would disrupt the clubhouse, so Veeck decided to bring in veteran manager Bill McKechnie as an "adviser" to Boudreau. The team looked strong in spring training; Gordon was playing with renewed vigor compared with his poor '46 performance. The infield defense was very strong—Gordon, Boudreau, and Keltner manned second, short, and third. Jim Hegan and Al Lopez were both fine defensive catchers. First baseman Eddie Robinson, a powerful slugger who missed most of the '46 campaign because of family troubles, was slotted for first base. Outfielder Dale Mitchell came up from the minor leagues and claimed the left field job. The rest of the outfield was manned by Catfish Metkovich, Pat Seerey, Hank Edwards, and Hal Peck. Defensively, the regulars were a strong group, but there were questions about how good the hitting would be.

The pitching staff also had some question marks. Feller was penciled in for his standard 300-plus strong innings. The Reynolds trade put a hole in the rotation, but the expected development of Bob Lemon, now a full-time pitcher, would cover that loss. Veeck liked Al Gettel and thought he'd do good work. Don Black, a live-armed pitcher with a serious drinking problem, had followed in the footsteps of Rollie Hemsley and was now sober, which could only help his performance. Red Embree could be counted on for 160-some innings of decent work, and even 37-year-old Mel Harder was still around for spot appearances. Much was riding on Feller. He was counted on to pitch to his usual standards, and the rest of the staff was based on "if": Tribe pitching would be strong if Lemon developed, if Gettel did as well for the Indians as he'd done for the Yankees, if Black stayed sober. Most experts felt that the Tribe was an improved club over 1946, but with only an outside chance as a challenge for the pennant. Fourth place and a record a bit above .500 was the consensus augury.

The Tribe got off to a good start, playing better than .500 ball in April and May, battling for second place. Feller was pitching well, leading the league in strikeouts, though not at the same blistering pace he'd kept in '46. The Indians and Feller received spats of national publicity throughout the spring, the Indians because Bill Veeck, after years of complaints from players, moved the fences in at cavernous Cleveland Stadium. "Now our players will have a chance to hit some home runs at home like the Red Sox and Yankees," he said. It would be good for attendance as well, as Veeck understood what modern owners have come to know: higher-scoring games draw people into the park.

Feller's publicity centered on his finances and the hangover from his tremendous pitching performance in '46. "Four-Alarm Fireballer" was a featured article in *All Sport* Magazine in April of

'47 and reviewed Feller's financial and professional accomplishments of the previous season. Asked if he could continue pressing
for strikeout records, Feller answered no. "From now on, I'm just
out to win ball games. Let the strikeouts take care of themselves. If
they come in bunches, all right. If they don't, what of that?" The
Indians, or at least trainer Lefty Weisman, expressed some concern
that Feller had worn himself down with the strikeout march and
the barnstorming tour in '46. "I'm hidin' your baseball uniforms at
my house until it's time for spring practice," Weisman playfully
told Feller at the conclusion of the barnstorming tour. Feller told
anyone who asked that his arm was fine, but observers had noticed
a drop in velocity late in '46, and many adopted a "wait-and-see"
approach for Feller in '47.

Finances were the main focus in a large *Saturday Evening Post*
feature on Feller on April 19th. The piece noted that Feller's salary,
attendance bonus, and endorsements could total as much as
$150,000 gross in '47. Yet his overall take-home pay after taxes
could be as little as $47,000, thanks to the heavy income tax burden
imposed by the Bureau of Internal Revenue. These high tax rates
were put in place to finance the Second World War and had yet to
be repealed. The article also discussed Feller's incorporation as
"Ro-Fel, Inc," which had been made necessary by insurance issues
from the barnstorming tour, and which had some tax advantages
as well. Feller was the first professional baseball player to incorporate in this way. He gave credit for his business creativity and success to both his father and Cy Slapnicka, but others credited Feller
himself with the way he'd developed into a successful modern
businessman. "He's a genius in being able to learn quickly," Alva
Bradley told the *Post*. "He always had a very good idea of his own
value. It usually was close to what we considered his value to us.
We had no trouble in contract discussions." Bill Veeck's experience
in dealing with Feller was similar. "Feller is the easiest ball player
I have ever dealt with, firm but fair."[2] Other owners, however, were
growing irritated by Feller's success. The barnstorming tour had
shown the potential earning power of players on their own, but
the owners wanted the players dependent on them. Already in the
spring of '47, there was grumbling in the ownership ranks about

restoring the 10-day barnstorming limit, or perhaps eliminating barnstorming altogether. Embarrassment and bad publicity about the paucity of the 1946 World Series player shares, especially in comparison with what the players on the Feller tour had made, had resulted in an increase of the World Series player's pool to a guaranteed minimum of $250,000, a rise of some $40,000 over the '46 take.[3]

Feller put much of his money into annuities, saving for retirement as well as the education of his growing family. There was the occasional luxury item, such as his cabin boat, a Cadillac for his use, a Buick for Virginia, a four-seat airplane, and the purchase of some land in Texas. This was still in sharp contrast to the spending habits of previous superstars like Babe Ruth; it seemed obvious that with such a sound business mind, Feller was set for life financially, despite the heavy tax burden. However, Feller wasn't content to merely own things; if he found he owned something that wasn't used much, he would sell it. For example, he discovered that he seldom had time to use the cabin cruiser he'd bought after the war, so he sold it (for a greater price than he'd originally bought it) rather than having it just sit around as an idle symbol of wealth.

Feller's business affairs continued to draw more national commentary during the spring than his pitching did. *Newsweek* weighed in with a feature article on June 2d focusing on Feller's endorsements and his new book. *Strikeout Story* was his first autobiography. Its first print run of 50,000 sold quickly and a second run of 25,000 was planned. The book was ghostwritten by Frank Gibbons of the *Cleveland Press*, though the two collaborated closely on the project. Many of the words and almost all the thoughts and themes were Feller's own.

His endorsements were also thriving. The Popsicle Company was happy with their promotional relationship with Feller, "the response to their 120,000 Bob Feller comic books and 75,000 Bob Feller bat pencils made them eager to renew their contract with him."[4] Other endorsement deals with General Mills cereal (Wheaties) and Wilson Sporting Goods were similarly successful. The magazine estimated that Feller had about $400,000 saved in bonds, annuities, and bank accounts. He was his own boss now, no longer dependent on his father, Slapnicka, or anyone else, on top of the world at age 28.

Feller's family life was also detailed by *Newsweek*. During the season, Feller lived with his family at the Tudor Arms, an expensive apartment/hotel complex in one of the richer sections of the city. Their apartment was filled with Virginia's books, mostly biographies and best-sellers. Her paintings hung on the walls. Bob himself was content to read technical works, mechanical journals, and aviation magazines, feeding his long-standing love of gadgets and contraptions.

The family was seldom in one place for long during the off-seasons, often spending time with Virginia's parents in Chicago, or Bob's mother in Van Meter, or visiting friends in various places across the country. They estimated that they had traveled some 100,000 miles by airplane, train, and car in 1946. The recently purchased ranch land in Texas was intended for a permanent home, though construction could not begin until the war-related shortage of housing materials cleared up.

Baseball on the field did get some mention in the *Newsweek* story, though it was secondary to the business and social descriptions. Feller rated Ted Williams as the toughest hitter in the game because of his outstanding batting eye. "He won't go after a slightly bad ball even with two strikes on him." DiMaggio was rated as tough, too, as well as Luke Appling, Johnny Pesky, Roy Cullenbine, and Stan Spence. Feller admitted that his biggest problem, even now with so much major league experience under his belt, was control. "I've tried everything," he said. "My control may stay with me through three straight games. In the next three games I'll do everything just as I did it before—and it all turns out wrong." He believed that one possible cause was variations in the height of the pitching mound throughout the American League. He claimed to be able to discern a difference of as much as an inch, and that some parks could vary as much as six inches from where they were supposed to be.

Sport Magazine got on the Feller biographical bandwagon in June as well, producing a 10-page feature story, including 13 photographs. This story dealt mainly with rehashing Feller's background, his beginnings on the farm, and his meteoric rise. His business affairs were also described in the standard terms. But *Sport* writer Ed Fitzgerald did pull in some intriguing nuggets worthy of our attention now. First, Fitzgerald claimed that, despite his huge income and wide-ranging business interests, none of the other Indians bore any resentment against him. Indeed, they admired Feller for what he'd been able to do, and related to him as a regular guy. At least, that was the perception in early 1947. Second, Feller admitted that he did not bear down in spring training play, feeling that it could burn out his arm to do so. Third, Fitzgerald overheard Feller have a brief discussion with another writer in regard to the rebellion against Ossie Vitt back in 1940. "Pretty bush league, wasn't it?" Feller mentioned to the other writer. "A little," was the reply. "About a hundred and one percent?" Feller growled back. Fitzgerald "definitely got the impression that he [Feller] regretted it [the Vitt affair] now." Feller also explained his method for determining his worth for the Indians in the yearly contract negotiations. "I keep a close check on every penny the club makes from Spring to Fall. Then I estimate carefully how much of that money they make out of my pitching. When it comes time to talk about next year's pay check, I have all the figures down. And I'm not usually far off, either."

The fact that Feller's contract negotiations were always smooth is testament to both the success of his method and its honesty.

Despite all the attention given to Feller's business affairs that spring, in the end it was his mound performance that drew the most notice, as it should have been. Feller was pitching well early in the year, well enough that former major league catcher Frank Bowerman, who caught for Christy Mathewson back in the 1900s and was regarded as a keen observer of the game, rated Feller as the "greatest pitcher baseball has yet seen" after watching him pitch a game in Yankee Stadium. Feller "has more physical equipment than I have seen in any other hurler in my time," Bowerman told *New York World Telegram* sportswriter Dan Daniel on May 7th. Indeed, Feller pitched some of his best baseball in late April and early May. He threw a one-hitter against the St. Louis Browns on

April 22d in Cleveland, allowing only a single base hit by Al Zarilla in the seventh inning of a 5–0 shutout win. He followed that up with another one-hitter, this one against the Red Sox in Cleveland on May 2d. This was a 2–0 win, the only hit a single by Johnny Pesky in the first inning. It was his 141st major league victory, and his incredible 10th one-hitter. In his first four starts, Feller allowed just one run in 35 innings.

It did not last. In May, things started to go wrong in Cleveland. The team went into a hitting slump. Hank Edwards got injured, and aside from Gordon and Boudreau, no one was hitting consistently well. By June 25th, the Indians were 10 games out of first place, struggling to stay around the .500 mark. Part of the decline was traced to Feller. After his one-hitter on May 2d, he also went into a slump, pitching poorly for the rest of the month of May, including four straight poor starts in the last two weeks of the month. It didn't take long for the rumors to start that Feller was tired, and that the barnstorming tour was at least partially responsible. The *Washington Post*'s Shirley Povich, who seldom had good words for Feller, fired the first national shot, claiming in an article headlined "Did Tour Play Hob for Bob" that "never before have American League hitters found Feller such a soft touch. His pitching this year has been strictly that of an in-and-outer."[5] Povich admitted that Feller remained a big attraction, but "when Feller can't produce 20 victories a year he'll slide into the category of just another pitcher who must haggle over an $18,000 contract." Feller denied there was anything wrong, blaming cold and rainy weather (which had plagued the Indians throughout the spring) for his weak pitching.

Feller began throwing better in early June. On June 13th, a Friday, pitching against the Athletics, Feller was outstanding for four innings, fanning nine of the first 11 men he faced. But on his final strikeout, he caught his foot in a hole in front of the pitching mound. This wrenched his knee, and pulled a muscle in his back. Unable to repeat his delivery consistently for the rest of the game, his velocity immediately dropped off. This was unfortunate. Long-time observers of Feller, including Cleveland sportswriters Frank Gibbons and Ed McAuley, felt that Feller in the first four innings of that game threw harder than he'd ever thrown in any previous game. Feller agreed. "It was the best stuff I ever had," he told me in 2002. He returned to make his next start, but was inconsistent for the next few weeks.

Attention on Feller's problems faded temporarily on July 3d when Bill Veeck announced that the Tribe was making an important addition to the roster. "We've signed a new ballplayer named Larry Doby. He's a Negro. He'll be a great ballplayer. He's a second baseman with the Newark Eagles in the Negro National League."

Jackie Robinson was tearing up the National League, making fools of those who'd doubted him, bearing up incredibly well under a torrent of racial insults from the stands and other players. But so far, no other team had been willing to give a black player a chance, owners and general managers wanting to stall as long as they could out of racism, fear, or general apathy. But not Bill Veeck. He'd been interested in signing black players before, though he waited until Robinson was established and obviously successful before making his move. He was already a maverick; those who supported integration feared that if Veeck were the first owner to bring in a black player, that the whole issue would be tarred as a publicity stunt, especially if the player failed. But with Robinson successful and the bookish Branch Rickey having cleared the way, Veeck was free to move.

He had considered signing one of the established Negro League veterans, but that could also be derided as a publicity stunt rather than a serious attempt to improve the team for the future. He decided instead to go with a relatively young, but very talented, prospect recommended by his scouts. Doby fit the bill. He was athletic, ran well, and had excellent power potential. He was also college educated, rather quiet, shy, and competitive, but not the sort of firebrand that Robinson could be. He was visibly nervous in his final game for the Eagles, muffing several routine plays, although he did hit a home run. He took the train from Newark to Chicago to join the team on July 5th.

Doby's debut was awkward. While some in the Indians clubhouse welcomed him, others refused to shake his hand. Feller was neither cold nor warm toward Doby. There was some indication that manager Boudreau resented Doby's presence at first, though this was more because Veeck hadn't consulted Boudreau before bringing Doby in; the two later became close friends. Doby struggled in his initial exposure with the Indians, hitting just .156 in 29 games for the rest of the season, being used primarily off the bench in a reserve role as a pinch hitter. Although Doby was not a success at first, Veeck's eye was on what he could do in the future.

By July, it was clear that the Indians were not going to contend, as the lack of hitting was proving critical. Feller stabilized after his rough May and early June stretch, but not enough to silence the doubters. In his last start before the All-Star Break, Feller left the game in the first inning, unable to continue because of back pain. X-rays revealed torn cartilage and a separated rib, originally caused by the June injury in Philadelphia. He was selected to the All-Star Game, but decided against pitching. He could still have attended, of course, but decided not to do so, saying it wouldn't be fair to the fans for him to appear but not pitch. For this he was roundly criticized when the second half of the season began, but this was only the beginning.

Although Feller was pitching better in the second half than he'd pitched in May and June, his velocity was down, and he was frequently less than overpowering. Most observers traced this to the barnstorming tour, apparently ignoring the impact of the back injury. Feller's barnstorming and outside business interests became a major issue for Cleveland sports fans. The issue exploded again on August 13th, when Feller announced that he had signed to pitch in the Cuban winter leagues. At the time, his record was "just" 14–9, and Cleveland fans took the news badly. Ownership was less than pleased as well, and Commissioner Chandler issued an edict preventing *any* major leaguer from playing in the Cuban winter league. Feller offered to turn all of his Cuban salary, estimated at $18,000, over to the newly established major league pension fund, but Chandler refused to reverse the decision. This defused the Cuban issue, but Feller returned to making arrangements for another barnstorming tour on the '46 model.

On August 23d, the *Cleveland News* published a pro/con feature entitled "Should Bob Feller Barnstorm?" On the pro side was former Indian outfielder Jeff Heath.

What's going on there up in Cleveland? I hear that the sports writers and the public are giving my old roommate, Bob Feller, quite a beating. No one knows better than I do that a Feller can be a hero one day and a bum the next, but I never thought it would happen to Bob.

The *News* has asked me to take the affirmative side of the question: Should Bob Feller Barnstorm?

Certainly he should. He has the perfect right to earn some extra money within the regulations set up by the commissioner. He has almost a duty to let himself be seen in towns off the big league beat. When Bob barnstorms, he makes money for himself, but he also makes thousands of new friends for baseball. His trip is swell promotional activity for the entire game.

Now people are staying that he hurt his arm on that trip and that, besides, he isn't doing so well this summer because he is giving so much time to arranging his barnstorming schedule.

Both arguments are silly. I made the tour with Bob last fall. . . . He worked only a few innings each day, and then he didn't have to strain himself any more than he would warming up on the sidelines.

As for the other point, anyone who has traveled with a big league team can tell you that the players have more spare time than the members of any other profession I can think of.

Bob could spend his time off the field sitting in movies, playing cards, maybe having a beer or two. Instead, he works on his barnstorming schedule. As a matter of fact, Bob is such a high-strung boy that I think it's good for him to have his mind occupied by outside activities.

It's true that Bob isn't having one of his best years. Heck, that can happen to anybody. Barnstorming has no effect whatever. Hal Newhouser didn't barnstorm, and look at his record [this year].

Heath's argument is correct on some grounds: Feller's organizational and business affairs were unlikely to have an actual negative impact on his pitching. He wasn't drinking beer or playing cards or chasing women, and he certainly didn't neglect his physical condition or forgo his duties to the Indians. It's also true that Hal Newhouser hadn't barnstormed, but was, like Feller, suffering a decline in effectiveness. A bad year could just be a bad year. On the other hand, to assert boldly as Heath did that the barnstorming tour had no effect at all is unsupportable.

The con position in the *News* piece was taken by one David F.

Reinthal, a season ticket holder for 10 years, and vice president of the Bamberger-Reinthal Company, a textile mill with a history of worker abuse, strikebreaking, and difficult labor relations.

Any public figure, whether a politician, movie actor, or baseball player has a certain obligation to the people who put him in the position he has attained. To some extent he is in a position where a great bit of his life cannot be ruled by his own desires. It is in this position that Bob Feller finds himself today.

Endowed with great natural ability and once considered the game's greatest pitcher, it still took the confidence and enthusiasm of the average baseball fan to put him in the position he has attained today. There is no question that Feller, through his poor season, plus his increasingly unfortunate habit of speaking the wrong thing at the wrong time, has alienated many of his fans who were once his loyal supporters. Now Feller should call off his latest postseason barnstorming tour in a gesture to regain the loyalty of his fans.

The Cleveland baseball fans do not begrudge Feller's astronomical salary of approximately $85,000 when they feel he earns this. This year the opinion is quite general that he has not earned it and much of the blame is being laid to the tour he took last year. Whether this tour hurt him or not, the fact remains that he is having a bad season and the fans feel that this barnstorming tour is the cause.

Further, Feller has an obligation to his fellow teammates. The Cleveland team has a chance to reach second place, which would mean approximately an additional $1,000 for each player. This $1,000 means little to Feller, but means considerable to the average player earning $6,000 or $7,000. Feller's poor season plus his concern about barnstorming have not been conducive to obtain this extra bonus for his fellow teammates.

Cleveland has waited 27 years for a pennant and will not be happy until they get one. Feller's actions have not been conducive toward this end. He personally can earn more and probably gain more personal prestige with a spectacular postseason tour, but the Cleveland fans and players want a pennant in Cleveland and feel Feller has let them down.

No one can blame Feller for wanting to earn as much money as is possible. This is only human and especially so in the case of a baseball player whose earning period is very limited, but Feller seems to have gone beyond this natural urge without regard for the loyalty or friendship of his fans, his teammates, and his employer. His first job is to win games for the Cleveland Baseball Team. Once he has proved that he can do this in as great numbers and in as spectacular a manner as he used to, then a barnstorming tour would be justified, but until this day Feller should content himself with his $85,000 and the confidence and loyalty of the people around him.

Reinthals' argument seems based entirely on the assumption that Feller was solely responsible for the Indians not contending in 1947. Feller was not pitching as well in '47 as he had in '46, but he was still effective overall, as we shall see. And his problems had nothing to do with the struggles of the offense, or inconsistent pitching from the other moundsmen. But Feller, as the most expensive man on the team and the biggest name, became the lightning rod for all criticism and resentment from long-frustrated Clevelanders.

Was there actually anything to the argument that Feller's barnstorming was responsible for his drop in '47? Heath's assertion of "absolutely not" is as specious as Reinthal's assertion of "of course." It is possible that the '46 tour was a factor to some extent, but the exact nature of it is impossible to pin down from this distance in time. The back injury suffered in the game against the Athletics was an obvious factor. The other charge, that Feller's business dealings and preparations for the '47 tour were inhibiting his performance for the Indians, was clearly unfair. Business affairs had not interfered during his excellent '46 season. In fact, fans and writers were amazed at how Feller was able to handle both the playing side and the business side of baseball that year. It was considered a point in his favor, a major contribution to his image as the All-American athlete/entrepreneur. But now, suddenly, it was the source of all problems. Feller himself later admitted that questions about him throwing too much were "valid," though he personally chose to ignore the critics and felt there was nothing seriously wrong with his arm. And the concern about his overattention to business affairs he rejected out of hand.

There were many critics to ignore, most of them not so well spoken as Reinthal, however. All three Cleveland papers were inundated with letters from angry fans, taking Feller to task for his subpar pitching, as well as his alleged greed. Catcalls from the stands were frequent on the occasions Feller struggled. The transition from hero to goat in the eyes of Tribe fans was quick and unmerciful. Ed McAuley called it a "fan eruption unequaled since the Vitt Rebellion days."[6]

Feller seemed at something of a loss to deal with it, huddling with Bill Veeck at one point for advice on public relations. "The only story," he said emerging from the meeting, "is that there is no story. This stuff about my outside activities is a big rhubarb and I'm not going to talk any more about it."

"We talked about the importance of good public relations for one thing," Veeck told McAuley. "I suggested that it is always well to try to anticipate the public reaction to any move or statement." The fans weren't the only ones complaining about barnstorming: the owners were too. Clark Griffith supposedly blamed Feller's '46 tour for the '47 slump of Mickey Vernon, though Vernon had always been inconsistent. Griffith was said to be the prime mover behind ownership attempts to reimpose strict limits on barnstorming. Ownership retained the 30-day window that Chandler had agreed to in 1946, but put back the start of barnstorming until October 8th, a decision that angered Feller. "No employer should be able to tell his men how much they can earn, or where and when they can earn it, once they've fulfilled their contract obligation for the season."[7] Feller blamed unnamed "bigwigs" for the flap, though the reaction of the Cleveland faithful was clearly on the side of the owners.

The season wound down with the Tribe playing well in September, finishing at 80–74. In fourth place, they were 17 games in back of the resurgent Yankees, but it was a big improvement over 1946 and the best record the Tribe had managed since '43. Joe Gordon had been everything hoped for, hitting .272 with 29 homers and providing steady defense. Boudreau was spectacular as usual with the glove, and contributed a .307 average and 45 doubles. Rookie Dale Mitchell hit .316. The rest of the offense was rather disappointing. Among the pitchers, Bob Lemon (3.45 ERA, 11 wins), Al Gettel (3.20 ERA, 11 wins), and Red Embree (8–11 record but solid 3.15 ERA) were quite effective. Reliever Eddie Klieman was the team's fireman, and would subsequently be awarded the league lead with 17 saves while posting a 3.03 ERA.

And what of Bob Feller, the huge disappointment, the man who, to some, was single-handedly responsible for the failure of the Indians to win the pennant?

He led the American League with 299 innings. He led the American League with 20 victories. He led the American League with 196 strikeouts. He led the league in games started. He led the league in shutouts. His 2.68 ERA ranked second in the league. Adjusted for park effects, it was 30 percent better than league average, which ranked sixth. He led the league in fewest hits and walks allowed per nine innings, something he accomplished only one other time in his career. He led the league in strikeouts per inning. By no reasonable measure could Feller's 1947 season be considered a failure. The criticism of him was grossly unfair.

Yet it was still there. Even Feller himself felt that something had changed; he'd struck out "only" 196 batters, a far cry from the 348 he'd fanned the previous year. Part of that was a simple reduction in workload from 371 innings to "just" 299. The sore back and strained knee from the game against the Athletics did seem to reduce the hop on his pitches. Another factor was league context: strikeouts were down across all of baseball in 1947. Feller had fanned 8.43 men per nine innings in 1946, compared with the American League average of 4.21. In 1947, the league average dropped to 3.72, and Feller's rate dropped to 5.90. His rate dropped more than the league rate did, although it was still high enough to lead the league. If Feller was really slipping, it was only in comparison with what he'd done in 1946.

Other things were not quite the same in 1947 as they were in 1946. After the conclusion of the World Series, Feller went barnstorming again, though the series was neither as heavily promoted nor as well attended as the '46 event. Feller's club was well stocked once again, featuring National League home run champ Ralph Kiner of the Pirates, Andy Pafko of the Cubs, first baseman Ferris Fain of the Athletics, and Feller's teammate, Ken Keltner. Pitching in back of Feller were 16-game winner Eddie Lopat of the White Sox, 10-game winner Bill McCahan of the Athletics, and 22-game winner Ewell Blackwell of the Cincinnati Reds, who had led the

National League with 193 strikeouts. Jeff Heath and Jim Hegan also participated.

The Feller troupe spent several days touring Mexico, where baseball was growing in popularity, despite the financial collapse of Jorge Pasquel's Mexican League. Local promoters took pains to provide "lavish" entertainment for Feller and company. At one point, disaster nearly struck when the local Mexican team the Americans were supposed to play suddenly disbanded. Thinking quickly, Feller contacted a friend, Ken Parker, who was running an All-Star barnstorming tour of Pacific Coast League players in California. Parker and his crew quickly flew to Mexico City to play Feller's squad, all expenses paid out of Feller's pocket.[8] It was a good club; the PCL stars, with some assistance from local Mexican stars, played the major leaguers to a split in the Mexican tour. Games were played in Mexico City, Tampico, Monterrey, and Torreaon. Feller remarked that the thin air and high altitude in Mexico City made it hard to throw his curveball properly, something that major league pitchers discovered to be equally true in Denver 50 years later.

Feller's tour concluded with contests against the Chet Brewer's Kansas City Royals Negro League barnstormers in California, with Satchel Paige the headline performer. Paige was backed by Kansas City Monarch catcher Joe Greene, plus infielder (and future major leaguer) Charlie Neal. Paige was brilliant; some observers felt he was angry that he hadn't gotten a chance yet in the major leagues and was taking his frustration out on Feller's club. Paige's attitude was understandable. Jackie Robinson had proven himself. The Indians had taken a chance on Larry Doby. The St. Louis Browns, disregarding the highly racist nature of their home city, brought in Hank Thompson and Willard Brown in mid-season trial, although they eventually sent both back to the Kansas City Monarchs. The Dodgers had signed Dan Bankhead, a successful Negro League pitcher, and had used him as a pinch-runner in the World Series. But no one had called for Satchel Paige.

Whether or not he had extra motivation, Paige made Feller's squad look awful. In five games against Feller's team, Paige threw 27 innings, allowing just 13 hits and three runs, a 1.00 runs-allowed

average. He fanned 44, and gave up only one walk. Feller, by contrast, was battered by Chet Brewer's club, throwing 18 innings, giving up 18 hits and nine runs, while fanning just nine. The worst
had been in a highly promoted "grudge" matchup between Feller
and Paige on November 2d. Both men would throw nine innings,
Feller telling the press beforehand that Paige was so old, he
couldn't stand up under the strain of pitching a full nine innings.
Unlike his comments about Jackie Robinson the year before, this
truly was tongue-in-cheek, a way to drum up publicity for the
game and intensify the rivalry. Satchel played along by claiming
that he might be 50. It worked: the game was a sell-out at Wrigley
Field in Los Angeles.

Both Paige and Feller threw nine innings on November 2d, but
the results were radically different: Paige threw a four-hit shutout,
and fanned 15. Feller was blasted for eight runs.[9] Could anyone
possibly doubt that Satchel Paige was a major league pitcher? Yet
the phone still didn't ring. Satchel went off to play winter ball in
the Caribbean. Feller went back home to his wife and son.

The 1947 tour was not a financial success. What had been a
large profit in 1946 turned into a $5,000 loss for Feller in '47. Atten-
dance was down some 100,000 from the previous year, which Feller blamed in part on the later start. Once the World Series was
over, it was hard to get people interested in baseball as attention
quickly turned to the gridiron. "Unless the rule is amended," Feller told *The Sporting News* on November 12th, "there is no use in
making tours."

The 1947 tour was indeed the last major barnstorming adventure of Feller's career. The rise of television brought major league
players into more and more households; it was no longer necessary
for stars to barnstorm to drum up interest in the game, or to give
fans in the boondocks a chance to see major leaguers in action. Integration of organized baseball eventually drove the Negro
Leagues and the various black touring clubs out of business. Occasional exhibition games continue to this day, of course, but the
great age of barnstorming was over.

Feller's barnstorming gave black players a chance to showcase
their talents against white counterparts. It also made a tremendous
amount of money for Feller. But while the '46 and '47 tours showed

Feller at his most creative and most business-savvy, they also may have exposed one of the weaknesses in his personality. This was not overt racism, as Jackie Robinson and others believed they perceived, but rather what many saw as a growing venality. As we have seen, Feller had always been interested in making money. In previous cases of alleged greed, such as the '46 confrontation with Clark Griffith, Feller's actions were not avaricious and one-sided as his detractors had said. But one alleged incident during the '47 tour casts this side of Feller's personality in the worst possible light.

Chet Brewer, running the Kansas City Royals touring team that Feller's All-Stars played in California, felt unfairly "cut out" of the business management of the exhibitions and kept on the sidelines by Feller's business managers and the local promoters. Suspicious that his players were being underpaid, he managed to acquire some ledger sheets from Feller's business people. Brewer noticed a problem: Satchel Paige was being underpaid. His contract called for 15 percent of the gate gross, but he was being paid out of the net receipts. This couldn't be an accident; the difference between what he was contractually owed and what he'd received was some $2,400, not a small sum. Brewer told Paige about it. Satchel then went to Feller and got the money. Paige apparently did not hold the incident against Feller, but Feller held it against Brewer. "Boy, Bob Feller hated me for a long time. I saw him once in an airport in Phoenix and he didn't even speak to me. He hated to pay Satchel that $2,400," remembered Brewer.[10]

I asked Feller about this incident in October of 2002. He said it was the first he'd heard of it, that he didn't know what Brewer was talking about, and that it was the tour promoters and the Kansas City management that were responsible for making sure everyone got paid. "Satchel got every dime that was coming to him," Feller told me. "He was a great guy and a good friend of mine." Feller went on to praise Brewer as a pitcher, but insisted he knew nothing of the incident to which Brewer refers.

Since both Paige and Brewer have passed on, getting a current account of this "he said, he said" dilemma is impossible. On the other hand, Feller did tell some of his Indians teammates about financial problems with Paige, though the details are different from

Brewer's ledger book story, at least according to Steve Gromek. "The story I heard [from Feller] was that Satch signed a contract with Feller, then realized how many people they were drawin' and he wanted to get more money."[11] Paige biographer Mark Ribowsky points out that Feller's version of his monetary disagreement with Satch seems "contrived to make Satch's well-known avarice and lack of responsibility the issue, not those account books."[12]

I will leave it to the reader whether to believe Brewer's story, or Feller's.

13

The Highs and the Lows

You can say what you want to about any particular athlete, and people could say what they wanted about me—
whether they loved me or hated me, whether they
thought I was a hero for pitching so much or thought I
was doing it only for the money, whether they thought I
was ducking an All-Star Game or was honestly injured.
But whatever you think about any athlete, you have no
way of knowing how it feels to go through the highs and
lows of the profession.

—Bob Feller

Despite his image as a publicity-driven showman, Bill Veeck
understood the necessity of long-term planning in baseball.
Looking toward the future, he felt that the Indians were a
better club than they'd shown in 1947. Certainly this was
true statistically: the club had scored 687 runs while allowing 588, which should have resulted in a much stronger record than
just 80–74—using Bill James' famous Pythagorean formula projected the '47 club to go 88–66. James' mathematical approach was
still some 30 years in the future, but it is evidence that the Tribe
was a better club than their won-loss record indicated, something
that Veeck felt intuitively. The Indians had had a long history of
underachievement throughout the Alva Bradley years, a record
that Veeck was determined not to repeat.

Something needed to be done to shake up the roster and the
clubhouse. Although Veeck was well aware that Lou Boudreau was
one of the best players in baseball, he'd never been 100 percent con-

vinced that his managerial skills were up to snuff. His handling of
the bullpen, in particular, seemed shaky. There was another concern as well: Boudreau's ankles were weak, occasionally kept him
on the sidelines, and could give out completely at any time. The
shortstop was approaching his 30th birthday, and his value on the
trade market would never be higher. Trading Boudreau, of course,
would be very difficult from a publicity standpoint, and might also
create problems in the clubhouse. But when the St. Louis Browns
approached Veeck during the World Series with a trade offer for
Boudreau, he felt he had to listen.

The Browns had been the basket case of the American League
for years. Some historically mediocre clubs, the White Sox for example, had access to decent amounts of revenue, but seemed to
lack the knack for finding good players or allocating their resources well. Other weaker teams, such the Senators and the Athletics, had some decent scouts and baseball brains, but lacked the
financial resources to consistently compete. The Browns, though,
combined both weaknesses into a package of consistent despair:
their front office was usually both inept and broke. The '47 club
had finished 59–95, featuring mediocre pitching and a very weak
offense. The three best players on the team were first baseman
Wally Judnich (.258, 18 homers), aging former Indian Jeff Heath
(.251, 27 homers), and shortstop Vern Stephens. Stephens had hit
15 homers with a .279 average, and had led the American League
in assists at shortstop. Best of all, he was just 26, entering his prime
years.

Veeck and Browns general manager Bill DeWitt began talking
during the World Series. The Browns wanted to shake up their own
roster, and were also looking for cash to ease their monetary problems. Veeck and DeWitt came up with a trade proposal that would
send Boudreau and $100,000 cash to St. Louis, in exchange for Ste-
phens, Judnich, and pitchers Jack Kramer and Ellis Kinder. Purely
on paper, the deal would make sense for Cleveland. Stephens
would replace Boudreau in the lineup, providing more power with
only a slight decline in defense. He was also younger. Judnich
would complement Eddie Robinson at first base very well, and
Kinder and Kramer would provide decent pitching reinforcement.

From the Browns perspective, the trade would give both financial relief and a needed big-name player to try and boost interest in the team. But the deal stalled when the Browns wanted enough extra cash included in the deal to pay Boudreau's salary for the next three years.

The financial terms could have been resolved, but what killed the trade was when word leaked out. Veeck had told some writers off the record about the pending transaction, but someone spilled the beans, and word got around Cleveland very quickly. Fans were enraged, to the point where Veeck was met by a hostile crowd at the airport when returning from his World Series trip. He quickly backed down, ensuring everyone that Boudreau's job, at shortstop and as manager, was safe for 1948. The main effect of the incident was to sour relations with Boudreau. The relationship between the owner and the manager was not to the point of outright hostility, but rather one of strained cordiality. Although Boudreau was given a two-year contract, it was apparent to all that, if the Indians did *not* improve in '48, that Boudreau probably wouldn't be back as manager.

Although the huge transaction with the Browns didn't come off, Veeck was still active on the trade market, as usual. Pitcher Red Embree was traded to the Yankees for outfielder Allie Clark, who'd hit .373 in limited action in '47. He picked up another outfielder, speedy glove man Thurman Tucker, from the White Sox. Although the Stephens/Boudreau trade had fallen through, Veeck went ahead and acquired Walt Judnich from the Browns in exchange for three minor leaguers and cash, then added Johnny Berardino in another cash transaction a few weeks later. Finally, pitcher Russ Christopher was purchased from Philadelphia during spring training. He'd been suffering from pneumonia, but Veeck was convinced he would recover, and considering he'd pitched well in '47 (2.90 ERA, 10 wins, 12 saves), it was a good gamble. Veeck also added famous Detroit slugger Hank Greenberg to the Tribe's front office, although it was rumored he could be activated at some point if an extra bat was needed. Hall of Famer Tris Speaker was brought in as an outfield coach; his main duty during spring training was to work with Larry Doby, who would move from infield to outfield on a full-time basis.

Bob Feller was still counted on as the Tribe's ace, but the bad publicity that hounded him in 1947 continued as '48 opened. "Feller Legend Bows to Materialism" opined *New York Post* sportswriter Jimmy Cannon in the January issue of *Baseball Digest*. Referring to his '46 and '47 barnstorming tours, Cannon wrote disdainfully, "It is the opinion of many that Feller has dissipated his greatness on these trips through the villages below the big leagues, and they make venomous remarks when you mention his record of twenty wins against eleven losses." At this point in baseball history, most "experts" judged a pitcher solely his won-loss record. As we saw in the previous chapter, Feller had pitched extremely well in 1947, despite all the criticisms of fans and press. Even if you ignore statistics like ERA, he was still the only pitcher in the American League to win 20 games. "But twenty isn't enough for Feller," wrote Cannon.

The complaints about Feller's performance don't hold water. They didn't at the time, as many grudgingly recognized, and they certainly don't from the distance of 50 years. But more disturbing was the shift in perceptions about him. It wasn't just the fans who started turning against Rapid Rob, but the players as well, according to Cannon. "When I go down into the dugout or sit with them in the clubhouses and hotel lobbies, the ball players talk of Feller with spiteful coldness. They no longer wonder at his great talent as a pitcher but are disgusted by his frantic chase of the buck." Other writers also recorded this resentment against Feller, though few active players would actually go on the record about it. Walker Cooper had allegedly challenged Feller while riding on a train with him early in 1947, accusing him of being "stingy and selfish." Feller took the abuse, then walked away without saying a word. Some of the players on the barnstorming tours were overheard by writers muttering about Feller's high-handedness. They compared their dealings with him with their dealings with ownership. Others, on the other hand, praised his business acumen and felt they'd been treated fairly. Cannon noted that the growing resentment against Feller was curious, because most of the players would be doing ex-

actly the same thing in his situation: maximizing their earning potential. But even some of those who understood Feller's position
felt he was jeopardizing his career. One who was willing to go on
the record about it was Rogers Hornsby, Feller's boyhood idol.
"Feller is a fellow who must win more games than anyone else—
strike out more—finish more than anyone else. He's got to do it
because he gets more money than anyone else in the game. He's
cutting his life right in half in exhibition games. He'd make more
money if he just pitched during the season and picked up what he
could with odds and ends and let the exhibition games go."

Although outwardly dismissive of such opinions, Feller was
not blind to the need to repair his reputation and reach out to the
community. In January, he spoke on national radio to announce
that he was helping organize a nationwide program to promote
understanding between young people and adults, and to recognize
and promote community service for the youth of the nation. On
February 12th, he held a press conference in the Mayflower Hotel
in New York City. There, he announced that the Popsicle Company
had put forth some $100,000 to help fund this drive against juvenile
delinquency. Feller chaired an advisory committee, consisting of
himself, Bob Hope, Perry Como, Father Flanagan of Boys Town,
Bishop B. J. Shiel of Chicago, and Walter F. White, famed civil rights
crusader and National Secretary of the NAACP. The program
would give awards to boys and girls for outstanding community
service, including certificates of achievement, gold medals, and
U.S. Savings Bonds. Feller acted as a spokesman for the campaign,
but made it clear to the press that he would devote his full time
during the playing season to the Indians, and that the project was
for community service, not a money-making venture.[1]

The attempted rehabilitation of Feller's image continued
throughout the spring. Feller announced that he was curtailing his
outside business interests. He finished up his second book, a manual for youngsters entitled *How to Pitch*, as well as a motion picture
short on the same subject, but he then devoted himself even more
than usual to physical conditioning. He dropped plans for any
1948 barnstorming, although skeptics believed this was mostly because the '47 tour had not been profitable. He told Cleveland writer

Hal Lebovitz that he had two goals for '48: to be the best possible pitcher, and to be the best possible father and husband.[2] The birth of a second son, Marty, pulled Bob into wanting to spend more time with his family. Feller told Lebovitz that the criticism of the fans over his '47 season was "silly," noting that Ted Williams had come in for similar criticism from Boston faithful, even though he'd also had a strong year. Magnification of the failure of superstars was all part of the game.

The Lebovitz article also presented a side of Feller to the public that was, to this point, rather unknown: his sense of humor. Feller was no cut-up, but he loved practical jokes, especially those involving gadgets or small explosive devices. These jokes could be pulled on anyone at any time. One of his favorite targets was sportswriter Ed McAuley. Lebovitz related one incident where McAuley, a cigar smoker, was riding a train with the club. Puffing a stogie, McAuley was suddenly surprised when ashes started flying around the compartment, a blizzard of cinders. Confused and embarrassed, he threw his cigar down, only to discover that the problem was not from his cigar, but rather from an air-blowing device that Feller had hidden behind him and was using to circulate the ashes. Another favorite item of Feller's was a miniature novelty guillotine, which seemed to "sever" fingers if you weren't watching carefully. The theme of Feller's humor would later be taken up again by Lebovitz in a *Sport* article given wide currency in the *Fireside Book of Baseball* in the 1970s.

Lebovitz emphasized two additional points about Feller. First, although he was the target of increasing criticism about greed, he could also be very generous to those in need. Way back in the late 1930s, Feller had quietly established a scholarship fund at Morningside College in Iowa for rural kids who had academic potential but needed a way off the farm. This was not something widely publicized at the time. Feller also offered financial assistance to the families of nine players from the Spokane, Washington, baseball team who'd been killed when their bus ran off an embankment in July of 1946. Feller and Dixie Walker had been the driving forces in seeing to it that the Professional Baseball Players Association provided some funds for the families involved. Second, Lebovitz denied the rumors spread by Jimmy Cannon and other out-of-town writers about other Indians players being disgruntled about Feller's salary. Lou Boudreau, for one, defended Feller. "The fact that Bob makes more dough doesn't bother me. I treat him just as I do the others. He doesn't want favors. He's always ready to pitch, always hustles, and never complains."

Of course, all the laudatory articles in the world would not restore Feller's image if he didn't pitch well. Things looked up in that regard as 1948 began.[3] The revamped Indians roster looked improved in all ways, with better offensive support for the pitching staff. Boudreau was even more focused than usual, perhaps trying to save his job. Feller's back seemed completely healed. Although his spring training performance was mediocre, as usual, his early regular season performances were very strong. Feller began the campaign on a positive note with an Opening Day 4–0 shutout of the St. Louis Browns on April 20th. Pitching before the largest Opening Day crowd in history (73,163), he fanned just three, but walked only two and allowed only two hits. His fastball wasn't superb in terms of velocity, but it had excellent movement, both his curve and slider were working well, and his command was unusually strong. "One of baseball safest bets is another great year for Feller," wrote Ed McAuley.[4]

McAuley was a talented sportswriter, but unfortunately he was not prescient in this case. Feller won his next start, holding the Red Sox down for a 4–1 win, giving up a home run to Ted Williams. The Indians were off to a torrid start, holding first place with an 11–4 record by May 10th. Everything was going better than expected. Feller was pitching well, and so were Bob Lemon and knuckleballing rookie southpaw Gene Bearden. Joe Gordon, Lou Boudreau, and Ken Keltner were all off to good starts. Larry Doby had adjusted very well to the outfield, and was hitting for both power and average and more than justifying Veeck's faith in him. But the Indians weren't running away with anything. The surprising Athletics were just percentage points behind them with a 12–5 record, and the Yankees were only a game back at 11–6.

The 1948 American League pennant chase quickly developed into one for the ages. Everything was clicking in Cleveland, but the

Athletics and Yankees kept pace, and Boston slowly crept up the standings. Feller continued strong pitching in May, holding a 5–2 record by May 20th, and just missing another no-hitter against Philadelphia. Although Feller was winning games and generally keeping the opposition controlled, observers noticed that his style was different from previous seasons. He seemed more and more reliant on the slider, using his curveball less than in the past. His fastball still moved well and had above-average velocity, but it wasn't as overpowering as in previous seasons. Feller seemed intent on tricking hitters, rather than just throwing the ball past them. Opposing managers, including Steve O'Neill of the Tigers, predicted that if Feller continued to rely on the slider, the league would catch up with him. "I hope he just keeps throwing those," one anonymous player told *The Sporting News.* "They're big round watermelons with nothing except heart."[5]

May 23d was a critical day: Bill Veeck was trying to set an attendance record in a doubleheader against the Yankees, advertising heavily in advance and scheduling Feller to start the first game. Rain kept the crowd down to "just" 78,400. The Tribe took a quick 4–0 lead, but Joe DiMaggio lined a fastball for a two-run homer in the fourth inning, bringing the Yankees to within a pair. In the sixth, "the Clipper" struck again, golfing a Feller slider out of the park for a three-run homer, giving the Yankees a 5–4 lead. Bob was removed in the seventh, with the Yankees going on to win the contest, dropping his record to 5–3. Although the Tribe came back to win the second game by a 5–1 score behind Don Black, the day was a portent of the tight race to come, as well as future struggles for Feller.

His next start, against the White Sox, was a defeat, losing 4–2. He followed that with 11 scoreless innings against the Senators on June 5th, but the Indians could not score either, eventually dropping the game 5–0. Five days later, Feller took the mound against the Red Sox in Fenway Park, and was slugged for eight runs in five innings. His velocity was noticeably down, and he was no longer fooling people with the slider. The 11 innings he'd thrown against the Senators probably had something to do with the loss of zip, even though Boudreau had given him an extra day of rest. But it was not enough; Rapid Rob was losing his rapidity. He came back on the 13th to pitch against the Yankees in New York, and was more effective, throwing five shutout innings before surrendering two runs and the lead in the sixth. The Indians lost 5–1, and Feller's record now stood at 5–6.

The good news, however, was that the Tribe still held first place. The offense continued to roll. The infield was especially sharp: all four men—Boudreau, Gordon, Keltner, and Eddie Robinson—were having strong offensive seasons along with their usual fine glovework. Boudreau liked to switch lineups and make frequent use of pinch hitters, so the outfield playing time was shared between .300 hitter Dale Mitchell, the surging Larry Doby, Thurman Tucker, Allie Clark, Hank Edwards, and Wally Judnich. Slugger Pat Seerey had been sent to the White Sox in early June in exchange for outfield defensive star Bob Kennedy. The roster was a good balance of players with power, players with speed, players with excellent fielding ability, and players with all three. On paper, and much of the time on the field, the Indians had clearly established themselves as the class act of the American League by June. But there were two sources of trouble. The pitching staff was erratic: Lemon and Bearden were pitching very well, but Feller was obviously laboring, and the rest of the staff was inconsistent. Since the Yankees and Athletics were refusing to fall out of the race, the Indians could not stand pat.

On June 15th, Veeck sent pitcher Bill Kennedy, who was not a major part of the staff, to the St. Louis Browns in exchange for pitcher Sam Zoldak. In addition, $100,000 in Cleveland funds accompanied Kennedy; the Browns needed the cash (as usual), and Veeck was willing to do anything to bolster the staff. Zoldak was a decent pitcher, though hardly worth what Veeck paid for him. However, the move proved to everyone that Veeck was serious about winning the pennant.

The same day as the Zoldak/Kennedy/$100,000 transaction, Bob Feller took the mound again, this time against the Red Sox in Cleveland. He was pitching with just two days' rest, a huge gamble on Boudreau's part, and it showed, as the Red Sox pounded him for six runs in a 7–5 win. The buzz after the game was that there was something wrong with Feller; speculation started up again in the Cleveland papers, as well as on the wire services. It didn't seem to occur to anyone that the problem may have been that he was starting after too little rest. Feller rebounded to pitch well on June 20th, giving up three runs early but settling down to defeat Philadelphia by a 4–3 score. This put his record at 6–7, and maintained the Tribe's 3.5 game lead in the standings.

Feller did okay in his next start, June 24th against the Yankees, holding the Bronx Bombers to four runs in nine innings. But Vic Raschi was too much for the lineup to handle; he tossed a shutout, sending the Indians and Feller to a 4–0 loss. Feller did much better on the 29th, allowing just one run in eight innings against the Tigers, fanning eight, showing the best velocity he'd presented in some time. On July 3d, Feller overpowered the Browns with an 8–2 victory, again showing very good stuff. He made an ineffective relief appearance in a July 5th doubleheader against the Tigers, giving up three runs and taking the loss.

The following day, Bill Veeck decided to bring in a new pitcher for a tryout: Satchel Paige.

Larry Doby was having an excellent season. The fans in Cleveland had accepted him, although the same was not true of all his teammates. Some still ignored him; he wasn't always flashed the proper signs, for example. Still, no one was downright hostile, and with his club more or less successfully integrated, Veeck decided to bring in more Negro League players. He'd had his eye on Paige for some time. At some point during the spring, he'd asked Feller—still regarded as an expert about African-American players despite the Jackie Robinson flap—if Paige still had enough left to pitch in the majors despite his advanced age. Feller gave him a positive recommendation, saying that while Satchel didn't throw as hard as he once did, his control was excellent. Paige easily passed his "tryout" with Boudreau and Hank Greenberg, showing above-average velocity, good breaking stuff, and superb command. He signed with the Indians the next day. The reaction in the baseball press was for the most part good, although there were dissenters. The press in Cleveland was generally positive, the main wonder being how the Indians would use Paige, and if he had sufficient stamina to help the club. The strongest negative national commentary came from *The Sporting News*, which questioned the Tribe's motives, deriding the move as a publicity stunt on the part of Veeck, and generally making themselves look both foolish and, in retrospect, racist. Paige's signing overshadowed Feller's strong pitching on the same day; he held the White Sox to two runs in a complete game victory. Satchel made his major league debut in relief on July 9th, and quickly showed his effectiveness against "professional" hitters, as if he hadn't done so on hundreds of other occasions.

Feller made one final start before the All-Star Break, losing a 3–2 complete game to the Browns. This lowered his record to nine wins and 10 losses, although his ERA, 3.57, was still some 50 points better than league average. The Indians ended the first half in first place, with a half-game lead over the Athletics.

As usual, Feller was picked for the All-Star Game, although more for his superstar reputation than for his actual '48 performance. Feller was aware of this, but he felt he didn't really deserve the honor. For years, the story was that on the evening of July 9th, Bill Veeck and Lou Boudreau called Feller in and told him he should skip the game. He needed a rest, they supposedly said. Teammate Bob Lemon had also been chosen, and Veeck wasn't wild about having two of his key pitchers risk injury or other mishap for the sake of the game. Feller, remembering the '47 debacle, was uncertain about the plan; he didn't want to take more heat from the fans. Feller later claimed that Veeck had tried to convince him to fake an injury. "Wrap your finger in a bandage," Veeck said, "and tell the press you cut yourself on a razor blade or got hit with a buzzsaw."[6] Feller rejected the phony-injury plan, but eventually gave in to Veeck's "request," with the proviso that Veeck take the blame for the decision should the fans get upset.

On the following morning, the Indians announced that Feller "would not be available" for the All-Star Game, though the reason was left unclear. News went out on the wire services. During the afternoon, word leaked that Feller's withdrawal was "voluntary." Hearing this, Feller was furious about the way the situation was being handled, and went to Veeck complaining that the fans would condemn him. Veeck quickly issued a statement claiming direct responsibility for the decision, attempting to absolve Bob of blame. He reiterated the statement the next day, but it was too late. American League manager Bucky Harris, who had selected Feller for the squad, was furious. Baseball owners, meeting in St. Louis for the game, took the opportunity to criticize the maverick Veeck, claiming that he was lying to protect Feller. An unidentified owner spread a rumor, apparently unfounded, that Veeck was planning on selling the club. Veeck, usually cheerful, shot back at critics in an irritated tone, telling Cleveland beat writers that "our first concern is trying to win the flag," and implying that Bucky Harris had picked both Feller and Lemon in an attempt to sabotage the Indians for the second half. "We were the only club in the American League from which Harris chose two starting pitchers," he said angrily.[7]

This did not mollify the critics. Commissioner Chandler issued a terse statement: "In the future, all players selected for the All-Star Game will be on the scene in uniform, if physically possible." *The Sporting News*, whose coverage of Feller was usually laudatory, inveighed with a harsh editorial on July 21st, accusing the righthander of ignoring the wishes of the fans and of indifference toward the major league players whose pensions the game would fund. The editorial page rejected Veeck's explanations, taking Feller to task for greed. "Baseball has given to Feller financial independence and position," wrote publisher J. Taylor Spink. "What he has done in the latest two All-Star Games is regarded by many as shabby recompense for the vast benefits the game has bestowed on him."[8] Cleveland writers, McAuley in particular, defended Feller, McAuley submitting a timeline to *The Sporting News* for publication on the 28th, showing how the events had been misconstrued. But the negative interpretation of the event fit too nicely with the spreading legend of Feller's greed in the baseball consciousness.

For decades, Feller maintained the version of the story listed above, but when I asked him to confirm the details in October of 2002, he confessed to me that it actually *was* his idea to skip the game, and that Veeck had agreed to cover for him. "It was my idea. I had had a lousy year, and I didn't deserve to go. It was just for old times' sake," he told me. He would hear catcalls and boos about the All-Star Games for the rest of his career.

Feller's first start in the second half, July 16th in Philadelphia, was a disaster. Booed and taunted unmercifully (one banner in the stadium read, "Feller the Quitter"), Feller was knocked out of the game in the first inning, possessing neither velocity nor command. He started again three days later in Washington and did better, allowing three runs in six innings to receive a no-decision in a game the Indians won in extra innings. Feller's next start, July 22d against the Yankees, did not go well. He gave up six runs in five innings before being relieved by Paige. It was his 12th loss, and his ERA was rising. Rumors circulated that Feller might be removed from the rotation, although his traditional ineffectiveness out of the bullpen, punctuated by a poor relief outing against Boston on the 24th, mitigated that possibility. (Feller usually did not pitch well when used in relief. Thus it seemed more likely that he would return to effectiveness if left in the rotation to work his problems.)

The Indians had a bad habit of fading in the second half, and it looked like this would happen once again. Although Philadelphia was slowly dropping out of the race, the Red Sox were surging, and the Yankees remained ever dangerous. On the 27th, the Indians played a doubleheader against the Athletics in Cleveland. Feller started the first game, which was a surprise since Boudreau had announced beforehand that the assignment would go to Ed Klieman, normally a reliever. Feller did not pitch well, giving up five runs in five innings. But it was enough for the victory, as the Tribe pounded out 15 hits in a 10–5 triumph, granting Feller his 10th win and boosting his record to 10–12.

By now even Feller was admitting that he was not throwing well. On the 28th, he went to visit Dr. Austin, the bonesetter who had fixed his arm way back in 1937. No major trouble was found; there was no magic fix this time around. Feller gave up four runs in six innings in his next start, a no-decision against the Red Sox in a game that the Tribe eventually won in extra innings.

On August 1st, four teams still had an excellent shot at the American League pennant. The Tribe was now tied for third place with the Yankees, but just two games behind the first-place Red Sox. The Athletics were in second, just a half game back.

It was 10 days until Feller started again, this time against the Yankees in the first game of a critical four-game set. He was more effective this time, lacking his best fastball but showing better command and movement on his breaking stuff than in recent games. He gave up three runs in six and a third innings. The bullpen almost blew the game, but in the end the Tribe prevailed, granting Feller his 11th win. The pennant chase continued to seesaw; this win put the Indians back in first place, though just half a game ahead of Philadelphia.

Feller was ineffective August 10th, losing to the Tigers by a 7–3 score, then he made a mediocre relief appearance against the Browns on the 12th, giving up two runs in two innings of bullpen work. It didn't matter, as the Tribe coasted to a 26–3 win. Feller pitched again on the 14th, scattering 11 hits in a complete game 6–2 win over the White Sox. Feller was hit hard in his next outing, August 22d against the White Sox, taking the loss in an 8–1 defeat. The pennant chase was still a tight four-team affair, and the Indians desperately needed Feller to return to his previous form. Lou Boudreau admitted as much, stating publicly that the Indians needed Feller to rebound if they were to win the pennant.

On August 27th, Feller took the mound in Yankee Stadium. The Yanks scored a run in the second inning, but then Feller settled down. His stuff was almost back to previous standards in this contest; his fastball was very good, his curve was sharp, and his command was excellent. He had decided to throw fewer sliders, relying more on the curveball. The plate umpire told Gordon Cobbledick after the game that, although he felt Feller had looked finished earlier in the season, he was back to his old form in this game and had never pitched better.[9] After only two days' rest, Boudreau then used Feller in a relief outing against the Senators on the 29th, which helped result in a 3–2 defeat.

Boudreau's management of the pitching staff was now being questioned by the beat writers and, privately, by Bill Veeck. It was felt that Boudreau had overworked Feller earlier in the season, and his deployment of the bullpen was frequently called into question.

Rumors about his job security surfaced once again; if the Indians failed to win the pennant (they were back to 1.5 games behind again on the 31st), Lou's neck was on the line.

September seemed to right the ship, at least for Feller. He threw a strong nine-strikeout game against the Athletics on the 2d, winning the game 8–1 and bringing his record back to .500 at 14–14. He then threw a seven-inning shutout in the second game of a doubleheader against the Browns on the 5th, but despite his apparent return to effectiveness, the Indians were in trouble. A dropoff in the hitting attack and trouble in the bullpen had cost them several recent close games, and by September 7th they were four and a half games out of first place.

On September 9th, Feller pitched another strong game, this time holding the Tigers to one run in seven innings, before being removed for a pinch hitter in a game the Indians eventually won 3–2 in extra innings. That gave Feller four strong starts in a row. Pitching next on three days' rest against the Browns, Feller was again effective, holding St. Louis to three runs in nine innings. Unfortunately, the opposition pitching was effective as well, holding the Tribe to three runs of their own. The game ended in a 12-inning tie, called on account of darkness. Cleveland Stadium had lights, but (as ludicrous as it seems) it was against baseball rules to use them to finish a game begun under natural light. The game would have to be replayed.

The recent spate of doubleheaders and extra-inning games had depleted Cleveland's pitching staff, so Boudreau turned to Don Black to start the makeup game. Black had a good arm, but had never been a consistently effective pitcher, and hadn't been trusted by Boudreau with major assignments for several weeks. Tragically, Black collapsed in the first inning, a victim of a cerebral hemorrhage. He survived but never pitched again, and would die 10 years later at the age of 42. The incident badly shook all who witnessed it; Feller later wrote that it helped put the pennant race in perspective. "How can this happen to a young and healthy guy only 32 years old, especially a professional athlete in peak physical condition? Nobody ever knows the answers to questions like that."[10]

Feller's next appearance was on the 17th, and a fine one it was, an 11-strikeout 4–1 victory over the Washington Senators. Whatever had ailed him earlier in the season seemed a thing of the past; the zip on his pitches was back, and he seemed primed for the pennant charge. The Indians, nearly given up for dead a week earlier, were suddenly back in the thick of things, as both the Red Sox and Yankees fell into slumps. By the 20th, they were only a half game out of first place.

The Indians designated the game of the 23d against the Red Sox as "Don Black Night." All proceeds from the game would go to Black and his family, to cover his medical expenses and provide some financial cushion should his playing career be over. A huge crowd of over 70,000 packed the stadium, and gave Feller, the starting pitcher, a huge ovation. His recent spate of strong pitching, as well as the emotionality of the occasion, overrode whatever rough feelings Clevelanders still harbored for Bob. It was one of his best games of the season. His curveball was unhittable, and his fastball hopped despite the cold weather; he allowed just four hits in a 5–2 win. The Indians had now won eight straight games, and the victory moved the Tribe into first place.

The schedule favored the Indians at this point. They had to face the Tigers and White Sox to finish the season, while the Yankees and Red Sox were slated to face each other five times. The race was a three-way tie for first place on the 24th. Lou Boudreau scheduled Feller to start two more games to finish the season, the 26th against the Tigers in Detroit, then the 30th against the Tigers in Cleveland. The other four games would be split between Bob Lemon and Gene Bearden. The rest of the staff, including Paige, who had contributed several critical starts in August, was detailed for bullpen work.

Dueling Hal Newhouser on the 26th, Feller benefited by three early Indians runs. His stuff was very good; he held the Tigers to five hits and won the game 4–1. It was his 18th win, and he looked very much like the Feller of old. The Yankees and Red Sox, meanwhile, were beating each other up and had fallen into a second place tie. Interestingly, Boudreau made a critical decision, cancelling Lemon's scheduled Tuesday start and moving Bearden up to pitch on the 28th and Feller on the 29th. For a knuckleballer like Bearden, this wasn't a huge problem, but moving Feller up to pitch on short rest was controversial. The decision was made because Boudreau was concerned about Lemon, who was exhausted from the long season and hadn't thrown well lately. Bearden justified the first part of the move on the 28th by shackling the White Sox with an 11–0 victory.

Boudreau's gamble almost backfired on the 29th, as Feller came to the mound with little stuff in his arsenal. He battled, however, giving up 10 hits and two runs to the Chicagoans, but winning the game by a 5–2 mark. It was clear, though, that the game had been a close call; Feller had not been in top form. But things looked good for the World Series: the Indians were up by two games in the loss column with three to play, and a well-rested Bob Lemon would pitch against the Tigers on Friday.

It did not turn out as planned, however. Lemon pitched well, holding a 3–2 lead going into the ninth inning. But two errors, three walks, and a single led to three Detroit runs, and the Bengals went on to a 5–3 win. Boudreau was later criticized for leaving an obviously tired Lemon in the game too long, despite the fact that the bullpen was rested and ready for action. With the Yankees and Red Sox playing each other, the pennant couldn't be decided for another day.

Boston defeated New York on Saturday to eliminate the Yankees, while Gene Bearden defeated the Tigers, tossing a brilliant 8–0 shutout. This put the Tribe ahead of the Red Sox by one game, with one game left to play. If the Indians won on Sunday, they won the pennant no matter what. If the Indians lost and the Red Sox beat the Yankees, the season would end in a tie, necessitating a one-game playoff, to be played in Boston (the result of a coin flip a few weeks before).

Another huge crowd filled Municipal Stadium on the afternoon of October 3d to watch Bob Feller defeat Hal Newhouser and clinch the pennant for the Tribe. It would be the capping triumph of Feller's career—at least that was the script. The Tigers apparently failed to read their lines correctly.

Feller had nothing. His pitches had neither velocity nor movement. He escaped the first two innings unscathed, but the wheels came off in the third, as the Tigers battered him for three runs. Boudreau, who'd shown a great reluctance to pull his pitchers in previous games, yanked Feller quickly in favor of Sam Zoldak, but the damage was done. The Tigers went on to a 7–1 victory. Meanwhile, in Boston, the Red Sox nailed the Yankees to the wall with a 10–5 win.

The regular season had ended in a tie.

Lou Boudreau faced a difficult decision in picking a starter for the playoff game. Feller was considered, but rejected on the grounds that he seldom pitched well in Fenway Park. Besides, he'd pitched the day before and gotten his socks knocked off. Bob Lemon was another option and was the most likely choice according to the press. But he had worn down in September and appeared physically exhausted. The third option was Gene Bearden, who had pitched a lot recently, but felt fine physically. The main fear about using Bearden was that left-handers faced a handicap in Fenway Park. Boudreau decided that, all things considered, Bearden was the best choice. He asked his players for their opinion; the clubhouse agreed and deferred to his judgment. Boston manager Joe McCarthy pulled a surprise of his own, starting veteran ex-Indian Denny Galehouse instead of the widely anticipated Mel Parnell. Lou Boudreau often played hunches, and they often failed to work. But his decision to start Bearden was inspired. The knuckleballer shut down the Red Sox effectively, while Galehouse was hit hard, and the Indians went on to an 8–3 victory.

Cleveland went crazy; the Indians had finally won a pennant. Their opponent in the World Series would be Boston, the Boston Braves. The Braves had been starved for success even more than the Indians, not having won a pennant since 1914. The Braves had gone 91–62, winning the National League by 6.5 games over the St. Louis Cardinals. Their big stars were second baseman Eddie Stanky, shortstop Alvin Dark, third baseman Bob Elliot, and the excellent pitching duo of Johnny Sain and Warren Spahn. The Braves had considerably less offensive firepower than Cleveland, plus a weaker bench; the Indians were given a slight edge in pitching by most experts. The Tribe was the stronger team, but anything can happen in a short series, and Boston had home field advantage.

Feller was tapped to start the first game in Boston on October 6th. It was the game he'd been waiting for his entire life, the contest dreamed about long ago back in Iowa: the chance to pitch in the World Series. Feller was disappointed in his poor start against the Tigers on the last day of the regular season, and vowed that the World Series would be different. Indeed it was.

In the first inning, it was obvious that Feller had his good stuff: his fastball was hopping, his curve bending, his command solid. He retired the first 11 Boston hitters with ease before yielding a walk in the fourth inning, then a single in the fifth. He retired nine more in a row after Marvin Rickert's single. Feller had the game well in hand . . . or he would have, except for the fact that the Indians were being handcuffed by Johnny Sain nearly as easily as Feller was shutting down the Browns. The Tribe had four hits but no runs against Sain by the seventh inning. Feller had a one-hitter going. It was a classic pitcher's duel, one of the best in postseason history.

It came to the bottom of the eighth, still scoreless. Feller walked leadoff hitter Bill Salkeld. Phil Masi was pinch runner. Mike McCormick then sacrificed Masi to second base. Lou Boudreau came to the mound, ordering Feller to walk Eddie Stanky, Boston's number-eight hitter, to set up the double play with the pitcher coming to bat. Feller thought it was a bad idea. "I can get Stanky," he argued.[11] But Boudreau insisted, and Feller obeyed his manager's wishes, walking the peppery infielder. Sain, the next hitter, did not hit a double-play grounder as Boudreau wanted, but instead hit a fly ball to right field for the second out.

This brought leadoff man Tommy Holmes to the plate, a dangerous left-handed hitter, who'd ranked third in the National League batting hunt that year with a .325 average. It was a hazardous situation; a single would give the Braves a 1–0 lead, enough to give them the win the way Sain was pitching. Holmes was a contact hitter who seldom struck out and was not easy to overpower.

Boudreau gave Feller a signal: pickoff play at second base. This was something the Indians had been practicing for years; Feller and Boudreau were masters at catching unwary runners off the bag at second. Masi was apparently unwary; he had a large lead.

Feller whirled toward second base and fired. Boudreau caught the ball; Masi was out by at least a foot. Everyone in the park thought so.

Except the man who counted: umpire Bill Stewart. A National League umpire who was unaware that the Indians pulled this trick on occasion, he was startled by the play and called Masi "safe."

On the next pitch, Holmes made contact with a pitch and singled to left field, scoring Masi. The Braves had a 1–0 lead. Feller got the next hitter out, but the Indians had to score at least a run in the top of the ninth off Sain in order to tie the game. They failed to do so, giving the Braves a 1–0 victory and game one of the Series.

The game was a bitter disappointment for the Tribe and Feller. Bob had pitched his heart out, and newspaper photos the next day confirmed what everyone who saw the game knew: Masi had been out, the umpire had blown the call. The inning should have been over. A correct call would not have guaranteed an Indians victory, of course, not with Sain pitching as well as he was. He deserved to win the game as much as Feller did.

The Indians badly needed a victory in the second game, and they got it from Bob Lemon, who outpitched Warren Spahn to take a 4–1 win and put the series back in Cleveland tied at a game apiece. More victories followed in game three and game four, Bearden pitching a five-hit shutout in the first contest, and Steve Gromek outdueling Spahn in the second game 2–1. This gave the Indians a commanding three-games-to-one lead going into the fifth game, with Feller tapped to start.

Feller had been robbed of glory in the first game; here was his chance at redemption, to win the World Series for himself and the Cleveland Indians. On paper, it looked like a good bet for the Indians. Feller's opponent was Nelson Potter, a 36-year-old with good control, but not the best pitcher the Braves had to offer. Boston manager Billy Southworth was saving Warren Spahn for game six, should the Braves manage to get the Series back to Boston.

It was obvious from the beginning of the game that Feller was not in top form. The velocity and movement he exhibited in the first game were not there. He gave up three runs in the first inning, then another in the third before settling down somewhat. The Indians scored a run in the first, then got to Potter in the fourth inning, Southworth bringing in Spahn to relieve and try to save the game. Feller gave up a run in the sixth inning, with the game heading into the top of the seventh tied at five apiece.

Boudreau's decision to let Feller start the top of the seventh was highly questionable. He was not pitching well, and the bullpen was well rested, each previous contest having been a complete game. But start the seventh inning Feller did, and it was a disaster. Feller quickly gave up a run on two singles and a sacrifice. He was finally relieved by Ed Klieman, then Russ Christopher, then Satchel Paige. By the time the inning was over, the Braves had scored six runs. Spahn closed out the contest, winning the game 11–5.

Feller was crushed. He'd had his chance in two World Series games now, and had failed to win either contest. Some disappointed Tribe fans blamed him; the catcalls he'd heard earlier in the year during the All-Star controversy came back. But the press defended Feller, Gordon Cobbledick in the *Plain Dealer* going so far as to blame Boudreau for Feller's loss in game five. "It was obvious as early as the third inning that unless he suddenly found his missing fast ball that Feller would be beaten. It was obvious that Boudreau was tempting fate when he allowed him to stay in the game until that beating became a reality. . . . The Braves might have beaten any pitcher whom Boudreau could have used in relief of Feller, but Boudreau owed it to the game and to the record crowd to make them beat the best he had. That's what he failed most lamentably to do."[12] To his credit, Feller always took the blame for the game-five loss, but Cobbledick's analysis was essentially correct. There was no reason, other than sentimentality, for Boudreau to stick with an ineffective Feller for so long, not with the bullpen as rested as it was.

In the end, it did not matter. The Indians pulled out a game six victory over the Braves, Bob Lemon and Gene Bearden combining to defeat Bill Voiselle and Warren Spahn in a classic 4–3 triumph. This gave the Indians their first World Series win since 1920, taking the sting off the game-five defeat, not to mention all the years of disappointment. Cleveland was joyous.

The '48 Indians were one of the best teams of the immediate postwar era. Lou Boudreau, for all the justified second-guessing about his managerial decisions, had a great season at shortstop, hitting .355, with 18 homers, 106 RBI, 98 walks, and only *nine* strikeouts. Joe Gordon (32 homers, 124 RBI), Ken Keltner (31 homers, 119 RBI), Larry Doby (.301, 14 homers, 54 walks), and Dale Mitchell (.336 average) were the big offensive standouts, with Allie Clark, Walt Judnich, and Eddie Robinson providing additional offensive support. The bullpen, for all of Boudreau's hesitancy to use it in close games, put up good numbers. Russ Christopher "saved" 17 games with a 2.90 ERA. Steve Gromek (2.84), Sam Zoldak (2.80), Eddie Klieman (2.59), and the venerable Satchel Paige (2.47) made up the best middle-relief corps in the league. Gene Bearden went 20–7 and led the American League with a 2.43 ERA. Bob Lemon emerged as the staff workhorse, winning 20, posting a 2.82 ERA, and leading the American League in both innings pitched and shutouts. By the end of the season, it was Lemon who was considered to be Cleveland's ace.

As we have seen from the commentary above, Bob Feller's season was erratic. In some games, he was his overpowering old self. In others, he was weak. His overall numbers for the season were not bad: he won 19 games, with 15 losses. His 3.56 ERA was 14 percent above league average when adjusted for park effects, not up to his normal standards, but still good. He ranked fourth in victories, as well as second in the league with 280.6 innings pitched. He led the league in games started. His strikeout rate was down again, though he still led the circuit with 164. His strikeout-per-game rate ranked second. For all the complaints, Feller was still an above-average pitcher in 1948, but the slip in his game hinted at in his '47 numbers was now there for all to see. Those who saw him pitch frequently were of no doubt that the fastball was fading. "Hail and Farewell—Feller's Fastball," wrote Franklin Lewis in the *Cleveland Press*. Bob was still a good pitcher, but he could no longer be counted on as the ace of the staff, and he needed to make the transition from pure power to a more finessed style of pitching in order to remain successful.

14

The Twilight Gathers

Becoming number one is easier than remaining number one.

—Bill Bradley

There would be no barnstorming for Bob Feller in 1948. He appeared in one exhibition contest on October 16th in Van Meter, throwing seven shutout innings for the Northwest Iowa All-Stars as part of "Feller Day" in his hometown. The *Des Moines Register* noted that attendance for the event was down somewhat from previous years; only some 1,500 people showed up, though this was blamed on cold, drizzly weather more than anything else. Feller told local reporters that it would be his last bit of pitching before spring. The winter would be "a vacation from baseball for me," though reporter Leighton Housh noted evidence of Feller's determination to right whatever had gone wrong for him in '48. "Now he must re-establish himself as baseball's No. 1 pitcher. He doesn't say so, but you get the idea that he is already proceeding toward the objective."[1] Giving his arm a nice long rest over the winter was an obvious step.

Feller gave an interview to the *Fort Worth Star-Telegram* on January 16th, discussing his new ranch home in Texas and his liking for the Texas winter climate; it was more conducive to physical training and maximized the kids' chance to play outside. To the surprise of sportswriter Gene Gregston, he was not bitter about the botched umpire call on the pickoff play that hurt him in game one of the World Series. "Umpires are bound to make mistakes just like anyone else. After all, it's just a game." Feller was uncertain at this time if Bill Veeck would cut his salary. "If I am cut, I won't have too much kick coming because of the bad year I had," he admitted matter-of-factly.

Indeed, Feller did receive a pay cut, the first in his career. His contract in '48 had called for a $50,000 base salary, with attendance clauses that took his pay all the way to $80,000. In mid-January, Bill Veeck made an offer, undisclosed publicly, to Feller. The right-hander promptly rejected it. Both businessmen were able to compromise, coming to agreement on February 8th. Feller would take a $10,000 cut in his base salary, dropping it to $40,000, but the attendance bonus would remain, making it possible for Feller to earn $70,000. "I expected to take a cut this year," Feller told Ed McAuley. "I didn't have too good a season in 1948. Some of the other fellows had the best years of their lives and are entitled to whatever increases were being passed out by the club." For his part, Veeck refused to confirm or deny that Feller remained the highest-paid Indian, but did wish that all his players "were as reasonable" as Feller when negotiating contracts.[2] Feller was no longer the highest-paid player in baseball as a whole, that honor now going to Joe DiMaggio and his deal for $90,000.

Despite his willingness to take a pay cut without much complaint, the signing of Feller's new contract invited more criticisms of his personality. W. C. Heinz in the *New York Sun* wrote a long article about Feller's character on February 8th, reviving and expanding on the theme that he was alienated from the other players. The article is worth quoting at length.

> How can one expect a Feller to be a regular guy? The day he is born his father makes up his mind that this babe in the bassinet will be a great pitcher. The father had once wanted to be a great pitcher himself, and so at an age when the boy Bob might be just growing up with the other kids, being one of them and learning to live with them, he is out in the pasture behind the barn and the father is teaching him how to throw a baseball.
> You cannot criticize this kind of determination, either on he part of the father or the son. Certainly the contract Bob Feller signs today in Cleveland . . . constitutes a testimonial to many of the habits in which we in this country believe. It is a tribute to

ambition, determination, hard work, and ability, and yet even as these qualities mark one boy as one apart from other boys so they have marked the man.

They do not like Bob Feller. They like him, yes, as a pitcher, but not as a person, and they are the players who play with him and against him, and they are the fans. On the Cleveland ball club he is a loner. . . . When he has a bad day they are quick to boo him, even in Cleveland, for he has failed to build up a reservoir of good will upon which, in moments of frustration, to draw.

This must, in a way, be very difficult for Feller to understand. He lives cleanly. Two days after Pearl Harbor he enlisted. . . . While he did not give up his life he was willing to give it, and he gave four seasons out of what, because he is an athlete, must have been a comparatively short career.

The players and the fans know all this about him. They know . . . that when those members of the Spokane, Wash. team died in that bus crash Feller offered financial assistance to their families. He annually awards a college scholarship. He has made many hospital appearances, sponsored many good causes, and yet, when he is the losing pitcher in the first world series game in which he appears, when he is knocked out of the box in his second turn, there is rejoicing everywhere.

They do not like it the way Feller makes money. He not only makes it by pitching, but by endorsing sporting goods, a cereal, an ice cream, a shaving cream, a hair tonic, a peanut butter. He is an author and he has sponsored barnstorming tours. Other baseball players, of course, have made money by some of these means. None has made as much money by as many means. He is the first to be incorporated, and for this they do not like him—for this and one other reason.

Very little has been written about this other reason, but nevertheless it has become clear. It is the big reason, as it was on a day last season when Feller was warming up at the Yankee Stadium and a newspaper photographer walked off the field from the Indian dugout speaking of Feller and swearing.

"What happened?" somebody said.

"What happened?" the photographer said, "There were a half a dozen of us out there, and we asked him if he would mind posing for us a minute. Do you know what he said?"

"No."

"He said, 'Why should I pose for you guys for nothing? I get paid for posing for _____.'"

The photographer named the breakfast food which featured Feller in its advertisements. He said that he and the other photographers waited for Feller to pose for the commercial photographs, and then they flashed their bulbs in his face.

"We didn't have any plates in our cameras," he said, "We didn't want his picture. We did it just to get even."[3]

Heinz's piece does more than just relate an anecdote about Feller's increasingly public obsession with money. He touches on the fact that Feller, from an early age, was *different* from his peers, isolated in a way by the seriousness with which he took what to most kids was just a game. What to Feller was just honesty about the way he felt came across as bluntness, even rudeness in the minds of others. His inability to consider why people could resent his outside activities was a reflection of this alienation.

As usual, Bill Veeck was active with his roster in the off-season. Eddie Robinson and Ed Klieman were traded to the Senators for Mickey Vernon and Early Wynn. Several promising players from the farm system were expected to compete for jobs, including pitcher Mike Garcia, infielders Ray Boone, Bobby Avila, and Al Rosen, plus Cuban outfielder Minnie Minoso. Although Boudreau, Keltner, and Gordon were all on the wrong side of 30, there seemed plenty of talent in place to cover for them if they declined suddenly. Lemon and Bearden were still around, of course, along with Bob Feller. Although some questioned whether Feller wasn't due for further decline, others were confident that he would rebound. Feller himself had no doubts: a winter of relaxation to clear his mind and rest his arm would, he felt, restore his previous vigor and consistency. One concern in the mind of Feller, and the Cleveland beat writers, was the bullpen. Russ Christopher, plagued with respiratory and cardiac trouble, had retired. Former relief ace Klieman had been traded. Queried about the condition of the relief corps, Feller suggested that Satchel Paige could be the new bullpen mainstay, in a conversation with *Cleveland Press* writer Franklin Lewis. "Ol' Satch can still throw that ball. He's got plenty left."[4]

Feller was characteristically honest about his relatively weak '48 season, but insisted he would come back strong in '49. *Sport Magazine* featured an article by Feller called "Who Says I'm Finished" in their April issue.

He pointed out that, despite his occasional problems, he did win 19 games. "I've never heard of a pitcher being hounded out of the league because he could only win 19 games." He admitted that his velocity was down at times, and that his control occasionally gave him trouble. He also admitted getting "too cute" and out-smarting himself on occasion. "I will leave the cute stuff to Satchel Paige" in the future, he wrote. Feller also admitted that the mid-season All-Star Game–related booing possibly got to him. For '49, Feller wrote that while he was not as "consistently fast" as he used to be, he still threw hard, and with more attention paid to his phys-ical conditioning (it's hard to see how he could improve that), he expected to rebound. He would go back to using his slider again, though he would try not to rely on one pitch to the exclusion of the others.

As usual, Feller was slated as the Opening Day starter, April 19th against the Browns in St. Louis. While warming up, he felt a twinge in his shoulder, but decided to pitch through it. It was a mistake; he had nothing, and lasted just two innings before the shoulder pain became serious enough for him to leave the game. Examination revealed a strained shoulder muscle, possibly, the doctors felt, related to the back injury back in 1947. Rest was pre-scribed.

Feller was out of action for the rest of April, not returning to the mound until May 5th. He pitched reasonably well in his first start back from the injury, against the Red Sox, allowing three runs and six hits and earning the victory, although he pitched without his best stuff. It wasn't until May 15th that the Indians felt confi-dent enough in his arm to send him back to the mound again, but the result was two ineffective innings against the White Sox in an eventual 10–0 loss.

By that point, the Indians were already in trouble. The hitters weren't hitting. Lou Boudreau was out with a broken finger, and other injuries were crippling the pitching staff. Feller was obvi-ously not healthy. Bob Lemon had torn cartilage in his rib cage and was out for several weeks. Gene Bearden, the surprise hero of 1948, had lost control of his knuckleball, and was getting hammered on a regular basis. Early Wynn and rookie Mike Garcia were holding their own, but without Feller and Lemon, the Tribe was without a genuine ace in the rotation. There was also trouble in the bullpen;

not even Satchel Paige was pitching as well as expected. By the end of May, the Indians had dropped to seven games behind the Yankees, and the club seemed lifeless.

On June 1st, Feller returned to the starting rotation. Again, he was without his best stuff, yielding 12 hits, although he gave up just 3 runs to the Red Sox. It wasn't enough, as the sinking offense couldn't come through, losing the game 3–1. Four days later, Feller was hit with poor run support again, losing 3–0 to Philadelphia. Still, he'd pitched decently, and it looked as if the worst was past him.

This hope proved premature; the Yankees knocked Feller out of the box in the first inning on June 11th, tagging him for seven runs.

As the Indians sank in the standings, Feller occasionally put some good games together, but was unable to develop any sort of consistency. His velocity was clearly down. Even in the games he pitched well, it was mainly through reliance on his curveball. He ran off three strong starts on the 14th, 19th, and 24th of June, but was then hammered on the 28th, giving up seven runs in five innings to the Tigers. He pitched well again on the 3d of July, winning a 3–2 game against Detroit, then beat the Browns on the 9th, winning 7–4 but showing very mediocre stuff. Feller was blasted on July 15th, hit hard in an 8–0 loss to Philadelphia. Despite Feller's inconsistency, the Indians had crawled back into the race, keeping their record over .500 and making a fight of the pennant. At the All-Star Break, Feller was a .500 pitcher with a 6–6 record, while the Indians were 44–32, five-and-a-half games behind the Yankees in second place.

For the first time since he became a regular pitcher in 1938, Feller was not selected for the All-Star Team. He hadn't pitched well enough to go, obviously, and the fallout from '48 prevented any sort of nostalgia selection.

On July 20th, Feller was scheduled to start against the Yankees in New York. It was the 14th anniversary of his major league debut. UPI ran a story asking if Feller, looking for his 184th career win, could possibly get to 200 victories before being declared "washed up." It was a question asked by many people after the game, for the Bronx Bombers slaughtered Feller, tagging him for two singles, a hit batsman, a walk, and a home run before he was mercifully removed from the game by Boudreau. The subject of Feller's place in the rotation was raised by Franklin Lewis of the *Press*.

> Boudreau's insistence upon starting Feller is understandable on the one hand and puzzling on the other. Louie remembers the Feller of old and he feels Feller knows how to pitch. Then there is always the chance Feller will come bouncing back, even as he did when the Indians needed him so desperately a year ago. The puzzle is based on his use of Feller over Mike Garcia in New York in view of the records. . . . Garcia could have pitched ahead of Feller in the New York series and on his season's labors out-ranked Feller.[5]

Lewis, who considered himself a friend of Feller, went on to say that he'd been "urging Feller for a year to change his pitching style." He was throwing too many pitches belt-high down the middle, and while his fastball was still above average (both Yankees and Red Sox hitters told Lewis it was still one of the best in the league), it no longer had the overpowering extra "hop." In previous seasons, Feller had often been a victim of poor run support and bad luck, but this was not true this year, Lewis concluded. His record was "one of a guy who needs to switch" his mode of pitching.

Feller remained a .500 pitcher for the rest of the year, alternating rough outings with good ones. The Indians kept over .500, but were unable to mount a serious challenge to the Yankees in defense of their World Championship. The club finished 89–65, eight games behind New York. They posted a .578 winning percentage, a solid season but a disappointing one. The offense had taken a big step backward. Outfielders Larry Doby (.280, 24 homers) and Dale Mitchell (.317, 23 triples) had strong seasons, and new first baseman Mickey Vernon did well (.291, 18 homers). But the rest of the bats were very disappointing. On the pitching staff, Bob Lemon returned from his rib injury in good form, eventually winning 22 games and posting an excellent 2.99 ERA. Rookie Garcia won 14 with a 2.35 ERA.

Feller finished with his most mediocre numbers to date: a 15–14 record and a 3.75 ERA. His ERA was just 6 percent above league average, and the injury limited him to 211 innings and 108 strikeouts. His name, for the first time since well before the Second World War, did not appear on the leader boards of any of the major statistical categories. Based on both the numbers and pitching reputation, Bob Feller was now merely a slightly-above-average pitcher.

Following this disappointing campaign, there were changes coming to Cleveland. Rumors had swirled all summer that the club was for sale. Bill Veeck vigorously denied them, but in the end the gossip proved accurate; the club was sold to a group headed by insurance executive Ellis Ryan. Veeck's Cleveland years had been successful in every way, especially financially, but he wanted to go out on top; the failure of the '49 club to win the pennant may have had something to do with it, but Veeck was anything but predictable. Hank Greenberg, who'd spent the last three years in the Cleveland front office, was named general manager by Ryan.

Satchel Paige, who'd thrown 83 innings and posted a solid 3.04 ERA, was released.

Feller decided to take one final stab at barnstorming in November of '49, leading a tour of major leaguers in an exhibition series in California. Luke Easter, a black player signed by Veeck, had made his debut for the Indians in '49. He had prodigious power, and Feller tapped him as the main attraction for the tour. At one point during the tour, with attendance at a disappointing level, Feller pulled Ralph Kiner out of a sand bunker on a golf course and talked him into playing to try and spur additional interest. Despite this effort, the exhibition series was not well attended, averaging only 3,000 fans per game, and ended up being a money loser. "This fall exhibition business used to be quite a deal, but the way things are going this fall the players are just getting a nice trip out of it," complained Feller.[6] Although the tour was not a monetary success, from a baseball perspective it went well. Bob actually threw harder during this exhibition tour than he had during most of the regular season. He told Vincent X. Flaherty in the *Los Angeles Examiner* that his arm "never felt better," and that if he had had the same stuff for the Tribe during the regular season that he had now, "I would have won a lot more games for the Indians this year."

This brief barnstorming revival was possibly an attempt by Bob to make up for expected salary cut in 1950. No one, especially Feller, expected the Indians to pay him what he'd earned in '49. Still, cutting the salary of an established star was never an easy task politically. "Feller is and always has been a special case," noted Ed McAuley in the *Cleveland News*. Feller had been the centerpiece of the franchise, especially during the Bradley years, when he was the main attraction drawing fans to the gate.[7] The attendance bonus clause in his contract had become an unwanted artifact from those days. With Feller apparently in decline, rumor had it that the Indians were considering reducing or dropping this clause. Although baseball rules limited the maximum salary cut to 25 percent, the rule did not cover bonus clauses. The Indians could theoretically renew Feller's $40,000 salary, but drop the attendance dividend, which would cut his overall takings in half without violating the rules. Of course, doing so unilaterally would be highly disrespectful to Feller. "I'm glad I won't have to sit on the club's side of the desk when the negotiations get under way," concluded McAuley.

Speculation that Feller might play hardball with the new ownership was stifled on January 18, 1950, when Feller flew his plane out to Cleveland and suggested himself that the Indians eliminate the attendance bounty. In exchange for this concession, his base salary would rise from $40,000 to $50,000, but his total take would still be some $20,000 less than the previous season. The Indians quickly agreed to the suggestion, General Manager Greenberg commenting good-naturedly, "Certainly, Bob took a cut. It makes up for all those times I took a cut at his fast ball and missed connections."[8] Feller, however, predicted that a similar cut would not take place in 1951. "I don't consider myself permanently out of the 20-victory class. If I had been in peak condition all year and had had a little better luck, I'd have been a lot more help to the team." He was still the second-highest-paid player on the team, behind shortstop/manager Boudreau, and obviously intended to do well enough in 1950 to return to his previous status.

Feller's season got off to a slow start because of a virus; he missed almost two weeks of spring training with severe flu-like symptoms. He recovered in time to pitch against the Giants in exhi-

bition play in Shreveport, Louisiana, and was blasted by Leo Durocher's club. Durocher, perhaps unwisely, revealed that Feller
was tipping his pitches once again. "I could call every curve and
fast ball he was throwing. He was tipping off his pitches as plain
as anything. But when anybody offers him advice, he brushes it
aside."[9] Feller, meanwhile predicted confidently that he would win
20 games.

The Indians were a club in transition. The new administration
retained Boudreau as manager, but shifted some new blood into
the lineup, including Luke Easter at first base, Ray Boone at shortstop, and Al Rosen at third. Boudreau, his ankles aching, reduced
himself to part-time play. Rookie Bobby Avila would split time
with Joe Gordon at second base. Lemon, Wynn, Feller, and Garcia
made up the starting rotation, considered one of the stronger ag-
gregations in the league as long as everyone pitched up to ability.

Feller was much more consistent in 1950 than he'd been in
1949. He kept his ERA in the low- to mid-3.00s throughout the
season, punctuating his year with the occasional outstanding
game. Although Feller did not regain the form of his peak years,
his velocity was better than it had been in '49. He also benefited by
using his erratic slider less, concentrating on changing speeds with
his curveball. Poor run support gave him just four victories by mid-
June, although Feller was generally satisfied with how well he'd
pitched. "I have to pitch to my spots," he told Dan Daniel. "I
would like to return to that testing machine in Washington. . . . I
certainly could not pump it in that fast right now, but I think that
I could surprise some people. For a few pitches, I can still fire that
ball."[10] Opponents agreed. Although the Red Sox knocked Feller
out of the box in the first inning of his start on June 2d, they praised
his velocity. "He walked me, but he had good stuff," said Dom
DiMaggio. "He was wild, but he had plenty," commented Johnny
Pesky. "He was just as good as ever," opined Vern Stephens.[11] The
Red Sox could afford to be gracious, since they'd beaten him. But
Feller showed the comments were genuine by pitching a 3–2 complete game victory in Yankee Stadium the next time out, taking a
three-hit shutout into the ninth inning and throttling the New
Yorkers with his moving fastball and knee-buckling curve.

Feller fired another strong game on June 18th, holding the Philadelphia Athletics to just two hits and no runs, posting his first shutout since 1948. He fanned just two, but was in command of the game throughout. "Teammates as well as opponents agree that he is a much better pitcher this year than last," wrote Ed McAuley, "They attribute the improvement not only to his unhampered physical condition, but to his frank admission that he no longer has the speed which won him the nickname of Rapid Robert."[12] On July 2d, Feller beat the Tigers to record his 200th career victory.

Feller pitched well enough to draw an All-Star nod; this time there was no controversy. He pitched two-thirds of an inning in a game won by the National League 4–3 in 14 innings. Feller slumped a bit in August, but picked up the pace down the stretch, being particularly impressive in September. He won four out of six starts, throwing five complete games, and allowed a total of just four runs in his last 27 innings.

The Indians were above .500 and in contention all year, but were never able to mount a strong challenge to the Yankees. The Tribe finished 92–62, with a .592 winning percentage, which was good for fourth place, six games behind New York. Al Rosen led the league with 37 homers, while Luke Easter (28 homers), Ray Boone (.301), and Larry Doby (.326, 25 homers) provided more offense. The pitching was solid as well. Bob Lemon led the league with 23 wins; Early Wynn won 18 with a 3.20 ERA.

Feller failed to reach his goal of 20 victories, but generally pitched very well. He finished 16–11 with a 3.43 ERA, his ERA 27 percent better than league average when adjusted for park effect, his best showing since 1947. He started 34 games, completed 16, and fanned 119 men. His three shutouts ranked second in the league, and he finished third in the ERA race. Four of his 11 defeats were complete games decided by one run. Observers noted that he had completed the transition from overpowering hard thrower to polished pitcher. His command still gave problems at times, as shown by his 103 walks, but he'd learned how to survive without his best stuff. He may not have been the best pitcher in baseball anymore, but he was one of the best. At least, that is what an objective observer would say; Feller still heard catcalls from the stands and read complaints in the papers that he was washed up and should retire. In 1951, he resolved things would be different. "I was going to shut some people up."[13]

Feller devoted the 1950 off-season to conditioning and family time. His third son, Bruce, was born in November. Feller spent his work time doing extra physical training, wanting to get into the best physical shape of his career in order to prove the doubters wrong in '51. Financially, Feller came to terms quickly in mid-January, signing another contract for $50,000. There was a touch of controversy about this, some writers and fans noticing that Feller had won fewer games than Bob Lemon or Early Wynn, but was still getting paid more. But, as Franklin Lewis pointed out in the *Press* on February 7th, Feller remained one of the best attendance attractions in the game, even if his attendance bonus had been eliminated. He was worth "every penny" the Tribe paid him. Besides, he'd earned $50,000 in 1950 and had pitched well; cutting his salary after a good season made no sense. The fact that Feller didn't expect or demand an increase was another point in his favor; he knew his worth to the club.

Although the Indians had had a good season in '50, it wasn't good enough for GM Hank Greenberg and the front office. Major changes were felt necessary to keep pace with the Yankees. Lou Boudreau was gone, fired as manager and released as a player; he signed with the Red Sox as a player/coach. The new field boss was Al Lopez, former major league catcher who'd been traded to the Indians in '47. Ex-Indian hurler Mel Harder was brought in as pitching coach, a role he'd filled unofficially in the past. Given his quiet, mentoring personality and deep knowledge of pitching, this was considered a good move. Bobby Avila took over at second base full time from Joe Gordon. The starting rotation remained Lemon, Feller, Wynn, and Garcia, and the Indians were projected to contend for the pennant again, though the powerful Yankees under Casey Stengel were still the favorites.

Although he suffered through a poor spring training (as usual), Feller got off the starting line quickly in 1951, winning 10 of his first 11 starts. His achievement was all the more impressive because he was injured during much of this time. On May 8th, Feller was pouring water into a whirlpool bath at Cleveland Stadium, wanting to ease his stiff back with a nice soak after a long workout. The hose he was using to fill the tub slipped, spraying scalding water all over his body. The team physician diagnosed first- and second-degree burns on Feller's chest, torso, and legs. Speculation in the press and in the front office was that Feller would miss at least three weeks due to his painful injury, but he appeared in uniform the next day, and missed only one start. His next outing was a complete game victory, a painful one, but Bob insisted on remaining in the game even though the Indians were coasting to an 11–2 win over the White Sox. The burns gradually healed, though it was necessary to cover them in cotton on days he pitched. Taking the bandages off after the game was awful. "Our trainer . . . got half sick pulling the cotton wrapping off my raw flesh after the game."[14]

By early June, commentary on Feller's excellent pitching spread through the national press. A UPI story on June 11th discussed his improvement. At this point, he stood 8–1 and led the American League with a 1.71 ERA. Feller traced his stronger pitching to the final healing of his back injury. A calcium deposit in his back that had formed at the spot where the muscle had pulled away from the rib had bothered him for two years. "Until this year," Feller told UPI, "I couldn't throw a ball naturally. There was always that pull when I came back. The doctors told me that the deposit would dissolve in time. Well it has. My motion is free and easy now." Although he hadn't regained the pure velocity of his youth, his fastball had its "hop" back, and his curve was better than ever. Observers also said he'd developed a much better feel for changing speeds and throwing strikes. "He pitches with his head now, not just his arm," said Hank Greenberg.

Opposing players interviewed by Harry Jones in the *Plain Dealer* on June 17th gave varying explanations for Feller's resurgence. Eddie Joost: "It's his control. He doesn't give you a good ball to hit at. He's really tough." Gus Zernial: "I never saw a better curve ball." Dave Philley: "He's got such good stuff. That fast ball does something." Mel Harder weighed in as well, saying that while Feller's curve seemed a bit sharper than the previous year, and that his fastball was perhaps a notch faster, the main reason he was pitching better was that he was ahead of the hitters more often. "It's his control. Now he's getting the ball over." Feller gave credit for his improvement to his teammates, noting that they were scoring runs for him, and that it was much easier to pitch when holding a big lead. The Tribe scored seven or more runs in seven of his first 10 starts, a welcome break from the long-standing tradition of Feller pitching in low-scoring contests.

Other writers noticed this phenomenon. Gerry Hern wrote in the *Boston Post* on June 19th, "What makes him big winner is that this year the lads are stroking the ball behind him. Big gobs of runs. In the past, Cleveland folks used to ask, 'Do those players resent him?' There is no reason to ask that now. Feller is now a popular figure with his teammates and other players. Many of them felt he showed his class when he came back after a severe scald received in the lockerroom." Other writers noticed this improved relationship between Feller and his teammates as well. "Feller is more popular among the players this year than ever before," wrote Frank Gibbons, crediting his insistence on pitching despite his burns for his improved reputation.[15] Drawing a direct path between this phenomenon and better run support is impossible, of course. Part of the run differential may have been because, at the height of his career, Feller often went up against the ace pitcher for the other team. Now, he often faced less-talented mound competition; Bob Lemon drew the enemy ace more frequently than in the past. On the other hand, some of Feller's most famous "lack of run support" games, his starts against Harry Eisenstat and Floyd Geibell, for example, weren't against ace pitchers, and in both cases the Indians were extremely motivated to play well as a team. Unless one posits a subconscious, and unprovable, resentment against Feller by his teammates, the idea that Feller got more runs in 1951 because his teammates liked him better is deceptive, even if it does make good copy.

On June 30th, Feller was passed up for the All-Star Game by manager Casey Stengel, despite the fact that he had a 10–2 record and was leading the league in ERA. The next day, Feller showed that, no matter what Stengel or anyone else thought, his performance was far from a fluke. Taking the mound in the first game of a doubleheader against the Tigers, Feller realized in the first inning that his curveball wasn't especially sharp that day, and that his fastball was only average. He switched to the slider instead, making frequent use of it as the game progressed. The Indians scored a run in the first inning, but Tigers starter Bob Cain settled down and was throwing well himself, making it a tight contest. In the top of the fourth, Tribe shortstop Ray Boone booted a ground ball by Johnny Lipon. Lipon stole second base, then moved to third on an errant pickoff attempt, Feller throwing the ball into center field. George Kell then drove Lipon in with a sacrifice fly to tie the score at 1–1.

The game remain tied in the fifth, the sixth, and the seventh. Feller used his fastball more in the late innings, finding that it had improved from earlier in the game, but the slider remained his key outpitch. By the top of the seventh, the crowd in excess of 40,000 was buzzing in anticipation. Could Feller throw his third no-hitter? Could the Indians score a run? The answer to the second question was answered in the bottom of the eighth, when Luke Easter singled in Sam Chapman to put Cleveland up 2–1.

Feller faced three tough hitters in the top of the ninth: Charlie Keller, George Kell, and Vic Wertz. Keller, who usually hit Feller well, was retired on a fly ball to right field on an 0–2 pitch. Kell flew out to left on a 1–2 pitch. Wertz was more difficult, working the count to 3–2, including a long foul ball smash that had home run distance. But Feller then caught Wertz looking with a slider on the outside corner, ending the game and giving himself his third career no-hitter. He walked three and fanned five.

Bob gave credit to his teammates for the achievement, singling out strong defensive plays made by Bobby Avila, Ray Boone, and Al Rosen in particular. He also had high praise for catcher Jim Hegan. "Jim called just about a perfect game and I didn't have to shake him off once. Boone, Avila, Rosen, they all came through with beautiful plays."[16] The game tied Feller with Cy Young and Larry Corcoran with three career no-hitters, which stood as the record until it was surpassed by Sandy Koufax in the 1960s. Cy Young himself happened to be listening to the game on the radio, and was approached by several reporters for his comments about

Feller. Young told of advice he'd given Feller earlier in his career. "The boy was trying to overpower all the hitters. I told him he'd never get away with it in the long run. I told him to mix up his stuff more, don't show 'em your overhand fastball every time. Johnson was tops. Feller isn't too far away."[17]

One man who also commented on the no-hitter was Casey Stengel, who'd come in for some criticism for leaving Feller off the All-Star team. Stengel had selected Bob Lemon instead, regarded by most as a superior pitcher overall to Feller at this point in their careers. "How did I know the guy would pitch a no-hitter? I'm better off dead!" Stengel said.[18] Feller apparently held no hard feelings about the All-Star slight. "He doesn't give an Iowa hoot," wrote Franklin Lewis after asking Feller about the issue.[19] Feller later commented that, in one way, being left out of the All-Star Game actually turned out for the best, since he received a great outpouring of support from Indians fans. "I would have liked to have made the team, but believe me, it was worth losing out just to have the experience of being on the sympathetic side of an argument for a change."[20] It was a welcome switch from the heckling he'd been getting in recent years.

The good feelings engendered by the no-hitter were not shared by everyone. Shirley Povich of the *Washington Post* hit Feller with a negative article just a few days after the no-hitter, mocking him as a "poor, downtrodden wage slave" on July 6th. This centered on Feller's complaint, made as the Tribe's player representative, that team owners were unfairly limiting the earning power of major league players by refusing to let them play winter ball in Cuba. The rule allowed Cuban players to play winter ball in their homeland, but players native to the United States were prohibited from doing so. Feller complained that it wasn't fair to either the North Americans or the Cubans. "The present rule is a simple matter of dollars and cents for the club owners. They get these Latin American players for peanut salaries with the argument that they are allowing them to boost their income by playing winter ball," Feller protested. Feller's point of view was that either everyone should be allowed to play winter ball, or no one should. Povich pointed out that, at least in the case of the Senators, the Cubans were not being taken advantage of. Clark Griffith payed Cuban players like Connie Marrero and Sandy Consuegra "more than most American players receive from their clubs at the same stage of service." Povich accepted ownership arguments that the ban existed in order to prevent "their more valuable chattels" from hurting themselves in winter ball. He attacked Feller, accusing him of "resentment of the dough the Cubans are picking up" and claiming that Feller had no genuine concern for his fellow players.

The latter charge, at least, was unfair, but Povich had a long history of interpreting anything Feller said or did in the most negative way possible.

While Feller's relationship with the fans in Cleveland had flipped between love and hate over the years, the love was in full force through most of '51. On August 13th, the Tribe honored him with "Bob Feller Night" at the park. He received the key to the city from Cleveland mayor Thomas Burke, as well as a silver tea set from the club and a silver punch bowl from his teammates inscribed with their signatures. The Indians printed up a special "newspaper" for the occasion, titled *The Strikeout Story*, featuring a rundown of Feller's career and exploits. He gave a brief speech, giving his teammates special credit for his achievements, concluding, "I hope I don't disappoint you."[21] Feller then took the mound after the ceremony, defeating the Tigers 2–1 in a complete game victory. It was his 19th victory of the season, running up his record to a stunning 19–4.

His next start, against the Senators on the 21st, was his 20th win, a six-hit shutout against the Senators. "Truth is, I even surprised my self," he told reporters after the game.[22] He told them he had three goals entering the season: to win 20 games (accomplished), to throw another no-hitter (accomplished), and to win the World Series. "I've got to win at least 25 if we are to win the pennant. And if we don't win this year, we'll have only ourselves to blame."

The Indians had been in second place most of the season, but the Yankees proved to be too strong. Feller won only two of his remaining starts, losing four. The Indians finished with a strong record yet again, 93–61, a .604 winning percentage. But they ranked second behind the Yankees, missing the pennant by five games.

The '51 Tribe featured both strong hitting and strong pitching. Luke Easter (.270, 27 homers, 103 RBI), Bobby Avila (.304), Al Rosen (24 homers, 102 RBI), and Larry Doby (.295, 20 homers, 101 walks) were the offensive leaders. But the pitching staff was even better, leading the league in ERA and featuring three 20-game winners: Mike Garcia (20–13, 3.15 ERA), Early Wynn (20–13, 3.02 ERA), and Feller. Bob Lemon, considered the actual ace of the team by most experts, was the victim of poor run support for a change, posting a 3.52 ERA but going 17–14, leading the league in losses.

As for Feller, he led the American League with 22 wins while losing eight. His .733 winning percentage ranked third in the circuit. He ranked fifth in the league with 249.6 innings pitched. However, despite the much better won-loss record, Feller's pitching in 1951 was actually not quite as good as it had been in 1950. Rough starts at the end of the season increased Feller's ERA from it's mid-season lows. He still finished with an ERA of 3.50, but this was only 8 percent better than the league average when adjusted for park effect. His 3.48 mark in 1950, however, had been a full 27 percent better than league. Feller was effective in 1951, but the big improvement in his won-loss record was a matter of superior run support and better luck. Still, no one can deny that it was a strong campaign, especially in the first half. But the contrast between 1951 and the previous few seasons was not as strong as the won-loss record implied.

This was not the way people saw it at the time, however. Feller's "comeback" was considered one of the top stories of the 1951 season. The Cleveland Baseball Writers named Feller "Man of the Year," honoring him with a postseason ceremony. The ceremony program dedication shows how Feller was perceived in Cleveland at the end of the '51 season, by both the writers and the fans.

> Because:
> He made such a brilliant comeback after three relatively lean years had caused some to believe he was nearing the end of his trail;
> He was the outstanding pitcher in the American League, winning

the greatest number of games (22) and compiling the highest percentage (.733);
He pitched a third no-hit game, a feat performed only twice before in baseball history and not at all since the turn of the century;
He established a new modern record for total victories in a Cleveland uniform, 230, breaking the mark of 224 held by Mel Harder;
He sought, as player representative of the Indians, to improve the lot of his fellow workman and to uphold the dignity of the game;
He set a shining example for the youth of America, both as a sportsman and as a citizen;
Because of all this . . .
The Cleveland Chapter, Baseball Writers Association of America, is proud to announce it has chosen as "Man of the Year" in Cleveland baseball for 1951, Bob Feller.

Bob Feller had come back, back into the good graces of the fans and, for the most part, the writers. He had made the final transition from thrower to pitcher. Whether it would last was another matter entirely.

15

Dusk

Do what you can, with what you have, where you are.
—Theodore Roosevelt

1951 was a good season for Bob Feller on and off the field. At the end of the campaign, he returned to Van Meter to pitch in an exhibition game, the funds raised being used to construct a new community center. There had been a movement afoot to name it the "Bob Feller Building," but Feller vetoed this proposal. "It's the town's building. Everybody worked to erect it and I insisted my name be kept out."[1] This project went well, but it did not take long for him to step back into controversy. Feller would not barnstorm in '51, but he did spend the late fall and winter giving speeches and making appearances across the continent. In October, he visited Toronto, serving as the main attraction in the Toronto Minor Baseball Association's annual meeting at a local club. There he would speak and sign autographs for some 450 Canadian children.

Feller made a strong positive impression on *Toronto Globe and Mail* writer Hal Walker, influencing him with this "absolute frankness in speech, his sincerity, and friendliness."[2] But while Feller came across well personally, his words did not translate well into print. Feller mourned the death of barnstorming, pointing out that a recent tour promoted by a friend had lost some $70,000, and tracing the decline in the popularity of such exhibition contests to the integration of the major leagues. "This [racial rivalry] used to constitute real grudge fights on the diamond. Now the boys just go through the motions." Feller then criticized the All-Star Game, deriding it as "a lot of nonsense." He pointed out that many players feigned injuries to get out of playing, and even those who did not "merely want to pick up a wrist watch and the other gifts you get."

Ouch. He further described the Indians infield as "poor," and said that the team had been lucky to finish in second place, given the erratic defense and inconsistent hitting.

Although the Toronto reporter did not seem offended by Feller's comments, the same was not true south of the border. *The Sporting News* published an account of the Toronto interview on October 17th, which set off yet another round of bad publicity for Feller, nationwide in terms of his All-Star comment, and in Cleveland because of his statement about the Tribe. On return to the United States, Feller was interviewed by Hal Lebovitz for *The Sporting News,* and attempted to clarify and explain his comments. "All Star Game 'Just Nonsense'? Feller Denies He Said It That Way," screamed the headline on October 31st. Lebovitz pointed out that Feller's habit of blunt talking had resulted in similar controversies before, but that Feller usually "takes the blows as smilingly as he does praise." But this time Feller responded directly with a denial that he'd said what the Toronto writer claimed he'd said, adding an endorsement of the value of the All-Star Game. "My words were misinterpreted. I never used the word 'nonsense.' In fact, I never thought of it. I see three great values in the All-Star Game. First, it stirs up tremendous baseball publicity. Second, it has a very worthy purpose, the player's pension fund. Lastly, it is a great exhibition." The middle point was in response to critics who said he didn't care about the pension fund that the All-Star Game helped finance. Feller elaborated further, trying to explain how his comment had been taken out of context. "Now mind you, I said 'exhibition.' I didn't say it was a great contest. And that's how I think the reporter misinterpreted my remarks and came up with the word 'nonsense.' Perhaps I should have elaborated. 'The All-Star Game is a joke—from a competitive standpoint.'" Feller went on, saying that the game served a great purpose, but that as a competition to prove which league was superior, it was "a joke."

As for the comment about the Indians infield being poor, Feller issued a flat denial. "That, I never said. That, I never thought. That, I don't believe." He stated everyone on the club was responsible for their failure to beat the Yankees, including himself, but that he had not singled out the infielders. He mentioned that Luke Easter's bad knee had prevented him from playing up to his full potential, that Al Rosen and Larry Doby had had "ordinary" seasons, and that Ray Boone had hit in bad luck all year. He also pointed out his own failure to pitch well down the stretch as a major contributing factor.

It's impossible from this distance to know if Feller was truly misquoted, and even then it was a "he said, he said" situation. In any event, the controversy blew over relatively quickly, but was yet another example of how Feller's bluntness worked to his disadvantage in public relations.

As 1952 approached, attention turned to Feller's prospects for the upcoming campaign. Speaking to the Cleveland baseball writers on the day he was honored as Man of the Year, Feller gave this list of his remaining baseball ambitions: "I'd like to win my 300th game, I'd like to become the only pitcher with four no-hitters, and most of all, I'd like to help our club get into another World's Series."[3] It looked as if all three goals were achievable. He had 230 wins to his credit entering the '52 season. Feller's 22-win campaign in '51 implied that he had plenty left, enough to at least get close to 300 wins should he pitch for three or four more seasons. He'd thrown a no-hitter in '51, and pitched several other games with stuff that was good enough to shut any team down. His contract was renewed for $50,000. And finally, the Indians had won 89 or more games for four seasons in a row. They had one of the best starting rotations in baseball, and enough hitters to be dangerous every day. It was surely only a matter of time before they put everything together at once and pushed past the Yankees.

But this would not be in 1952.

The season got off to an inauspicious start in spring training. Feller was hit for three runs in the first inning of an exhibition game against the Pittsburgh Pirates. His velocity was weak enough that Al Lopez complained to some reporters that Feller had been lobbing the ball. "I hate to see a pitcher lob 'em in," Lopez said.[4]

Reminded that Feller seldom pitched well in spring training, concentrating more on conditioning his legs than in firing the ball in games that didn't count, Lopez answered, "I know Bob has had his own timetable for working into pitching condition and he has always been successful with it. I wouldn't want to change him." But it was apparent that Feller's attitude bothered Lopez on some level. "I never had a fraction of Bob's ability, of course, but as long as I played, I wanted to look good every time out. That was my kind of pride, I guess. But Feller has worked out over all these years a conditioning program which he thinks is best for him."

This particular language passed uncommented in the Cleveland press, but Lopez's phrasing in that last sentence possibly gives away what he truly thought about Feller's conditioning program. Rumors spread that Lopez felt Feller was not giving his best effort, but that wasn't what the manager had been trying to say. "Bob is the last guy in the world to be charged with loafing. He's the hardest working player I've ever seen," he said in response to the rumors. Overall, Lopez admired Feller's work ethic, but it seems likely he did not completely approve of Feller's approach to physical training. Feller himself rejected criticism of his spring program. "That doesn't bother me. I never dog it. I pitch as well as I can with the stuff I have in that particular start, but if my arm isn't right, I don't risk hurting it just to give the fans a show." His job was to win games for the Indians from April through September, not in March. This irritated the "fans in Podunk" who came out to see spring exhibition games, Ed McAuley wrote condescendingly, but it was best for the Tribe.

Despite the spring controversy, Feller began the season in strong fashion, winning three of his first five starts. On April 23d, Feller matched up against Bob Cain in St. Louis. Cain had been with the Tigers the year before, and was Feller's opponent in his no-hitter. On the 23d, both Feller and Cain reprised their pitching-duel roles. Feller threw a one-hitter, giving up a triple to Bobby Young in the first inning; Young later scored on a ground ball. But Cain *also* threw a one-hitter, and in his case kept the Indians shut down completely in the run column, earning a 1–0 victory for the Browns. It was the first time in major league history that both pitchers threw a one-hitter in the same game. It was the 11th one-hitter of Feller's career.

It appeared at this time that Feller's 1952 season would be a reprise of 1951. He was pitching well, and the Tribe was in the thick of the pennant hunt once again. But as the saying goes, it was only April. Feller's next start did not go as well as his losing masterpiece against the Browns: he gave up nine runs and 18 hits against Philadelphia, although he pitched the entire game and was the victor in a 21–9 slugfest. In retrospect, leaving Feller in to pitch an entire game under these circumstances—the Indians well ahead and Feller not having his best stuff—was a questionable decision on the part of Al Lopez, for following this game Feller tipped into a slump. While Feller had won three of his first five starts, he proceeded to win only six more starts over the rest of the season. And unlike some of his previous bouts of "bad" pitching, it was not a matter of poor run support or rotten luck. By mid-season, Feller was pitching genuinely poor baseball. His velocity was down considerably, and his fastball was but a shadow of its former self. The good command he'd shown in '51 was absent; he was unable to consistently get ahead of hitters with his curveball and slider. Al Lopez tried to compensate by giving Feller extra rest, skipping him in the rotation occasionally and putting a greater burden on Wynn, Garcia, and Lemon. But it was to no avail.

By the end of the summer, Feller's pitching had gotten bad enough that he was publicly considered a "sacrifice" when the Indians went up against Philadelphia's Bobby Shantz on August 26th. Shantz was having a great year (he ended up leading the league with 24 wins), and was considered the best pitcher in baseball that season by most observers. Feller pitched a strong game, taking a 2–0 lead into the eighth inning, but he was making a maximum effort, exhausting himself in the process, and it was obvious that the strain of the poor season was taking a toll on him. The first hitter in the top of the eighth, Billy Hitchcock, worked the count to 2–1 against Feller. Feller came in with a slider; the pitch was called "ball three" by plate umpire Grover Froese. Feller was enraged by the call. The pitch appeared to be a clear strike, at least to both Feller and Indians catcher Joe Tipton. "In all the years of observing

Mr. Robert never have I seen him charge an umpire on a question-able call," wrote Hal Lebovitz.[5] Feller rushed the umpire, scream-ing that the pitch had been perfect. He had to be restrained by Tipton, as well as manager Lopez, who removed him from the game. "I was running out of gas," Feller admitted afterward. The Tribe eventually won the game in 11 innings. It was one of a very few times Feller ever lost his cool on the diamond. "I have seen him express mild surprise at an umpire's decision," wrote Lebovitz, "but a violent demonstration, never." His own physical exhaus-tion, combined with the humiliation of a poor season, had put Fel-ler on the emotional edge. Lopez lost confidence in him from this point; Feller started just one game in September. When the Indians and Yankees met for a critical September matchup late in the year, it was Mike Garcia who got the call to pitch the crucial, possibly pennant-deciding game, not Bob Feller. Garcia, Lemon, and Wynn took all the starts down the final stretch. Any illusion that Feller might still be the ace of the club was dispelled.

Once again the Tribe fell short of the Yankees in '52, and Feller's poor season was a major contributing factor. The team led the league in runs scored, getting strong production out of Luke Easter (31 homers), Bobby Avila (.300, 12 steals, 11 triples), Al Rosen (.302, 28 homers), Larry Doby (.278, 32 homers), and Dale Mitchell (.323). The pitching was also excellent, as three Indians starters won 22 or more games: Early Wynn (23–12, 2.90), Mike Garcia (22–11, 2.37), and Bob Lemon (22–11, 2.50). The Big Three starters were collec-tively picked as "Men of the Year" by the Cleveland baseball writ-ers. The Indians finished only two games behind the Yankees, and Feller's weak performance was held to blame by many. He finished 9–13 with a 4.73 ERA in 30 starts, easily the poorest season of his career to that point. He fanned just 81 in 192 innings. He gave up 219 hits. His ERA was 30 percent *below* league average, the worst mark of his career. Although some writers blamed poor defensive support for Feller's troubles, it was a simply horrible season, made worse by the knowledge that, if he'd been able to pitch even aver-age baseball, the Indians would probably have won the pennant. It was the first major taste of failure in Bob Feller's entire life to that point. "I didn't know what it was like to have a losing season, and my disappointment was compounded because I was having that kind of year on a team that was a big winner."⁶

Feller was under no illusions about what 1952 meant, as was made clear in a pair of wire service articles that circulated in early December. "No question about it. 300 seems out of the question," Feller said when asked if he still had a chance to meet his career victory goal. He expected to pitch three more seasons, and now very much doubted he would be able to achieve the coveted 300 mark. He further told UPI that he was trying to develop a new pitch, a knuckleball, to add something extra to his repertoire, since his fastball was gone and his other pitches had been less than effective in '52. He told reporters he would stay in the game as long as he felt he could still be a useful pitcher, but would not hang around too long and lose his baseball dignity.

Feller took time off in November to tour Europe with Virginia, the couple sailing aboard the Cunard liner *Mauretania*. The Fellers found that, aside from a few reporters' questions in England and a bit of attention in Holland, there was little baseball interest in Europe. This caused some mild amusement when dealing with customs. "My passport caused some raised eyebrows. Under occupation I was listed as a professional ball player and the examiners had no idea what that was."⁷

The couple rented a car and drove throughout Western Europe. The trip was enjoyable, a "once in a lifetime experience," though a severe storm encountered by *Mauretania* on the return trip resulted in some bumps and bruises, including an injured elbow for Virginia.

The hot topic of conversation in Cleveland during the winter was Feller's status. Again, the Tribe looked to have a strong team on the field in '53, but to match the Yankees, a comeback by Feller was critical. "I haven't given a sports talk this winter without being asked from the floor, 'What do you expect of Feller?'" wrote Ed McAuley. "If he can regain his control, he will be a useful member of the staff. If he can't, this may be his last year in the Wigwam."⁸

McAuley noted that, despite Bob's poor pitching in '52, there had been few complaints from the fans about his salary, as opposed to the severe abuse Feller had taken from angry boosters over monetary matters in the late forties.

There were rumors, going into contract negotiation season, that the Indians would impose the maximum 25 percent salary cut on Feller. On February 3d, Feller met with Hank Greenberg to discuss contract terms. The meeting took seven minutes, the two parties coming to agreement on a contract for $40,000, representing a 20 percent cut from his '52 take. Greenberg told reporters that Feller was never in danger of the maximum cut; no Indian was. "When you tell a fellow you're reducing his salary 25 per cent, you sound as if you'd like to cut him even deeper if you could. It's not good psychology."[9] Feller had no complaints about the contract. He was still one of the best-paid players in the American League, and he vowed he would improve his performance in '53. He said he still had enough on the ball to win, but had to improve his command; this would be the focus of his preparation for '53.

Others agreed. One anonymous teammate told Gordon Cobbledick in February that Feller still had enough stuff to be successful, but "was so conscious of the loss of much of his old speed" that he tried too hard to "shave the corners of the plate paper-thin with every pitch." Cobbledick concurred with this assessment, writing in the *Plain Dealer* that he wasn't ready to quit on Feller, and that Indians fans shouldn't either. Feller approached the task at hand with renewed vigor, increasing the intensity of his calisthenics program even more. This was his standard reaction to struggles; he'd increased his workout load to attempt to fix pitching problems before. But Feller felt that as he aged, conditioning was even more important than it had been in the past. In addition to more workouts, he also tried more "positive thinking." He would not resign himself to failure.

Whatever the reason, Feller did improve in 1953. While his fastball did not come back, he was able to throw his breaking pitches and an improved changeup for strikes more often. He did not break out the knuckleball he'd discussed over the winter, finding his curveball and slider adequate to keep hitters off balance. Feller was not used in full rotation, and Al Lopez made sure he had plenty of rest. Although the Indians maintained a good winning pace throughout the season, the '53 campaign was not as tight as the '52 race had been. The Tribe played well at 92–62, a .597 winning percentage, but the Yankees won 99 games and took the pennant handily.

Press attention for Bob in '53 was focused less on his pitching than on other affairs. He achieved the dubious honor of injuring White Sox second baseman Nellie Fox in Washington on August 2d, even though he was several hundred miles away at the time. In Washington, Feller had used his locker to perform chin-ups as part of his exercise routine. The White Sox came into D.C. following the Indians, the Tribe moving on to Philadelphia, and Fox took over the locker that had been used by Feller. As Fox reached up to get some toothpaste, he accidentally pulled the locker down on top of himself, injuring his legs in the process. The locker was sunk in concrete, normally preventing it from moving, but it had been loosened by Feller's exercises.[10]

A second and more important event also happened in August. For years, Feller had been campaigning to allow major league players full access to winter ball employment. Commissioner Ford Frick finally announced a "compromise" proposal: three players from each team would be allowed to play winter ball, provided they had permission from the commissioner's office as well as their own clubs. Feller rejected this. "Is it fair to say to one fellow, 'you can go,' and to his roomate, 'you can't go?' Why discriminate? If one major leaguer is allowed to play winter ball, every major leaguer should have the same permission."[11] Feller went on to say that the Office of the Commissioner should be more than just a mouthpiece for the owners. He suggested that the players be allowed to participate in the selection of the commissioner, since the office was supposed to represent all interested in the game: owners, players, and fans.

On the mound, Feller finished the season with a 10–7 record, making 25 starts and throwing 176 innings. His ERA of 3.59 was 5 percent better than league average, not outstanding of course, but much better than in '52. His numbers weren't much different than those posted by the other Tribe pitchers. Lemon went 21–15 with a 3.36 ERA, and Garcia 18–9 with a 3.24 ERA, more effective than

Feller but not by a huge amount. Early Wynn, 17–12 but with a 3.93 ERA, was actually less effective on a per-inning basis than Feller, though he pitched almost 80 more innings and started nine more games. Bob no longer had the stamina to pitch as frequently as his teammates; or at least, Al Lopez didn't think so.

The season over, Feller returned to the Hot Stove circuit, giving speeches and making personal appearances, often on behalf of the Indians. He was satisfied that he'd proven his value to the club, removing the bitter taste of 1952. He felt he had at least two or three more years of decent pitching ahead of him and had grown to accept his new role as respected veteran spot starter, rather than league-dominating mound ace. Feller did vow, however, that he would not stick around too long: "I will not try to outdo Satchel Paige," he told the Connecticut Sportsman's Show in February.[12] Although the career statistical records he'd wanted were out of reach, there was still a good chance the Tribe could reach the World Series within the next year or two, giving Bob a shot at redeeming himself for failing to win a game in 1948.

Feller's tendency to say exactly what was on his mind got him in trouble yet again on the fall speaking tour. Speaking at the Buffalo Jewish Center in late October, he warned that while the Indians were still a good club, he was concerned that the need for more hitting from first base, outfield, and catcher would put them at a disadvantage in the pennant chase. The Yankees were still the team to beat, though several of their pitchers were old. Both the White Sox and Red Sox were improving. The Indians, if they didn't improve to match the competition, could fall into the second division, he told the Buffalo audience. Feller's critique of the Indians was valid. Luke Easter was 37 years old, still dangerous with the bat, but limited to just 68 games in '53 by injury. His replacement, Bill Glynn, was a weak hitter. Catcher Jim Hegan was skilled defensively and worked well with the pitching staff, but he was not a good hitter, and his nonthreatening stick put an additional drag on the offense. Aside from Larry Doby, the Indians lacked punch from the outfield. Feller was right to be concerned about the Tribe's weaknesses, but his honest comments in Buffalo, as his honest comments had done so often before, provoked a backlash at home, as well as some crowing among Yankee fans in New York.

Again, Feller was forced to clarify his comments on return to Cleveland. "I won't say I was misquoted," he told Hal Lebovitz, always a sympathetic ear. "I will say that I was misunderstood."[13] He pointed out that he didn't say the Indians were destined to fall to the second division; he said it was possible, and that the statement was based on the assumption that the Yankees didn't falter, that the White Sox and Red Sox improved, and that the Indians did nothing to solve their problems. "For what it's worth, I just as easily could have said we'll win the pennant." Feller emphasized that teams are always saying they'll win, and it was more honest, and more meaningful, to give an accurate assessment. "Why should we go around saying we're going to win? Let the Yanks do the boasting—and then we'll try to knock them off. You never hear Frank Leahy say Notre Dame is going to win."

Feller's itinerary that fall and winter was a busy one. He made more than 50 appearances across the eastern half of the country, ranging from the East Coast, into upstate New York and Canada, down south to Texas, back up north to Iowa. Most of his personal appearances were done gratis; for some, his expenses were paid. He traveled for the most part in his own aircraft, a Beechcraft Bonanza, enabling him to schedule appearances without having to worry about airline reservations or passenger train timetables. He was, commented *The Sporting News*, acting as an unofficial ambassador for the game, stirring up interest and promoting both the Indians and major league baseball as a whole.

One favorite topic in these appearances was television, which was a short-term problem for the game, but in Feller's opinion presented great long-term opportunity. "Eventually we'll learn how to live with it [television]. The monster some day will be a tremendous boon and make baseball better than ever."

In January, Feller settled on a 1954 contract for $35,000, a slight cut from his '53 earnings, but reasonable given his reduced workload. The Tribe was still relying on Wynn, Lemon, and Garcia to anchor the rotation. Feller would be used as a spot starter, especially on Sunday doubleheaders. The front office added left-hander

Art Houtteman to fill out the rotation. To provide bullpen support, they promoted a pair of pitchers from the minors, Don Mossi and Ray Narleski. They even signed veteran Hal Newhouser, former Tiger ace, on his last legs but still effective when kept within his limits. Aware of the need for the offensive boost that Feller desired, the Indians also picked up outfielders Dave Philley and Al Smith, and were on the lookout for additional help at first base as the season began.

April 13th marked the beginning of the season. By the end of the month, the Indians were 6–6 and in fourth place. Feller had yet to start a game.

His first opportunity came on May 2d when he opened the first game of a Sunday doubleheader against the Senators. It resulted in a 6–4 Cleveland victory, though a no-decision for Feller. His next outing was two weeks later, another doubleheader opening, this time against the Athletics. This was another Tribe victory, albeit a hard-fought one, 12–7. Neither of Feller's first two starts had been impressive. He'd made it into just the fourth inning in the first game and into just the third inning in the second. People began wondering if Feller was completely through. Again, the rumor mill churned. This time, word spread through Cleveland that Al Lopez had wanted to release Feller in spring training, rumors that the front office did little to try and dispel. Supposedly, Lopez had been talked out of the action by GM Hank Greenberg, who was worried about fan reaction to the move, especially given the fact that Feller had pitched decently in '53. Dumping Feller would have to wait, although if he continued to pitch poorly, that time might not be far off.

But Feller avoided the reaper by winning his next start against the Baltimore Orioles (formerly the St. Louis Browns) on May 23d by a 14–3 score, tossing a strong complete game. He beat the Athletics on June 6th and then the Red Sox on June 12th. The Tribe won nine in a row in mid-June, solidifying their hold on first place. Feller was throwing well, and Lemon, Wynn, and Garcia were all in top form. The offense had improved, especially after the acquisition of Vic Wertz from Baltimore, brought in to provide a better bat at first base.

By July, even long-time Feller skeptics like Shirley Povich were impressed with his performance. "One of the more fascinating facts in American League affairs this year is the resurgence of the Old Man of the Cleveland Indians, Bob Feller, as a winning pitcher. At 35, when most pitchers have had it, Feller is writing a comeback story that has few parallels," Povich wrote in the July 21st *Washington Post*. By this point, Feller was 7–1 and had won six starts in a row in convincing fashion. He'd allowed a grand total of seven runs in his last six starts, noted Povich, and he'd been winning games not with junk pitches, but with a suddenly revived fastball. It wasn't back to 1940, or even 1950, standards, but it had returned to above-average velocity according to American League hitters. Feller also altered the grip on occasion to get extra sink on the pitch, in situations where a ground ball was needed. He even broke out the knuckleball a handful of times, using it as a changeup. The sinker, combined with his standard curveball, slider, and better control, made him a nasty opponent once again. "He can't pitch every fourth day like the others," Al Lopez told Povich, "but give him five days rest and he'll give you the best job."

Feller had told Lopez several times he was willing to work more often, but Lopez was adverse to pushing Feller too far. The rest of the team was doing "the best job" as well. There was no reason to squeeze any more innings out of Feller than necessary. The Tribe took sole possession of first place with Feller's victory on June 12th, and never looked back. The Yankees had a marvelous season, winning 103 games, but the Indians were even better, coasting to an incredible 111–43 record, including 11 straight wins in September that drove a stake through the Yankees' hopes. The .721 winning percentage set a new American League team record.

Everything went right for the Indians in 1954. Bobby Avila hit .341. Al Rosen hit .300 with 24 homers and 102 RBI. Larry Doby led the league with 32 homers and 126 RBI. Wertz knocked 14 homers after joining the team. The two new outfielders provided mixed results. Dave Philley hit a disappointing .226, but contributed 12 homers. Al Smith hit .281. Even Jim Hegan contributed to the offense, hitting just .234 but slugging 11 homers. The Indians led the

American League with 156 homers, and finished second behind the Yankees with 746 runs scored.

But it was the pitching staff that truly shone. Lemon and Wynn tied for the league lead with 23 victories apiece, and both also posted excellent 2.72 ERAs. Mike Garcia won "just" 19, but led the league with a 2.64 ERA. Art Houtemann was an effective fourth starter, winning 15 games and posting a 3.35 ERA. In the bullpen, the trio of Don Mossi (1.94, seven saves), Ray Narleski (2.22, 13 saves), and the distinguished Hal Newhouser (2.49, seven saves) did excellent work. Bob Feller made just 19 starts, kept on long rest by Lopez, but he pitched quite well, going 13–3 for an .813 winning percentage. His 3.09 ERA was 19 percent better than league average when adjusted for park effects, a solid performance.

The Indians were opposed in the World Series by the New York Giants, managed by Leo Durocher. Willie Mays was the big star here, and he'd had a marvelous season, hitting .345 with 41 homers and 13 triples, leading the National League in both batting average and slugging percentage. The Giants featured other dangerous hitters like shortstop Alvin Dark (.293, 20 homers), third baseman Hank Thompson (.263, 26 homers), and Negro League veteran Monte Irvin (.262, 19 homers). National League ERA champ Johnny Antonelli (2.29, 21 wins) anchored the pitching staff. Ruben Gomez and Sal Maglie were also good starters, and the denizens of the Polo Grounds featured a strong bullpen, starting with Hoyt Wilhelm and Marv Grissom. The Giants had won 97 games and were a very good team, but the Indians were considered clearly better in the minds of most experts. They had a more balanced hitting attack, and the pitching was stronger. Antonelli was considered equal to any of the Cleveland aces, but neither Gomez nor Maglie were.

The series opened in New York. Al Lopez scheduled Bob Lemon to start game one, and tapped Early Wynn to begin game two. Feller was scheduled to start game three, the first contest in Cleveland; Mike Garcia was set for game four. After that, the rotation would depend on how the Series went, assuming it went beyond four games. Feller was primed for game three; he knew it was probably his last chance to win a World Series game.

The Indians took an early 2–0 lead behind Lemon in the first game, but the Giants came back to tie the game in the bottom of the third. This contest was made famous by Willie Mays, who made a spectacular running catch to snare a long drive off Vic Wertz's bat in the ninth inning, with two men on, saving a run and the game for the Giants. It was a great play, etched in baseball memory forever by constant replays ever since on television and film, though some observers, Al Lopez and Feller included, felt they'd seen better, even from Willie. Feller especially pointed out a tremendous catch earlier in the year by Larry Doby as a superior play. But what made Mays' play special was the context: to save a World Series game. A pinch-hit homer by Dusty Rhodes in the bottom of the tenth sealed the victory for the Giants, defeating Bob Lemon and putting the series in New York's favor by a game.

Early Wynn pitched well for the Indians in game two, holding the Giants to three runs in seven innings. But Johnny Antonelli pitched better, holding the Indians to just one run, putting New York up two games to none.

Al Lopez was now faced with a difficult decision. The Indians were going home to Cleveland, out of the Polo Grounds and away from the short distances down the lines that seemed to favor pull hitters like Dusty Rhodes (who'd also homered in game two). But winning the third contest was crucial, and although Feller had pitched effectively in the regular season, Lopez was more confident in Mike Garcia. He moved Garcia up a day, naming him to start game three. If the Indians won game three, Feller might start game four, although this was uncertain. If the Indians lost, Bob Lemon would start the must-win game four, and Feller would be bumped from the starting plans entirely.

Lopez's decision to start Garcia backfired, as the Giants raked him for four runs in three innings. Houtteman, Narleski, and Mossi made relief appearances, but the Indians, despite an attempt at a late rally, were unable to solve Ruben Gomez and Hoyt Wilhelm. The Giants came away with a 6–2 win, putting the series at 3–0 and sticking the Indians in a very tight corner. Bob Lemon would *definitely* start game four, and Feller's chance of even appearing in the series seemed remote.

Lemon was not at his best in game four. The Giants scored three runs off Lemon in the first three innings, then knocked four more off Lemon and Newhouser in the fifth. The Indians, meanwhile, scored three off Don Liddle in the fifth, but were otherwise shut down. Don Mossi came in to pitch for the Tribe in the sixth inning, then Mike Garcia was brought in to hurl the eighth and ninth. But the Indians were unable to overcome Liddle, Wilhelm, and Johnny Antonelli, losing the game 7–4, and the Giants completed a stunning World Series sweep.

Like everyone else in Cleveland, Feller was crushed. It took some time for the pain to set in, it had all happened so fast. Losing the World Series was bad enough, but to lose it in such a way, being *swept*, especially after a 111-win season, was ignominious. For Feller, there was an extra disappointment: he hadn't pitched at all. To his credit, Feller never publicly expressed any bitterness about the issue, but it had to hurt. From a second-guessing perspective, Lopez's decision to start Garcia rather than Feller in game three was certainly defensible. Garcia *was* a better pitcher at that point, even Feller agreed. Moving Lemon up to pitch game four is also understandable, although sending in Feller to try and stop the sweep would have had a certain poetic beauty. But what many people at the time didn't understand, and what Feller himself questioned, was why Feller didn't get to pitch out of the bullpen in the last two innings of game four, rather than Mike Garcia, who had started the previous game. This did not appear a matter of "saving" Feller for a theoretical game five, as Early Wynn would have started that game. Al Lopez never explained why he didn't use Feller at all in the World Series until the late 1990s, when he said simply that Feller "wasn't that good of a pitcher anymore."[14] He simply didn't trust him to pitch in big games. Despite his 13 wins and solid overall performance in the regular season, Lopez had lacked confidence in Feller to pitch when it most counted.

The sadness of losing the World Series paled in comparison to what came a few weeks later. Lena Feller had been forced to cancel her scheduled trip to the World Series, staying back in Iowa because of chest pains; although Lena was not a smoker, her doctor believed it might be lung cancer. Diagnosis at the Mayo Clinic confirmed the problem as advanced lung cancer, and Lena was given only a short time to live. Bob went out to Iowa to be with his mother and sister. Lena Feller passed away in her home in Van Meter on December 3d, with her family at her side. It was her 61st birthday.

As did the passing of his father back in 1942, the death of Bob's mother drew national attention, including an obituary in *The Sporting News*. Both this article and the *Cleveland Press* notice mentioned the support she'd shown her son over the years, reviewing the tremendous influence his parents had had on Feller growing up. They also discussed an incident from Mothers' Day, 1939, when Lena had been hit in the head by a foul ball while watching Bob pitch in Comiskey Park. "Tell Bob not to leave the game," she had instructed the medical personnel as they were taking her to the hospital for stitches to her forehead. With his mother gone, Bob no longer had reason to keep the Van Meter property. He considered keeping it as a vacation and retirement home, but ultimately sold it to avoid paying property tax on a home he did not use.

After the death of his mother, Feller returned to the speaker circuit, making appearances across the East and Midwest as he'd done the previous winter. He used his own aircraft frequently, in one instance flying his own plane to a luncheon in Rochester, New York, even though all commercial aircraft had been grounded by a snowstorm. Feller turned his failure to appear in the '54 series into a joke, telling the crowd, "As far as the World Series with the Giants is concerned, I had absolutely nothing to do with it."[15] He predicted that the Tribe would contend again in '55, although the Yankees, as always, would put up tough competition.

Feller continued his unofficial ambassadorial duties during the spring. On March 19th, he appeared on NBC television, acting in a well-received baseball comedy sketch with comedian George Gobel. According to reviews of the show, he "handled his lines like a pro"; Gobel chimed in that Feller "pitched a no-hitter with his acting." The purpose of the sketch, according to Gobel, was to "remind his watchers that baseball is an important part of the American way of life," exactly the kind of thing that Feller was always interested in promoting.[16]

Feller also weighed in on a controversy involving the spitball. Commissioner Ford Frick had proposed rescinding the ban on spitballs, in an attempt to help the pitchers and shorten the length of games, which had crept up over two and a half hours on average. Most players were opposed. Feller told the *San Francisco Examiner* that allowing the spitball would do nothing to solve the problems of the game, and would even be counterproductive. Feller predicted that if the spitter were legalized, many pitchers would try to use it without having mastery of the art, and "more players would be hit, more walks given, and the games would be longer instead of shorter."[17] Ultimately, the proposal was dropped.

General Manager Hank Greenberg was faced with a dilemma heading into the season. The Indians had failed in the World Series, badly, so standing pat wasn't a great option, at least politically. On the other hand, how do you improve a team that won 111 games in the regular season? Greenberg decided to add additional power, bringing in aging slugger Ralph Kiner. The pitching staff was bolstered by the addition of fireballing southpaw Herb Score, a 22-year-old with a terrific fastball who drew comparisons to Feller at the same age. Feller himself would be assigned to spot-starter duties once again. It had worked well in '54.

The beginning of the '55 campaign was an auspicious one for Bob. His first start, April 16th in Comiskey Park, was not a success, losing 9–4 to the White Sox and Billy Pierce. But his next outing, May 1st against the Red Sox, was a masterpiece. Sox catcher Sammy White blooped a pitch into center field in the top of the seventh inning, a clean single from a scoring standpoint, though not a well-struck ball. Feller's velocity was pretty good in this game, and his fastball had solid sinking action, complementing his curve and slider nicely. Feller kept the Red Sox off-balance and didn't give up a single hit after White's base hit. He won the game 2–0 before 26,579 fans, notching his 12th career one-hitter. Feller credited his success in part to good game calling by Jim Hegan, and also mentioned that, after his bad game in Comiskey Park, he had stepped up his calisthenics program yet again. It was "as good as any game I ever pitched," an assessment with which the reporters and fans who saw the game concurred.[18]

But Bob was unable to sustain this success. His next start, against the Athletics on May 8th, resulted in a 9–6 win for the Tribe, but he had neither the stuff nor the control he'd shown against the Red Sox. It wasn't until May 31st that he got another chance to pitch, this time shutting down the Orioles to win 2–1. But consecutive mediocre games against the Senators, a 6–4 loss on June 4th, and a 7–0 defeat on the 15th seemed to rob Al Lopez of any confidence he retained in Feller. He started just four more times the rest of June and July, before being sent to the bullpen for the rest of the season.

By this time, Feller was relying mostly on his sinker to get hitters out, which proved fairly useful coming out of the bullpen. He pitched in seven consecutive relief outings in July and August without allowing a run. Al Lopez denied that he had given up on using Feller as a starter. "I'll use him in spots," he told Frank Gibbons in mid-August.[19] But the actions of the manager belied his words. Feller made just one start in September, as part of a doubleheader.

The Indians were in a tight pennant race with the Yankees, ultimately falling short by three games. Rookie Score led the American League with a Feller-esque 245 strikeouts, while Bob Lemon and Early Wynn also posted strong seasons. Feller's numbers weren't bad overall. He went 4–4 with a 3.47 ERA, his ERA being 15 percent better than league average. But a sign of his decline could be found in his strikeout rate. In 83 innings, he struck out just 25, while walking 31. He made 11 starts and 14 relief appearances.

Feller chafed at the lack of usage, although he kept his mouth shut until the end of the year. He finally spoke out on September 26th. "I want to be able to take a regular turn again and prove I can still win consistently," he told the *Des Moines Register*.[20] "I could have pitched 200 innings or more. . . . I'd hate to leave Cleveland, but if they aren't going to let me pitch, I'll be better off somewhere else."

Feller admitted that he and Lopez seldom spoke now. For his part, Lopez shrugged off or merely ignored questions from reporters about Feller's lack of pitching time.

His future with the Indians was on Feller's mind heading into fall and winter, but there were larger issues on his plate as well. He became state chairman for the Ohio March of Dimes, fighting the scourge of polio. This was not a hands-off or merely honorary post; Feller was so heavily involved in the organization that he had a separate office built on his Gates Mills estate, so that he could work on the fund drive without distraction. Although they still owned the land in Texas, the Feller family had decided by now to live in Cleveland year-round to be closer to Bob's speaking engagements. Virginia didn't like Texas, and the ranch home had been adopted as their "permanent residence" primarily for tax purposes anyhow.

The March of Dimes was time-consuming, but it was Bob's service as American League Player Representative that got most of the press attention that winter. Working with NL Representative Robin Roberts, Feller pressed the owners for a say in the selection of the commissioner, a stronger commitment to the pension plan, an increase in the minimum wage, and permission to play winter ball. Feller and Roberts were particularly worried about lack of player input in negotiations for television and radio contracts. But their bargaining position was limited by the fact that the players were not organized as a true union; strikes were out of the question, for example. "We simply want to be treated fairly," said Feller, "not in the high-handed manner that has been so common in past relations."[21] Feller felt that the owners took the players for granted. "In the past the owners have invited us to lunch, filled our mouths with food, and said we were nice fellows. Then they stuck bats in our hands and said 'Go to work.'" In response to criticism that it was the owners who put the most money at stake in baseball, Feller said, "The owners put up the capital, yes. All we put up is our lives."

Among other reforms, Feller and Roberts pushed for some form of arbitration to settle salary disputes. Feller even believed that, at some point, limited free agency could be established to deal with the basic unfairness of the reserve clause. "Perhaps after three or four or five years [of service], a player would be able to shop around for another offer," he said.[22] Feller believed that there was nothing wrong with the labor situation that honest negotiation by reasonable, fair-minded men couldn't solve. These goals could be achieved through honest bargaining, in his view. But despite meetings over the winter with Commissioner Frick, little came of any of this. The baseball owners were not, in fact, reasonable or fairminded men. Until such time as the players were willing to take the formal step of threatening the owners with labor action, they remained little more than chattel in the eyes of most magnates.

But labor action at this point in history was out of the question in the minds of most players. Asked by reporters about the possibility of a strike during spring training, Feller was horrified. "No, no . . . There couldn't possibly be any such thing . . . nobody ever thought of it and nobody ever will."[23] Feller was visionary in many ways, but he failed to appreciate at first how strongly the owners would dig in their heels, and how much more militant the players would become in reacting to owner intransigence. The irony is that, had the owners gone along with some of the proposals suggested by Feller in the 1950s, the history of labor relations in baseball would probably have been much less disastrous, and ultimately more beneficial to the owners in the long run. "The people who made the union so strong," says Feller, "were the owners, by being so arrogant and not giving in on the smaller things we asked for."[24]

While negotiating with the owners and raising money for the March of Dimes, Feller took another step toward securing his future. He became president of a local insurance firm, George H. Olmstead & Company. As usual, this was more than just an honorary post; he quickly began learning the insurance business, preparing for his career after baseball. Despite all his varied business ventures, he continued his physical training and workouts, preparing for the '56 season.

There was considerable speculation about whether or not Feller would be with the Indians as the season approached. It was clear that Al Lopez had no faith in Feller and wanted to use other pitchers, but Hank Greenberg hesitated to simply release him. There were rumors about possible trades, although by early February, Feller had told Greenberg that he wanted to finish his career in Cleveland. He finally signed a 1956 contract for $25,000, although

Greenberg made it clear to him that it was up to Lopez how often and in what capacity Feller would be used.

During spring training, Feller seemed aware that this was his last go around the diamond. He had numerous ideas on how to improve baseball, ideas he wanted in the public mind. He gave interviews in March to national publications *Look* and *Parade*. "I'll never quit baseball," he told *Look*, seeing it as his goal to work to improve the lot of players who hadn't made as much money as he had during his career. He was trying to get the owners on board for a proposal to help fund college education for players, enabling them to make a living after they left the game. For those not interested in college coursework, an "employment and guidance" bureau could be established in each major league city, pairing up ballplayers with local businessmen to teach them a trade. Many players were "one-string violins," lacking outside business skills and entirely dependent on the game for income. Such players were in danger of becoming paupers once their careers ended. Feller wanted to prevent that.

In *Parade*, Feller praised the recent adoption of the Cy Young Award for pitchers, and suggested a change in the way the MVP Award was determined. Pointing out that baseball writers often select favorites or made bizarre choices on their ballots, he proposed a committee system to vote on the award. The committee could consist of one fan for each team, a player from each team, the manager of each team, a reporter for each team, and eight umpires from each league. It was an intriguing proposal, though of course it was not adopted.

Feller's ideas to improve baseball were pushed out of the pages in early April, when news leaked from the Indians front office that Feller's slot on the pitching staff was in danger. "Greenberg, Lopez Want to Drop Feller," blared the front-page headline in the *Cleveland Press* on April 10th. Feller was actually throwing well in spring training, but Lopez wanted to carry younger pitchers north, and Feller was taking up a valuable roster spot. Franklin Lewis followed his scoop up the next day, adding more details to the controversy. Basically, the Indians wanted Feller to leave, but hoped he would retire on his own volition. From Greenberg's perspective, it came down to money. Feller wasn't likely to pitch enough to justify his salary, although the GM didn't want to say this on the record, and was uncomfortable with the idea of trading Feller, given the expected fan reaction. Lopez wanted younger pitchers able to hold up under a greater workload, though he had "nothing to say about it" when asked on the record. Feller insisted that he still had enough left to be an effective pitcher and only wanted a chance to prove himself, although Lewis pointed out that Feller had "plenty" else to say off the record about the situation. Lewis concluded that "to keep from straining relations while a baseball season is on, none of the principals has any desire to make honest statements, so you can discount nearly all the love-and-kisses quotations you might read." Some of these "love-and-kisses" quotations popped up in *The Sporting News* on April 18th, when Lopez told Hal Lebovitz that Feller's spring work had earned him the number five spot in the starting rotation. "Everybody has to make the club. Feller has had a fine spring and he has made it."

Indeed, Feller did make the club, though Lopez's designation of Feller as the fifth starter was apparently just an affectionate smooch. Feller made one start in April and one start in May before being sent to the bullpen. He seldom worked in games of any meaning, essentially deployed as a mop-up pitcher. He was not especially effective when he did pitch. Feller got in one spot start on September 15th, though by this time letting him pitch was safe, as the Tribe was 11 games back of the Yankees and out of the race. One highlight of the season for Bob was September 9th, designated as "Bob Feller Day" in Cleveland. He was honored with a marching band, a new car, various personal gifts, and a telegram from President Eisenhower.

> It is a pleasure to join your many fans and friends as they honor you today. Your outstanding record in baseball, together with your war record in the United States Navy and your peace-time record in many charities and community projects, makes a fine example of American manhood.
>
> > Best wishes for future honors and service.
> > Dwight D. Eisenhower
> > President of the United States

Feller made one final start, on the last day of the season, September 30th. He lost to the Tigers 8–4, throwing a complete game, but failing to strike out a hitter. The Indians finished 88–66, in second place. Feller's final numbers were an 0–4 record and a 4.97 ERA.

Al Lopez resigned to take the managerial post for the Chicago White Sox.

The fall was filled with rumors. Few expected Feller to be pitching for the Indians in '57, but what would happen to him? Would Feller retire voluntarily? Would he be released? Would he be traded? After weeks of speculation, the answer finally came on December 28th. Feller met with Hank Greenberg to discuss his future. After the meeting, he announced to the assembled reporters that he would, in fact, retire. Three clubs, rumored to be the Athletics, the Orioles, and the Tigers, had offered Feller pitching contracts, but Bob had no intention of leaving Cleveland, where his family was now firmly settled. His playing days were over. Greenberg offered him a job in the Indians' front office, but Feller turned that down, too. He would devote his time to the insurance business, as well as the presidency of the newly formed Major League Baseball Players' Association.

This chapter of the storybook had finally ended.

16

Image and Legend

The prospect of retirement wasn't as hard for me to take
as it is for most players because I knew I would still be in
baseball.

—Bob Feller, *Now Pitching: Bob Feller*, p. 211

Retirement for Bob Feller was not a quiet sojourn into the
sunset. He was no longer busy on the pitching mound, but
he was determined to remain active and visible in the game.

As he'd done for several years, he toured the nation
during the winter, giving speeches to various groups. He
used self-deprecating humor when discussing his retirement. "I
decided to retire after getting on a plane one day," he told the Boston chapter of Baseball Writer's Association. "It was one of those
new DC-7Bs, and the pilot looked young to me. Then I got to thinking that a few times last year my catcher was Earl Averill, Jr., whose
dad played with us when I broke in. So I retired."[1] For the baseball
season, he signed a contract with Motorola, acting as "Consultant
on Youth Activities." He would tour the nation during the spring
and summer, conducting workout camps and baseball seminars
for children under the Motorola aegis. From Motorola's perspective, it would be excellent "community relations" publicity. For
Feller, it was a chance to continue his unofficial role as baseball
promotion diplomat. He also continued his work in fighting for increased pensions as president of the Player's Association, and
pledged strong support for Little League programs.

Feller received a great deal of press attention in the spring, mostly retrospectives on the triumphs of his career. He used this platform to press for public support on his favorite issues, especially the player's pension plan, the future of the game in the television age, and the importance of youth programs. Again, he emphasized the need for cooperation between the players and the owners in making the game thrive. He also predicted, in the spring of 1957, that baseball would run into antitrust problems, and eventually be forced to modify the reserve clause, at least to some extent. "They'll water down the rules and operate as they always have, but it might help some of the ordinary ball players who can be covered up for seven years before they're free game for the draft."[2]

Feller crisscrossed the country. He was in Omaha on March 8th through the 10th, then in Phoenix from the 14th through the 18th, then flew to Florida. He put in appearances at several major league camps. He gave pitching clinics for Motorola merchants in many towns, giving interviews to local press all the way. He appeared in Tucson, Phoenix, San Diego, Tampa, Jacksonville, Savannah, Mobile, Cedar Rapids, Little Rock, and Nashville. He teamed up with Rollie Hemsley to run a baseball clinic in Columbus, Ohio, in May. He advised young pitchers to base their success on the fastball and curve, avoiding the slider until their arms were fully mature. As for the spitball, "it's cheating, and if you can't get along without it, you don't belong in competition."[3] At one point, Feller traveled more than 2,500 miles in five days to host clinics.

Although Feller's travel plans centered on the Motorola youth program, he became increasingly vocal about labor issues. He came out in favor of a plan to expose all players to a draft after three years in the minors if they weren't placed on the 40-man roster, a forerunner to today's Rule 5 draft. He was invited to testify before a congressional committee investigating baseball's antitrust status. Feller spoke before the committee on June 25th, blasting baseball owners for operating a monopoly and for abusing players as "pawns." He called the reserve clause unfair, and proposed its replacement with his suggested three-year rule.

The owners, and some others, did not take kindly to Feller's criticism. Press commentary was mixed, some writers feeling that

Feller's critique of the owners was justified, while others questioned Feller's motives in attacking his former benefactors. Harold Kaese, writing in the *Boston Globe*, was typical of the latter. "In considering Feller's testimony at Washington, it should be remembered that the ex-pitcher's philosophy seemed to be: Anything that's bad for my income is bad for baseball. His reference to owners as 'arrogant' made those on the inside laugh. Feller could be pretty arrogant himself."[4] Kaese went on to bring up the '47 and '48 All-Star Game debacles, then identified Feller as the "ringleader" in the '40 rebellion against Ossie Vitt. He also said that many of the players who barnstormed with Feller in the mid-40s, Johnny Sain in particular, vowed never to do so again because of Feller's high-handed manner.

Feller's defenders, meanwhile, pointed out that his own contract negotiations with the Indians had generally gone smoothly, and that he had good personal relations with all three Indians ownership groups he'd dealt with, Bill Veeck and Alva Bradley in particular. One of the things that stuck most in Feller's craw was baseball's refusal to increase the minimum salary beyond $6,000, an issue that obviously had never impacted Feller personally.

Although Feller's critics took the opportunity to attack him for greed and hypocrisy after his testimony, ownership quickly showed that they took a back seat to no one in pettiness. The day after Feller's testimony before Congress, he was notified that the Motorola baseball clinic he was scheduled to give on July 9th in Los Angeles would have to be moved to a new venue or cancelled. Wrigley Field, which Motorola had booked well in advance for the event, was suddenly "unavailable." The stadium was the home of the Los Angeles Angels of the Pacific Coast League, and was owned by the Brooklyn Dodgers. "They really threw us out of there," Feller told Franklin Lewis. "We had planned this clinic, and had been granted the date . . . we had a tieup with a Los Angeles newspaper. All of a sudden we get word that the clinic is out of Wrigley Field. The reason is pretty obvious."[5] The Angels and Dodgers claimed the event had never been scheduled, and that the park was not available because the Dodgers needed to conduct a workout for two high school pitchers they were interested in signing. This was a poor excuse, and although baseball denied there was any reprisal involved, it was generally assumed by everyone outside of ownership ranks that Feller was being punished for his impertinence before Congress.

On August 4th, Feller took his campaign to a new level, appearing on the ABC Television program *The Mike Wallace Interview*. Wallace's pitbull reputation existed long before his days on *60 Minutes*, and he grilled Feller about his stand on the reserve clause. His first question got to the heart of the issue raised by Feller's critics: what right did he, in particular, have to criticize the game?

> WALLACE: Bob, first of all let me ask you this, and I think it's something that may be puzzling to a lot of baseball's fans. In your top years with the Indians, you made about $80,000 a year and your entire earnings from baseball have been estimated at close to a million dollars. Now in view of your phenomenal success, how can you charge that ball players are getting a bum deal from their bosses?
>
> FELLER: As far as I'm concerned, Mike, the setup is wrong. It's not a matter of how much they make. It's the structure. The principle that a ball player is not in a strong bargaining position, especially the ball player that was not blessed with a good arm, a good eye. I was very fortunate and very fortunate to have a father to develop it, but the average ball players' life is only approximately four and three quarters years in the major leagues, and they make much less than some of the real lucky fellows like DiMaggio, Williams, Musial, Roberts.[6]

Feller went on, explaining the reserve clause in simple language, and criticizing the unfair nature of it. The player was essentially obligated to his original signing club for life, unless his rights were traded or he was released. But the club was only obligated to give him 30 days' pay in the event of that release. The contrast between the lifetime obligation of the player, and the 30-day obligation of the club, was clearly un-American in Feller's view. Feller brought up the concept of free agency. "I think during a baseball player's career sometime if he's unhappy on account of his salary or other conditions, not necessarily salary, he should have a chance to make a choice, and I arbitrarily say three years plus an option of two more to give the ball club a chance to make the man happy, to trade him to a team of his choice. Otherwise he has no say-so what part of the country he plays, what team, what teammates, many other things."

Wallace countered, quoting Commissioner Frick, in an echo of our own modern labor problems, that even a limited form of free agency would set off a "wild scramble" for the best players, and that only the teams with the most money would be able to compete. Feller didn't buy that reasoning, pointing out that, even without free agency, the best players already gravitated toward the teams with the most money, simply because they had more resources to spend on scouting. Baseball judgment was as important as financial resources. In reference to the top players, Feller posed this question:

> FELLER: Well, Mike, where are they now? You live in New York . . . if you have 400 ball players free agents and you have more money than the sixteen other owners, you take your choice of 25 ball players . . . is that going to guarantee you a pennant? And if your number three man, the third on the list, his judgment perhaps might be better than yours . . . you can't pick any 25 of them any more than I could bet you even money you can't pick one out of ten pitchers who will win 20 games this year.

Wallace pointed out that, while several players had come out in defense of the reserve clause, including Stan Musial, Feller had no currently active players in his camp. Feller replied that many, many players resented the reserve clause but were not willing to say so publicly for fear of retaliation. Feller also linked the issue of player rights to the "social changes" underfoot in America. Baseball needed an "overhauling" to take account of these changes and to "put the ball player in a more advantageous bargaining position than he is today." In the course of the interview, Feller predicted that the spread of television would damage minor league baseball, that beer sales might need to be restricted to prevent fans in some parks from getting out of control, and that America needed to pay much more attention to the physical health of its youth, which was in danger of growing soft. Too many kids were spectators rather than participants.

Press reaction to the interview was generally positive, although some felt that Bob pulled his punches on some topics, and that Wallace was handicapped by not being "sufficiently acquainted" with baseball. Feller himself felt that Wallace had gone easy on him. "I thought he could have asked some tougher questions. I think he let me off easy . . . we hardly scratched the surface."[7] Still, there was enough in the interview to stir the pot, especially on the reserve clause. Some of Feller's closest admirers, Ed McAuley for example, felt that he was wrong on the topic of potential free agency and limiting the reserve clause. In the event of the adoption of free agency, McAuley wrote, "I'd bet that within a few years the strength of the league would be so tightly concentrated in the two or three teams at the top that the others would have to go out of business."[8]

The more things change, the more they stay the same.

Feller remained outspoken and active throughout the late fifties. The Indians brought him on board in '58 to act as a "super-salesman," not really a scout, but someone who would talk with players the Indians were attempting to sign, trying to convince them of the joys of playing in Cleveland. He was a frequent and favorite interviewee of *The Sporting News*, weighing in on a variety of topics. He warned of the dangers of a "no windup" fad being used by some young pitchers. He criticized the large bonuses being paid to very young prospects. "It seems inconsistent for a club to pay an untested youngster $100,000, while at the same time arguing with one of its regulars over a $500 difference in salary."[9]

He signed up with the Mutual Radio Network in 1958, helping broadcast the "Game of the Day." This turned out not to be Feller's cup of tea. "Once the world's greatest pitcher, Bob Feller has become the world's worst sportscaster," wrote one wag.[10] His vocal delivery was awkward, and he had trouble with the rhythm of calling a baseball game from the press box, rather than throwing one from the pitcher's box. "Mr. Feller seems to panic if more than one athlete gets on base in the same inning," noted the *Denver Post*. He did, however, do a great job guessing the "caliber shot he expects the pitcher to fire next."[11]

Although the broadcast mike turned out not to be Feller's best mode of expression, he remained a frequent interviewee in the nation's newspapers, and remained highly sought-after on the speakers' circuit, often appearing at charity functions and fundraisers. He remained active as Ohio Chairman of the March of Dimes and continued working for his insurance firm, where his specialty was writing (and selling) insurance contracts for baseball bonus babies. Some 400 professional players had contracts through Feller at one point. He also served as a television spokesman for Grecian Formula. He coached for American Legion ball in Cleveland.

Feller made good copy. As in his playing days, his blunt manner of speaking, and occasional failure to turn on his inner speech censor, drew fire more than once. In May of 1959, he had some negative words for NL Player Rep Robin Roberts, questioning his judgment and wondering why Roberts "complains about the load of work he has to carry as the players' spokesman. If it's too much for him, why doesn't he resign?"[12] When asked about the decline in pitchers throwing complete games in 1960, he blamed it on lack of physical conditioning, implying that the younger generation wasn't in as good shape as his own had been. This charge was rejected by several coaches and scouts currently active in the game. Dodgers pitching coach Joe Becker pointed out that conditions were much different when Feller pitched, making direct comparisons difficult.[13]

In 1962, Feller was elected to the Hall of Fame. The buildup to his election saw a great deal of positive commentary, and not just from the Cleveland writers who usually praised him. Jimmy Cannon in the *New York Journal-American* acclaimed Feller's "chivalrous" attitude. An AP wire feature on January 21st ran in many national papers, running down his career highlights, and quoting Feller about his favorite baseball moments. He rated his second no-hitter, the '46 game against the Yankees, as his greatest thrill. Hal

Lebovitz asked about his family life. His oldest son, 16-year-old Steve, was playing second base for his Pony League club, while 14-year-old Marty preferred football; 11-year-old Bruce preferred playing music. "And all three watch television," said Bob. "I'm glad I was born before TV. If it had been there when I was a boy, all I probably would have done was milk the cows and watch TV."

Feller was elected on the first ballot, drawing 150 votes out of 160. He was elected along with Jackie Robinson; the two would be inducted together. The irony was not lost on Feller. In the *Saturday Evening Post* of January 27th, Feller wrote, "There is a certain irony in Robinson and me coming up for the Hall of Fame at the same time, because—and it pains me to confess this—I went on record as predicting that he would never make it in the big leagues. Just before Robinson came up with the Dodgers, I played an exhibition game against him. . . . I struck Jackie out three or four times on high fast balls, and I was sure he was just another one of those muscle bound football players." Jackie Robinson, for one, was not impressed with Feller's comments. "Feller was dead wrong when he made that statement 15 years ago, and he's still wrong. In the first place, I believe I faced him only twice that day. I got a double off him one time, and I don't know what I did the other time, but I didn't strike out. What makes me laugh is that Feller had no idea who I was." Nevertheless, relations in public between the two men were cordial at this point. Robinson waited at the airport for Feller to arrive in Cooperstown, then took him to dinner. "It's a pleasure to go hand in hand into the Hall of Fame with you," Robinson told Feller.[14]

In the *Post* article, Feller argued that the current Hall of Fame induction standards were skewed, and that players like Luke Appling and Red Ruffing deserved strong consideration. Directly comparing players across eras was made very hard by the different contexts. "Think of it this way," he told Dick Young. "The DC3 was the best plane of its day. The Jet 707 is the best plane today. You wouldn't dream of comparing them, would you?"[15] Less convincingly, Feller supported the induction of Candy Cummings for inventing the curveball, and George Blaeholder for inventing the slider. Feller also singled out Satchel Paige for high praise. "I believe that the Hall of Fame will never be complete until it finds a niche for Satchel." This was probably the first public acknowledgment by a major baseball figure that Paige deserved to be in the Hall of Fame.

Feller remained visible in the months before the ceremony, his activities garnering even more attention than normal because of the Hall of Fame honor. April 18th was declared "Bob Feller Hall of Fame Day" in Cleveland, given national exposure with a wire service photo of Feller accepting a celebratory plaque from an ancient Cy Slapnicka. Visiting Miami in May, Feller told local reporter Jimmy Burns that one of the biggest problems in baseball was slow games that turned off fans. He advised baseball to adopt the automatic intentional walk. He also blamed lack of foresight on the part of baseball owners in marketing the game. "Baseball brass was guilty from the commissioner's office down. . . . There should be promotions in conjunction with high schools and colleges to interest boys into become ball players."[16] He refined his views that players weren't as well conditioned as they were in his day, saying that the decrease in players who grew up on farms or with other manual labor backgrounds was partially responsible for the change. On the other hand, he also believed that modern players did benefit from better coaching, and were bigger and stronger than players in the past. Only in "mound durability" were modern players inferior.[17]

Feller, along with Robinson, Bill McKechnie, and Ed Roush, was inducted into the Hall on July 23d. He modestly told the gathered crowd that his plaque was incomplete, failing as it did to mention that he held the American League record for most walks given up in one season, 208 in 1938. Making the Hall of Fame, joining the immortals of his childhood, Ruth, Gehrig, Hornsby—it was one of the peak moments of Feller's life.

On the surface, everything was right in Feller's world. He was a successful executive. He was now formally honored as one of the absolute-best players in the history of the game. There had never been any doubt about that, but having the plaque in Cooperstown put the final icing on the cake. He had three strong sons. He had his detractors in the press and the public, but many admirers as well. He and his family were set for life financially, or so people on the outside believed. In reality, the Feller family, for all the outward appearance, was not a happy one, and Bob's financial condition was far more precarious than anyone at the time could have imagined. The reason for this was Virginia Feller's addiction to drugs.

The full details did not emerge until the publication of Bob's 1990 autobiography. Feller says his wife's problems were "an open secret" in Cleveland, though there are no hints of this at all in contemporary accounts of his family life. Indeed, contemporary accounts always refer to Virginia's beauty, intelligence, grace, and charm. The Fellers did an excellent job keeping up appearances. Virginia's problems apparently started as early as 1946–47. Addicted to barbiturates and amphetamines, Virginia became very hard to live with, staying up all hours of the night. Bob tried everything possible to help her with the problem, taking her to the Mayo Clinic on several occasions to try and "dry her out," but it never worked completely. He was at first at a total loss about how to deal with her troubles; it was far beyond anything he'd had to face growing up. He eventually resolved to deal with it by doing everything possible to protect his children, hiring a live-in maid to watch the kids when he was away, and socking away as much money as possible in investments to save for their education.

> Anyone who has been dealt that hand knows the emotional burden is even worse than the financial one. . . . I had never experienced the problem in my own family. Now here was my own wife getting hooked. People who do that pose a grave danger not only to themselves but to those around them. I fought hard to prevent that. . . . I wasn't going to let anyone, not even my own wife, destroy my future or that of my sons, even if she seemed determined to destroy her own.[18]

Virginia's drug problem drained Feller both emotionally and financially. He felt powerless to help her, yet frustrated that she was apparently unwilling to help herself. Worse, he'd seen friends like Don Black and Rollie Hemsley pull themselves away from the bottle; why couldn't his own wife do the same with drugs? Was it a matter of lack of willpower? Or were the drugs simply too powerful? He did not know. Financially, the cost of both medical treatment and the cost of the drugs themselves became an increasingly heavy burden. "My problems came in bottles—those containing my wife's pills."[19] At one point, the situation grew so desperate that Feller had to hide her drugs for fear that she would overdose on them. When out of town, he would call every few days to let her know where her next batch was hidden.

Feller did his best to keep the income flowing, staying in the public eye as much as possible, and continuing to work the insurance business. But the cost of paying for the education of his three sons, combined with Virginia's increasing medical bills, slowly but steadily let the air out of the financial balloon. Feller estimates that Virginia's problems cost him "several hundred thousand dollars" over the years.[20]

But this was not apparent yet. Feller maintained his image as a prosperous insurance executive and baseball promoter as long as possible. He was especially active in promoting American Legion baseball in 1963. He was successful enough in preserving his image that, when baseball was looking for a new commissioner in 1964, Feller's name came up as a candidate. He drew the endorsement of *Sport Magazine* that May, the editors pushing Feller for the job because he understood both the business side and the baseball side of the game. "He is not blind to baseball's pressing problems—the blight of the minor leagues, the disorders caused by too rapid expansion, the television oversaturation, the threat posed by pro football. We are not saying that Feller has an answer for all these problems, but we do believe that he will attack them forcefully, directly, and with a vigor that has been too sadly lacking in baseball for too many years." Of course, the chance that Feller would actually be considered for the commissioner's post was beyond remote; he'd alienated too many owners by this point. In 1965, Feller was considered for the position of executive director of the reconstituted Players Association, which was destined to become the most powerful union in the history of professional sports. According to Marvin Miller, Feller campaigned "for the position like a man possessed, wooing everyone in sight until he became a big-league pest."[21] Again, Feller's directness and occasional lack of tact had alienated too many people.

One public hint of Feller's family troubles, though obvious only in retrospect, came through in an August 1965 article in the *Cleveland Press*. Feller predicted that Sandy Koufax would break his single season strikeout record. Feller was impressed with Koufax's arm, though he rejected attempts to compare Sandy directly to himself. "It's ridiculous to try to rate players who performed at different times. People used to discuss whether I threw harder than Walter Johnson. How can anyone tell? The only thing that ever matters is how you compare with your contemporaries. It's the same with me and Koufax. These are different players now, using different kinds of bats and gloves." But one major advantage that Koufax had was the fact that he was single. "Koufax is a bachelor, and don't think that doesn't make a difference. All he has to think about is striking people out. A married man has his family to worry about. He knows he shouldn't let it interfere with his work, but it does anyway."[22] On the surface, this is an innocuous enough comment, but with what we know now about Virginia's problems, it's clear what Feller had in mind when discussing family worries.

Feller received considerable media attention in 1966, the 30th anniversary of his appearance in the major leagues, but as the decade wore on, he drew less and less press attention. By this time the financial pressures were mounting, forcing Feller to dip into his long-term investments. At one point, he was forced to sell some of his baseball memorabilia to boost his cash flow. He remained active in the community. Influenced by his father's political values, Feller was a staunch anticommunist and became involved in Republican politics. He served as chairman of the "Frances P. Bolton for Congress Committee," campaigning for election to the 22d Congressional district of Ohio in 1968.

In 1969, a new controversy erupted, again involving Jackie Robinson. At baseball's 100th anniversary celebration in July, Feller was honored with the title of "Greatest Living Right-Handed Pitcher."

But the occasion was marred by a blowup involving him and Robinson. Asked about the state of race relations in baseball, Feller said, "I don't think baseball owes colored people anything. I don't think colored people owe baseball anything, either."[23] Told of Feller's comments, Robinson replied, "I don't think Bob has grown any more from 1947. He has his head in the sand."[24]

The war of words intensified. A few days later, Feller said, "Robinson has always been bush. He's always been a professional agitator more than anything else. He's just ticked off because baseball never rolled out the red carpet when he quit playing and offered him a soft front-office job." He reiterated that the tension between him and Jackie dated back to 1946, during the exhibition game where Robinson demanded "three times" more money than had been agreed. Two witnesses from the time, a San Diego sportswriter and the tour promoter, backed up Feller's account of the incident, but Robinson stood his ground. "It's a damn lie," he said. "He slurred my ability. The impression I got at that time was that he wasn't in favor of Mr. Rickey getting a Negro second baseman into the majors." Robinson went on, saying that his main problem with baseball now was that black players were prevented from getting equal opportunity for coaching and front office jobs once their careers were over.[25]

Feller disagreed, saying that postplaying jobs

> should depend on ability and color should have no bearing . . . and doesn't. There hasn't been any discrimination in baseball since Jackie first entered the game. I can understand what Jackie Robinson is saying, but I think he's wrong. Professional baseball has done as much for the colored players as they have done for baseball. I think baseball has done more for underprivileged people, for minority groups, than anything else. . . . Ability alone is what should count in the front office, too. I think there will be a Negro with that ability.[26]

Today, comments like that conjure up images of Al Campanis.[27] Feller honestly believed what he was saying, but his statement that there was no longer discrimination in baseball was ludicrous. He should have known better. It must be pointed out, however, that the statement that caused the most controversy in this entire episode was not Feller's claim that there was no discrimination in baseball front offices, but rather his final assessment of Robinson's character. "I was wrong about his playing ability, but I'm not wrong about this. Jackie Robinson is bush, always has been." It was not Feller's view of racial discrimination that was especially controversial; it was his personal feud with Jackie.[28]

From today's perspective, Feller's inability or unwillingness to see the continuing racial divide in baseball is easy to condemn. But at the time, his view was shared by the "quiet majority" of white Americans. This "majority" was opposed to overt discrimination but was unable to grapple intellectually or emotionally with the deeper racial divides not only in the game, but in society as a whole. In one sense, Robinson was right: Feller did have his head in the sand. But Jackie's implication that Feller was opposed to racial integration from the outset was flat wrong. As discussed earlier, within the context of the 1930s through the 1950s, Feller was progressive on the issue of race. By the 1960s, his views, while ignorant from our perspective today and from the perspective of the more enlightened Americans of the civil rights period, were the mainstream among white Americans who were neither crusaders nor sheet-wearing bigots. To say this does not excuse Feller. His failures in this matter were the failures of his generation, and of America as a whole. It is easy to say he should have known better; so should have everyone else.

Feller also had problems with modern players. In 1970, he said that flamboyant ballplayers like Joe Pepitone, Richie Allen, and Jim Bouton were hurting the game. "It's just unfortunate that there aren't enough good players today so that people like Pepitone could be sent to the minors," he told reporters in Albuquerque. "It's people like Pepitone, Jim Bouton, and Joe Namath who give sports a bad name."[29] He also said that Curt Flood wasn't the right person to challenge the reserve clause. "Flood is just a crusader. Baseball hasn't hurt him. . . . I think the case against the reserve clause would have been much more effective if some player hurt by baseball had taken it to court." Some detected a racial overtone to Feller's comments, but it seems more probable he was thinking of money. Flood had plenty of money ("He's selling his paintings for $1,000 each, so what does he care?"). Of course, Feller himself had money, yet he had been one of the foremost critics of the re-

serve clause in the late fifties. At the time, he was criticized for raising questions about baseball when baseball had been so good to
him. His response at the time, that it was the principle of the thing,
applied equally to Flood, but Feller did not make that connection.

Things at home with Virginia continued to deteriorate, financially and otherwise. They finally divorced in 1971. Feller was
forced to sell their Gates Mills home to pay debts and the divorce
settlement. He continued to make personal appearances, but he
was now out of the insurance business. A friend helped out by getting Feller a job with the Sheraton Hotel chain; his job was to book
sports business for the chain. This provided needed income, as
well as a rent-free place to live. In 1974, Feller married Anne
Thorpe, whom he'd met at church. Like Virginia before her, Anne
was not a baseball fan, a quality in women that Feller found attractive, for it meant that their interest in him was an honest one.

Gradually, Feller returned to financial stability, though the
process was painful at times. He toured the country doing sports
and autograph shows, occasionally pitching in Old Timers exhibition games. He visited Green Berets in Vietnam on a morale-build-
ing tour in 1971. "My job is to talk to the fans and the media and
smile a lot," he told a reporter in Peoria.[30] His job was to be Bob
Feller. During the early eighties, he drove around the country in
his 1974 Ford Maverick, selling memorabilia. At times, his attempts
to bring in money and regain financial stability took on overtones
that, depending on your point of view, were either unsavory or
tragic. An August 1984 report from Scripps-Howard news service,
titled "Tarnished: Bob Feller Reduced to Pitching Himself," details
one such incident at a Denver Old-Timers game. Feller was aggres-
sively selling autographs, with the reluctant cooperation of a local
sports card dealer. At one point, Feller and the dealer got into a
disagreement about the cost of signing photographs, the dispute
witnessed by the Scripps-Howard reporter and some fans. "He
uses these old-timer games as vehicles to pick up an extra couple
of hundred bucks," said the dealer. "I mean, this is one of the 10
best pitchers to ever play the game of baseball. It's sad, really sad."
Asked about Feller's financial condition, a friend said, "Nearly
everybody I know who has had [financial] problems can have it

traced back to bad habits, but Bob has always taken care of himself. He's just had an incredible string of bad luck." It wasn't bad luck, of course, but the fallout from Virginia's drug problems and the divorce. But "Feller's pride does not allow him to offer an explanation." There are many similar stories from this period.

By the mid-eighties, things were improving in Feller's life. He became head of the Cleveland Indians Speaker's Bureau. In 1988, the Cleveland Sports Legends Foundation honored Feller with the commission of a 10-foot bronze statue. It was eventually placed at Jacobs Field following the completion of that new venue for the Tribe in 1994. In 1990, he published *Now Pitching: Bob Feller*, his second autobiography. Also in 1990, a committee was formed in Van Meter to fund construction of a museum devoted to Feller's baseball exploits. Ground was broken in 1994; the museum was designed by Steve Feller, Bob's son, who had become an architect. The museum was opened in June of 1995, and contains a variety of displays of Feller memorabilia, including uniforms, newspapers, and trophies. A prize display is a Feller bat, used by Babe Ruth as a leaning post during his retirement ceremony in Yankee Stadium in June 1948. Another display of great pride to Feller is his Green Beret; he was made an honorary member of the organization in recognition of his service to our country. Feller is also forthrightly proud of the success of his three sons. Steve is an architect in Orlando; Marty is a CPA and paralegal; Bruce became a scientist.

Bob Feller turned 84 in November of 2002. He is still extremely active in the game, making speeches, touring the country with Anne, signing autographs, promoting his museum. His job, in 2003 as it was in 1983, as it was in 1963, and as it was in 1953, is to be Bob Feller.

17

Bob Feller Sabermetrics

Feller is the best pitcher living. I don't think anyone is ever going to throw a ball faster than he does. And his curve ball isn't human.

—Joe DiMaggio[1]

The first time I ever batted against him was in 1937, when he was only eighteen years old. He had such blinding speed and was so wild that everybody was afraid to go up to bat, including me. He had a very deceptive motion. You never knew where the ball was coming from or where it was going, and neither did he.

—Hank Greenberg[2]

He's the best I've ever seen, and I think the true test of his greatness lies in the fact that he can rise to any occasion.

—Lou Boudreau[3]

I faced Bob Feller. Of course, he was all through. With his wind up and delivery, I couldn't see the ball! I can just imagine how tough he was to hit against [earlier]. You couldn't see the ball!

—Bob Keegan[4]

I'll never forget the time I took Walter Johnson to Griffith Stadium to let him see Feller for the first time. You can imagine how curious I was to get the reaction of the greatest fireball thrower of the past at his first glimpse of the greatest fireball thrower of the present. Inning after inning went by as I waited for Walter to offer his comment.

About the fifth inning, Johnson said, "That kid sure is fast." About the eighth inning, he whistled softly and remarked, "He must be the fastest pitcher I ever watched."

I could contain myself no longer. "Walter," I said hesitantly, "would you say that Feller is faster than you were in your prime?"

Johnson sat there quietly for a moment and I could sense a deep inner struggle. His modesty was battling with his honesty. It was a tough battle but honesty emerged triumphant.

"No," he said.

—Shirley Povich[5]

Feller was fast. Real fast. He wasn't as fast as Grove, but he was 'meaner.' This is the reaction of a right-handed batter, don't forget. Grove was consistently faster, but I followed Grove, a southpaw, better than I did Feller, who was harder for me to hit.

—Joe Cronin[6]

How good, exactly, was Bob Feller? Was he the greatest right-handed pitcher in the history of the game?

Subjectively, there is little doubt that Feller had the best fastball in major league baseball from the time of his debut until early 1948. At that point, his fastball lost velocity, fading from the most dominant pitch in the game to merely an above-average one, forcing him to rely on his other offerings. Fortunately, he had one of the best curveballs in history as well, enabling him to survive when the fastball lost steam. In terms of historical comparisons, the issue is less clear. Feller's fastball was obviously one of the best in history, but was it *the* best?

It depends on whom you ask. A survey of 645 players, coaches, and managers taken in 1986 rated Feller's fastball as the best of all time, Bob garnering 22.5 percent of the vote.[7] Nolan Ryan came in second place with 20.4 percent, followed by Sandy Koufax (13.1), Walter Johnson (12.1), and Lefty Grove (4.2). This survey is more of a snapshot of reputation at the time it was taken than anything else. At the time Feller actually pitched, however, most observers felt that both Walter Johnson and Lefty Grove had been faster in their primes, though neither had as good a breaking ball as Feller did. We don't have any sort of accurate speed readings for Grove and Johnson, but we do for Feller; his 98.6 MPH mark in 1946 is regarded as a factual measure. As we discussed earlier in the book, this reading was taken as the pitched ball crossed the plate. On a modern radar gun, this would be equivalent to 101–102 mph. Considering that most people felt Feller threw harder when he first reached the majors than he did when this test was taken, Feller's peak velocity must have been incredible indeed.

Of course, there is more to pitching than sheer velocity. Feller tended to rely on pure power when he was young and gradually learned the art of changing speeds. He never had outstanding control, but his stuff was so good that he usually didn't need it. Even when the oomph was gone from his fastball in the early fifties, Feller was able to deceive hitters with his delivery and the movement on his pitches well enough to survive. Our subjective conclusion is that, "stuff-wise," Feller was likely one of the two or three best pitchers to ever play the game, and very possibly the best one still living. From a "pitchability" standpoint, in terms of changing speeds and throwing strikes, Feller was not one of the very best. He was not a Christy Mathewson or Greg Maddux, but he was plenty good enough, skilled enough at the art of pitching to do good work even when his best velocity was gone.

The objective, statistical record must be taken in two ways. First, in terms of final career totals, Feller does not rank among the absolute best in the game, though this is a function of his war service. As we noted in chapter 10, if the Second World War had not occurred, or if Feller had been able to stay out of it, he almost certainly would have exceeded 300 wins and 3,000 strikeouts by wide margins. The only thing that could have prevented it was injury, but Feller was remarkably durable, despite workloads that would be considered criminal in today's game. Still, we cannot know for certain what Feller would have accomplished had war not intervened. He could have gotten hurt, on the mound or in some sort of

fluke accident. Because of the war, even the best statistical measures cannot tell us exactly where Feller would rank on a career
basis.

Looking at Feller on a season-by-season basis does reveal intriguing data. See table 17.1 for the raw numbers. Anyone with a
passing familiarity with baseball numbers can interpret these results. Feller was immensely durable, threw very hard, and was a
winning pitcher. His control gave trouble at times, which was the
main reason he led the league in ERA only once.

You can find this statistical information in any baseball encyclopedia. But over the last 20 years, there has been a revolution in
baseball statistics. We now have a variety of new metrics to measure performance. Let's write up a new chart for Bob Feller, using
some of the new statistical measurements (see table 17.2).

TABLE 17.1.
Bob Feller Career Statistics

Year	G	IP	W	L	Pct.	H	R	ER	SO	BB	ERA
1936	14	62.0	5	3	.625	52	29	23	76	47	3.34
1937	26	148.7	9	7	.563	116	68	56	150	106	3.38
1938	39	277.7	17	11	.607	225	136	126	**240**	**208**	4.08
1939	39	**297.7**	**24**	9	.727	227	105	94	**246**	142	2.85
1940	**43**	**320.3**	**27**	11	.711	245	102	93	**261**	118	**2.62**
1941	**44**	**343.0**	**25**	13	.658	**284**	129	120	**260**	194	3.15
1942/43/44	In Military Service: United States Navy										
1945	9	72.0	5	3	.625	50	21	20	59	35	2.50
1946	**48**	**371.3**	**26**	15	.634	**277**	101	90	**348**	153	2.18
1947	42	**299.0**	**20**	11	.645	230	97	89	**196**	127	2.68
1948	44	280.3	19	15	.559	**255**	123	111	**164**	116	3.57
1949	36	211.0	15	14	.517	198	104	88	108	84	3.75
1950	35	247.0	16	11	.593	230	105	94	119	103	3.43
1951	33	250.7	**22**	8	.733	239	105	97	111	95	3.49
1952	30	192.7	9	13	.409	219	124	101	81	83	4.73
1953	25	176.7	10	7	.588	168	78	70	60	60	3.58
1954	19	140.0	13	3	.813	127	53	48	59	39	3.09
1955	25	83.0	4	4	.500	71	43	32	25	31	3.47
1956	19	58.0	0	4	.000	63	34	32	18	23	4.97
Totals	570	3,827	266	162	.621	3,271	1,557	1,384	2,581	1,764	3.25

Numbers in **bold** = league leader.

TABLE 17.2.
Bob Feller Sabermetrics

Year	G	IP	ERA	ERA+	ERC	TPI	WSH	K	02K	SIM	Comp
1936	14	62.0	3.34	151	3.98	1.1	6	76	143	x	
1937	26	148.7	3.38	136	3.41	1.9	13	150	257	960	L. Dierker
1938	39	277.7	4.08	114	3.84	1.4	22	**240**	**422**	942	S. King
1939	39	**297.7**	2.85	154	2.66	**5.6**	32	246	**430**	904	E. Chamberlain
1940	**43**	**320.3**	**2.62**	161	**2.32**	**6.1**	34	261	420	923	E. Chamberlain
1941	**44**	**343.0**	3.15	125	3.32	3.2	30	**260**	**452**	892	E. Chamberlain
1942/43/44		In Military Service: United States Navy									
1945	9	72.0	2.50	130	2.19	0.5	7	59	108	926	D. McLain
1946	**48**	**371.3**	2.18	151	2.29	4.9	32	**348**	**511**	920	D. Gooden
1947	42	**299.0**	2.68	130	2.66	3.1	23	**196**	**325**	920	D. Gooden
1948	44	280.3	3.57	114	3.38	0.7	15	**164**	**290**	892	H. Newhouser
1949	36	211.0	3.75	106	3.57	0.7	14	108	188	915	H. Newhouser
1950	35	247.0	3.43	127	3.61	1.7	19	119	199	896	H. Newhouser
1951	33	249.7	3.49	108	3.72	0.1	18	111	186	866	J. Palmer
1952	30	191.7	4.73	70	4.67	−3.0	1	81	122	857	S. Carlton
1953	25	175.7	3.58	105	3.47	0.1	10	60	94	866	S. Carlton
1954	19	140.0	3.08	119	3.07	0.9	11	59	89	870	J. Palmer
1955	25	83.0	3.47	115	3.16	0.1	4	25	35	885	J. Palmer
1956	19	58.0	4.97	85	4.61	0.6	1	18	24	883	J. Palmer
	570	3,827	3.25	122	3.19	28.5	292	2,581	3,908	889	J. Palmer

ERA+ = ERA normalized for league runs, adjusted for park factor, and expressed in unit of 100: an ERA+ of 136 is 36% better than league average. An ERA+ of 100 is exactly league average. An ERA+ of 85 is 15% below league average, and an ERA+ of 127 is 27% better than league average. Statistics found in *Total Baseball*.

ERC = Component ERA. Developed by Bill James and STATS, Inc., in the *All-Time Major League Handbook*. Estimates ERA by looking at individual components of a hitter's record. ERC tracks regular ERA very closely. When a pitcher's ERC is much better than his regular ERA, or much worse, he may have pitched in good (or bad) luck, or may have an exceptional skill (or weakness) that is difficult to measure statistically.

TPI = Total Player Index, another development of Pete Palmer's Linear Weights method, found in *Total Baseball*. One of the first actually useful attempts to express in one number all of a player's contributions on the field—a controversial statistic, especially when dealing with fielding evaluations.

WSH = Win Shares, new method developed by Bill James in 2001. See *Win Shares* for a detailed explanation of this system. In short, Win Shares attempts to answer, in one number, "How many games did this player win for his club?" The system theoretically accounts for all fielding, pitching, and hitting contributions, thus enabling direct comparisons between hitters and pitchers, as well as players across eras.

02K = Feller's projected strikeout total if he had pitched within the context of the 2002 American League season. Example: in 1941, Feller pitched 343 innings and struck out 260 hitters. His K/9IP ratio was 6.82. The 1941 American League K/9IP ratio was 3.59. Feller's K/9IP mark was 190% of league average. The K/9IP ratio in the 2002 American League was 6.25. 190% of 6.25 is 11.87 K/9IP. Thus, 260 hitters fanned in 343 innings in 1941 is equivalent to 452 hitters fanned in 343 innings in 2002. This is not any sort of major sabermetric breakthrough, but it does show exactly how much Feller was dominating the league by putting his numbers in terms that modern fans can immediately identify with. The 2002 American League strikeout leader was Pedro Martinez with 239 strikeouts in 199.3 innings pitched. His K/9IP mark was 10.8. Feller's strikeout rate of 11.87 comes out to 263 strikeouts in 199.3 innings.

SIM = Similarity Score: method developed by Bill James to compare players' seasons. Start with a thousand and then subtract the following deductions:
One point for each difference of 1 win.
One point for each difference of 2 losses.
One point for each difference of .002 in winning percentage (max. 100 points).
One point for each difference of .02 in ERA (max. 100 points).
One point for each difference of 10 games pitched.
One point for each difference of 20 starts.
One point for each difference of 20 complete games.
One point for each difference of 50 innings pitched.
One point for each difference of 50 hits allowed.
One point for each difference of 30 strikeouts.
One point for each difference of 10 walks.
One point for each difference of 5 shutouts.
One point for each difference of 3 saves.

If they throw with a different hand and are starters, subtract 10; relievers, 25. For relievers you halve the winning percentage penalty and the winning percentage penalty can be up to 1.5 times the wins and losses penalty. Relievers are defined as more relief appearances than starts and fewer than 4.00 innings per appearance.

Similarity scores were computed on the Baseball-Reference.com website. The Sim score listed on the chart is the highest number, the "most similar" season compiled by another player at the same age. The actual player is listed in the final column. Thus, Feller's 1937 season at age 18 was most similar to Larry Dierker's age-18 season, 1965, with a Sim score of 960. However, Sim scores do not adjust for ERA or league, and even then, any Sim score less than 910 is not truly similar.

Sources: John Thorn, Pete Palmer, with Michael Gershman, ed., *Total Baseball* (New York: Viking, 1995); Bill James, with Jim Henzler, *Win Shares* (Morton Grove Stats, 2002).

Feller's sabermetric numbers shed light on his record that may not be completely apparent from the raw numbers. Note that both Win Shares and TPI rate him as the best pitcher in the American League in 1939 and 1940. We've already noted that he would likely have won the Cy Young Award in both seasons if it had existed at that point. He finished third and second, respectively, in MVP voting in those years. We've also noted that Feller came in just sixth in the MVP voting after his incredible 1946 season, and would likely have lost Cy Young balloting to Hal Newhouser. Both TPI and Win Shares confirm that the writers had it right. Newhouser led league pitchers with a 7.1 TPI. He led league pitchers with 33 Win Shares compared with Feller's 32. Compare the league MVP balloting with the Win Shares totals as calculated by James, and TPI as calculated by Palmer (table 17.3).

TABLE 17.3.
1946 MVP Balloting with Win Shares and TPI

1946 MVP Balloting	Win Shares	TPI
1. Ted Williams	49	7.9
2. Hal Newhouser	33	7.1
3. Bobby Doerr	27	4.8
4. Johnny Pesky	34	4.2
5. Mickey Vernon	33	3.6
6. Bob Feller	32	4.9

If you prefer TPI, Feller should have ranked third. If you prefer Win Shares, he ranked fifth. Either way, both metrics agree with the writers: Feller wasn't the best player in the league in 1946, or the best pitcher. However, this should take nothing away from the accomplishment. Feller's '46 season stands as a triumph of human endurance.

I find the Similarity Scores interesting because they show how unusual Feller was. James has noted that the more "unique" the player in question, the lower his Sim Scores tend to be, the less similar he truly is to other players in other words. Feller's final career numbers are most similar to Jim Palmer's, but the career Sim Score of 889 means that they are not really all that much alike.

Feller was unique, an archetype.

18

Myth, Truth, and the Man

There will be stories told about Bob Feller, and they will begin with the truth, but they'll be embellished in the telling until in the end fat and fancy will be fused into one, shining whole, and then Feller will be a legend.

—Gordon Cobbledick

Biography is, by nature, an equivocal endeavor. None of us truly know what goes on in the mind of another person. Actions can be described, even analyzed, but the emotions, logic, and thoughts that motivate them are ephemeral, often even to the historical actor himself, especially in retrospect. Yet biography is one of the most compelling forms of historical writing, and will likely remain so as long as Western civilization endures. In the baseball world, there has been an explosion of biography over the last 20 years. Yet, as we noted in the introduction, Bob Feller has been almost ignored, despite the fact that he was one of the most crucial players of his era.

As we've shown through subjective anecdotes and objective statistics, Feller was one of the greatest players in history. Because of his war service, his final cumulative records don't reflect this to the extent they could. But at his peak, Feller was one of the two or three most dominating pitchers who ever lived. This much is well known to anyone with a baseball encyclopedia, but Feller's impact on the game was just as important outside the lines. As we have shown, he was the most aggressive businessman/athlete of his generation, the first player to incorporate, the most assertive of his peers in terms of outside business activity and endorsements. He was one of the most intelligent and articulate players of his era. He was the highest-paid player in the game for several years. Feller's barnstorming tours were both lucrative and legendary, and provided a showcase for Negro League players to prove they could compete on equal, or better, terms with the white players of organized baseball. He was a key figure in labor relations in the 1940s and 1950s, pushing for adoption of the pension plan, and a greater voice for the players in the way baseball was run. His outspoken critique of the reserve clause in the late 1950s helped crystallize in the public mind the unfairness of the relationship between players and owners. Feller vocally supported a form of free agency 20 years before it was adopted. Ideas he proposed to improve the lot of players, such as college scholarships, were eventually implemented in some form. He was probably the earliest to call for the consideration of Negro League players like Satchel Paige for the Hall of Fame. In terms of public promotion of the game, Bob Feller was one of the best ambassadors that baseball ever had, a role he still relishes to this day.

All this is part of the historical record, even if it hasn't received enough attention in recent years.

But there is more to Bob Feller than merely his accomplishments on and off the field. As important as they were, it is his personality that needs exposition, for it is his personality that has aroused the greatest controversy. There are those who worshiped the ground on which Feller walked. There are those who dislike and even despise the man. What explains this dichotomy?

Bob Feller's personality has many positive traits. He is both intelligent and imaginative. He can be quite charming; I have felt the pull of his dynamism myself. His volunteering for war service when he didn't need to do so shows his strong sense of patriotism. His work ethic is exceptional. Feller's activity schedule in "retirement" is busier than that of most people half his age. He has done enormous good work for charity over the years. He is often brutally honest about what he thinks and feels, a trait that has gotten him in trouble on more than one occasion, as we have shown, although honesty is generally not considered a negative personality trait. He can be very funny (he installed a special horn on his Cadillac that made a "Moooo" cow noise) and is fond of practical jokes. He once gave Satchel Paige an ice cream sandwich in the clubhouse . . . a sandwich in which the ice cream had been replaced with a bar of soap. Satchel took a bite; his false teeth remained in the soap.

Although some questioned Feller's motives, those who knew him best were convinced that his concern for the lot of his fellow players was genuine. "He would come home and worry about young players on the team," said Virginia Feller. "He would say they have wives and children and he didn't know how they could get along on their salaries."[1]

Friends who knew Feller back in his Van Meter days loved him. "A great guy . . . Bob wasn't cocky, but he was very confident," remembered his friend Fletcher Jennings.[2] Others who worked with or close to Feller during his Cleveland years were profuse in their admiration. The Cleveland beat writers praised him. Ed McAuley frequently used his platform in *The Sporting News* to defend Feller against rumors spread by out-of-town writers. Gordon Cobbledick called him a "champion" on and off the field, someone who was "extraordinary among men" even when he wasn't pitching well. Franklin Lewis described himself as a "Feller man," calling Feller the hardest worker he'd ever seen, and a fierce competitor who was often misunderstood and underappreciated. Others felt the same way. Alva Bradley, Feller's first owner, was quite fond of him. "I've always thought a lot of Bob. A very fine, very substantial young man."[3] Lou Brissie, Feller's teammate in 1953, said that Feller was the "man I've got more respect for than anybody else I've ever met in baseball. He's entitled to every nickel he was ever paid."[4] In 1947, Feller was ranked as the second-most-admired business executive under 40 by the American Business Institute of Research.[5] This is one image of Bob Feller: the All-American entrepreneurial athlete/patriot.

But as we have seen, there is another image of Feller. A good example of the darker view is found in the *Biographical History of Baseball*, which refers to Feller as having a "long suit in crankiness." "Feller's brilliant pitching career . . . was sandwiched between some brazen illegalities and a personal venality that would never qualify the right-hander as Mr. Charm," reads his bio.[6] There were those in Van Meter who felt Feller treated them coldly. Some in Cleveland felt he was rude, distant from other players, and alienated from the fans. As we've mentioned throughout the book, he was criticized for greed and venality, oftentimes by people who did not want to go public with their accusations, but occasionally by those who would, such as Walker Cooper, Chet Brewer, or Shirley Povich. His blunt habit of speaking and occasional lack of appreciation for the finer points of public relations enhanced this resentment. Admirers of Jackie Robinson over the years have accused Feller of racism in his critique of Jackie's playing ability. Certainly, it is clear from his own comments that Feller was insensitive to the difficult realities of race relations by the late 1960s. Coldness, venality, racism; this is the negative portrait of Feller and definitely *not* the all-American nice guy.

Which image is the correct one?

Having looked at Feller's life and career in context, we conclude that both myth-images of Feller contain elements of truth but are incomplete. The positive image has much to recommend it. Feller's general work ethic, sense of duty and patriotism, and love of baseball are undeniable. He has magnetism and charisma; even today his personality dominates any room. He can be extremely generous and gracious, with both his time and his money. His concern for children is genuine. Despite the accusations of racism, there is no question that he was ahead of his time on many aspects of race relations in baseball. Simply being willing to play against Negro players in exhibition games put Feller ahead of most of his contemporaries. He pushed Satchel Paige for the Hall of Fame before anyone else. On the other hand, it is true, as his own words from 1969 show, that Feller did not understand that African Americans weren't given full opportunity in the front offices once the color barrier came down on the field. Whether this was because of some form of innate racism, or a softer yet pernicious ignorance, is impossible for us to know. Not even Feller himself, with 30 years of memory editing, may know. In assessing Feller's personality, one can see the good points clearly. Of the bad points, the racism charge is, at best, a selective and distorted reading of the facts, and, at worst, completely unfair to Feller. He can only be judged within the context of his time. For every Jackie Robinson suspicious of Feller, there was a Monte Irvin who praised him. "Bob Feller did as much for integration of baseball as Happy Chandler, Jackie Robinson, and Branch Rickey by playing so many exhibition games with African American players immediately after World War II," says Irvin. Whatever Feller's flaws, he was not one of the bad guys when it came to race.

Ultimately, the negative image rests mostly on the venality charge, for which there is significant evidence that must be addressed. There is no doubt that Feller could be generous. But there is also no doubt that his "business sense" crossed the line into obnoxious at times. A story told by Frank Graham illustrates this well.

> The sports editor of a national magazine went to Cleveland in mid-season with a photographer to get some pictures to illustrate an article he was writing about Boudreau. Feller watched Boudreau going through the paces for the photographer before a game.
> "How much are you paying Lou for this?" he asked the editor.
> "Nothing," the editor said.
> "You couldn't do a story about me for nothing," Feller said.
> The editor looked at him in silence for a moment. Then he said, "You know, son, some day, just for fun, I may do a piece on you. If I do, you won't like it."[7]

The barnstorming tours of '46 and '47 seemed to be the high point of accusations regarding Feller's overt concern with money. Even if one accepts Chet Brewer's version of events, paying Satchel Paige out of the net rather than the gross likely had less to do with racism than simple greed. Apparently, many of the white players were also unhappy with the way business relations were handled on the barnstorming tours. His aggressive hawking of autographs and memorabilia during the 1980s and 1990s also turned a lot of people off, and has done much to sully his reputation in recent years.

On the other hand, to simply say that Feller was or is greedy ignores a lot of contrary evidence. As stated, he has been very generous with charity over the years, often quietly. Despite numerous opportunities and the lucre that would have come his way, he never endorsed alcohol or tobacco products, refusing the money and opposing those products on principle. It should be pointed out that Jackie Robinson was not averse to making a buck by endorsing cigarettes, yet he has never been accused of excess greed in so doing. Within the context of the time, a cigarette endorsement was not unusual. Feller was never a hard case in negotiations with ownership; a truly venal person would likely have been so. Feller didn't jump to the Mexican League despite the large amount of money offered. Finally, Feller passed up his biggest opportunity for a huge payday by choosing to remain with Cleveland when Commissioner Landis could have made him a free agent. Again, this was not the act of an utterly venal person. Loyalty means a lot to Bob Feller, and loyalty is not known as a character trait of the truly mercenary.

And yet, the negative evidence cannot be ignored any more than the positive evidence. None of this is meant to exculpate Feller; we seek to explain.

The Second World War looms large as a major turning point in Feller's life. It is clear that Feller was subtly changed by the war, "just a wee bit bitter," according to Franklin Lewis, "not bitter about the Japs or a sergeant or fate. Just bluntly, sharply dedicated to a program of financial recovery."[8] Feller was always concerned about being taken advantage of. After the war this became almost paranoia, as Clark Griffith found out. Before the war, Feller had a reputation for being honest, but reserved and quiet. If you asked him a question, you'd get an honest answer, perhaps one too honest. But the question had to be asked first. After the war, the honesty remained, but the reservations were gone; he would tell you exactly what he thought, when he thought it, on his own terms, as Ed McAuley pointed out as early as the spring of 1945.

Feller's war experience was the first factor in this shift in his behavior. The second factor seems likely to have been Feller's failing marriage to Virginia, which dramatically increased the financial and emotional pressure he was under. If he was to provide for his family in the way he wanted, the money had to be earned, and earned now, before his earning power, already reduced by the war years and dependent on his success on the field, disappeared entirely. Appearances, financial and otherwise, had to be kept up. There is a sense of Feller as a financial Sisyphus, continually working to achieve a security and stability that would never truly be his, dealing with the family problems in the only way he knew how: to make as much money as possible. The combination of Feller's war experience and Virginia's drug addiction made him highly assertive where monetary matters were concerned, far too assertive for the taste of some. If people didn't like it, that was their problem.

On the mound, Feller was a legend who will endure as long as baseball does. Off the mound, he was one of the most intelligent and creative baseball entrepreneurs in history. His personality is more complex than either the purely positive or the abjectly negative myths imply. The all-American athlete image contains a great deal of truth that his detractors ignore, while the negative image points out flaws in his personality that the all-American image papers over. Ultimately, Feller is far more interesting when considered as a whole human being. Feller was and is a man, a good man in very many ways, but not perfect, not a demigod. There is much to admire in Bob Feller, and much of what he takes criticism for is unfair. There are also things that we can rightfully criticize about him, though this is true of any of us who fall short of divinity.

NOTES

Chapter 1

1. Eugene N. Hastie, *Hastie's History of Dallas County* (Des Moines, Iowa: Wallace-Homestead, 1938), pp. 166–67.

2. *Dallas County Iowa Militia Lists 1869–1881* (Iowa Genealogical Society, 1996).

3. *Dallas County News*, November 16, 1932.

4. Ibid., June 12, 1933.

5. *Outside In: African American History in Iowa, 1838–2000* (State Historical Society of Iowa, 2001), p. 30.

6. Ibid., p. 76. In 1923, a young woman named Dottie Blagburn was removed from a Des Moines theatre when she refused to leave a "whites only" section. The theater owner was charged with violating the Iowa Civil Rights Act, and was convicted by an all-white jury. It is difficult to imagine such an outcome in most other states during this time, in the South especially, but also in the North.

7. Bob Feller, *Bob Feller's Strikeout Story* (New York: Grosset and Dunlap, 1947), p. 4. This work contains numerous details about Feller's early life that are not found in his second autobiography (see below).

8. *Saturday Evening Post*, February 20, 1937, p. 12.

9. *Strikeout Story*, p. 4.

10. Bob Feller, with Bill Gilbert, *Now Pitching: Bob Feller* (New York: Birch Lane, 1990), p. 32.

11. Ibid., p. 34

12. Bob Feller, with Burton Rocks, *Bob Feller's Little Black Book of Baseball Wisdom* (Chicago: Contemporary Books, 2001), p. 12.

13. *Now Pitching*, p. 33.

14. Ibid.

15. *Strikeout Story*, p. 9.

16. *Des Moines Tribune*, October 10, 1936, p. 4.

17. Ibid.

18. *Chicago Herald-Examiner*, April 28, 1937. Feller wrote a series of articles for this newspaper that spring, describing his early life and experiences.

19. *Little Black Book,* pp. 8–9.

20. *Strikeout Story,* p. 4.

21. Variations of this statement are found in numerous newspaper and magazine articles from Feller's early career. They tend to vary slightly, and it is unclear which quotation came first.

22. *Little Black Book,* p. 10.

23. *Saturday Evening Post,* February 20, 1937, p. 13.

24. *American Legion Magazine,* June 1947, p. 26.

25. Interview with author, October 18, 2002.

26. *Des Moines Tribune,* October 10, 1936, p. 4.

27. *Saturday Evening Post,* February 20, 1937, p. 12.

28. *Now Pitching,* p. 20.

29. *Chicago Herald-Examiner,* April 19, 1937.

30. *Chicago Herald-Examiner,* April 21, 1937.

31. Quoted in numerous sources.

32. *Strikeout Story,* p. 5.

33. *Des Moines Tribune-Capitol,* October 25, 1928.

34. *Now Pitching,* p. 21.

35. *Des Moines Tribune,* October 30, 1928.

36. *Little Black Book,* p. 4.

37. *Saturday Evening Post,* February 20, 1937, p. 12.

38. *Strikeout Story,* p. 7.

39. *American Legion Magazine,* June 1963, p. 15.

40. Ibid.

Chapter 2

1. *Little Black Book,* p. 5.

2. *Chicago Herald-Examiner,* April 22, 1937.

3. Hal Manders reached the major leagues with the Tigers in 1941. He pitched for them in '42, then again with the Tigers as well as the Cubs in '46. His career record was 3–1 in 30 games over 60 innings, with a 4.77 ERA.

4. Max England's career went nowhere, as he was "too wild" on and off the field, and failed to keep himself in shape, according to various Van Meter old-timers.

5. *Now Pitching,* p. 140.

6. *Strikeout Story,* p. 9.

7. *Little Black Book,* p. 8.

8. *Chicago Herald-Examiner,* April 23, 1937.

9. *Now Pitching,* p. 36. An April 22, 1937, newspaper article in the *Chicago Herald-Examiner* gives his strikeout total in this game as 23. Attempts to locate a contemporary account of this contest in the newspaper ar-

chives of the Iowa Historical Society failed, so I have opted for the lower strikeout total of 15.

10. Ibid. All sources agree on the details of this game.

11. *Chicago Herald-Examiner*, April 24, 1937.

12. Ibid.

13. Ibid.

14. *Saturday Evening Post*, February 20, 1937, p. 66.

15. *Now Pitching*, p. 18.

16. Ibid.

17. *Chicago Herald-Examiner*, April 26, 1937.

18. Ibid.

19. *Des Moines Tribune*, July 5, 1935, p. 7-A.

20. Ibid., July 26, 1935, p. 3-A.

21. Ibid., July 30, 1935, p. 2-A.

22. Ibid., August 9, 1935, p. 2-A.

23. Ibid., August 24, 1935, p. 1-A.

24. *Chicago Herald-Examiner*, April 26, 1937.

25. Ibid.

26. Ibid.

27. *Strikeout Story* refers to a game during the summer of 1935 in which Feller fanned 23 hitters in a game at Tipton, Iowa, but the date of this contest is uncertain. p. 13.

28. Ibid., April 27, 1937.

29. *Saturday Evening Post*, February 20, 1937, p. 66.

30. Ibid.

31. *Des Moines Tribune*, January 27, 1937.

32. Letter from Billy Evans to Pat Donahue, October 11, 1946. Found in *Sporting News* archives. See also "Who Discovered Bob Feller?" *Sporting News*, October 30, 1946.

33. *Strikeout Story*, pp. 11–12.

Chapter 3

1. *Des Moines Tribune*, March 23, 1936, p. A-3.

2. *Now Pitching*, p. 40.

3. *Strikeout Story*, p. 15.

4. *Chicago Herald-American*, April 28, 1937.

5. Ibid., April 25, 1937.

6. *Strikeout Story*, p. 15.

7. Ibid., p. 16.

8. Ibid., p. 17.

9. Ibid.

10. *Strikeout Story* says that Feller pitched just one game for the Rosen-

blums before making his famous exhibition start for the Indians, but the *Chicago Herald-Examiner* of April 28, 1937, and the *Cleveland Plain Dealer* of July 7 and July 14, 1936, give details of two pre-exhibition Feller Rosenblum starts.

11. *Dallas County News*, July 8, 1936.

12. *Strikeout Story*, p. 19.

13. *Cleveland Plain Dealer*, undated clipping found in *Sporting News* archives.

14. *Strikeout Story*, p. 20.

15. Ibid.

16. Ibid., p. 22.

17. Ibid.

18. *Cleveland Plain Dealer*, July 17, 1936, p. 17.

19. *Dallas County News*, July 8, 1936.

20. *Strikeout Story*, p. 23.

21. *Sporting News*, February 21, 1946, p. 9.

22. *Strikeout Story*, p. 24.

23. Interview with author, October 18, 2002.

24. Neil D. Isaacs, *Batboys and the World of Baseball* (Jackson: University of Mississippi Press, 1995), p. 98.

25. *Cleveland Plain Dealer*, July 20, 1936, p. 13.

26. *Strikeout Story*, p. 32.

27. Franklin Lewis, *The Cleveland Indians* (New York: G. P. Putnam, 1949), p. 195.

28. *Strikeout Story*, p. 33.

29. *Cleveland Plain Dealer*, August 3, 1936, p. 14.

30. Ibid., August 4, 1936, p. 16.

31. *Strikeout Story*, p. 36.

32. Ibid., p. 39.

33. *Cleveland Plain Dealer*, August 25, 1936, p. 17.

34. Ibid., August 26, 1936, p. 16.

35. Ibid., August 31, 1936, p. 17.

36. Ibid., September 4, 1936, p. 19.

37. *New York Times*, September 4, 1936, p. 12.

38. *Cleveland Plain Dealer*, September 8, 1936, p. 17.

39. *Strikeout Story*, p. 49.

40. *Cleveland Plain Dealer*, September 19, 1936, p. 20.

41. Ibid., September 24, 1936, p. 15.

42. Ibid., September 28, 1936, p. 16.

43. *Des Moines Tribune*, October 8, 1936.

44. Ibid.

Chapter 4

1. *Cleveland Plain Dealer*, September 13, 1936, p. 2-B

2. Ibid.

3. *Des Moines Tribune*, December 10, 1936.

4. *Cleveland News*, December 10, 1936, p. 14.

5. *Sporting News*, June 15, 1944.

6. *Plain Dealer*, September 25, 1936, p. 16.

7. *Strikeout Story*, p. 52.

8. Ibid., p. 55.

9. Ibid., p. 57.

10. *Cleveland Plain Dealer*, October 8, 1936, p. 20.

11. *Des Moines Register-Tribune*, June 30, 1957.

12. See David Pietrusza, *Judge and Jury: The Life and Times of Judge Kenesaw Mountain Landis* (South Bend, Ind.: Diamond Communications, 1998). Chapter 22 gives a detailed account of Landis fighting a rear-guard action against the development of the modern farm system, of which the Feller case was a major milestone.

13. Ibid., p. 354.

14. *Strikeout Story*, p. 58.

15. *Cleveland Indians*, p. 196.

16. *Cleveland Plain Dealer*, June 11, 1972, p. 2-C.

17. *Strikeout Story*, p. 58.

18. *Judge and Jury*, p. 354.

19. *Des Moines Tribune*, October 5, 1936.

20. Ibid.

21. *Des Moines Tribune*, October 8, 1936.

22. Interview with author, October 18, 2002.

23. *Des Moines Tribune*, October 10, 1936.

24. *Cleveland Plain Dealer*, October 20, 1936.

25. *Judge and Jury*, p. 355.

26. *Cleveland Plain Dealer*, December 1, 1936.

27. *Des Moines Tribune*, December 1, 1936.

28. Ibid.

29. *Des Moines Tribune*, December 10, 1936.

30. *Judge and Jury*, pp. 359–61.

31. *Des Moines Tribune*, December 11, 1936.

32. *Des Moines Tribune*, January 6, 1937.

33. *Strikeout Story*, p. 61.

34. Ibid.

Chapter 5

1. *Strikeout Story*, p. 62.

2. Mel Harder, interviewed in Nick Wilson, *Voices from the Pastime* (Jefferson, N.C.: McFarland, 2000), p. 89.

3. *Strikeout Story*, p. 64.

4. *New York Times*, March 12, 1937.

5. Ibid. March 11, 1937.
6. Ibid., March 12, 1937.
7. *New York Daily News*, March 10, 1937.
8. *Strikeout Story*, p. 65.
9. Dick Bartell, with Norman Macht, *Rowdy Richard* (Berkeley, Calif.: North Atlantic Books, 1987), p. 197.
10. *Strikeout Story*, p. 69.
11. *Now Pitching*, p. 47.
12. *Strikeout Story*, p. 73.
13. *Strikeout Story*, pp. 74–75.
14. *New York Times*, April 25, 1937.
15. *Now Pitching*, p. 50.
16. *New York Times*, May 11, 1937.
17. Ibid., May 16, 1937.
18. Ibid., May 18, 1937.
19. *Strikeout Story*, p. 79.
20. Ibid., p. 80.
21. Ibid.
22. Ibid., p. 83; also *Now Pitching*, p. 52.
23. *Now Pitching*, p. 54.
24. *New York Times*, September 28, 1937.

Chapter 6

1. *Cleveland Indians*, p. 200.
2. *Now Pitching*, p. 69.
3. *Strikeout Story*, p. 121.
4. Ibid., p. 128.
5. Ibid., p. 129.
6. Ibid., p. 135.
7. John Phillips, *The Crybaby Indians of 1940* (Cabin John, Md.: Capital, 1990), p. 1.
8. Ibid., p. 152.
9. *Sporting News*, September 14, 1939.
10. Ibid.
11. *New York Daily News*, August 25, 1939.
12. Ibid.
13. Ibid.

Chapter 7

1. *Strikeout Story*, p. 164.
2. *Sporting News*, May 2, 1940.

3. *Crybaby Indians of 1940*, p. 5.

4. *Sporting News*, May 2, 1940.

5. *Cleveland Indians*, p. 208; also, *Crybaby Indians of 1940*, p. 24.

6. *Crybaby Indians*, p. 25.

7. *Strikeout Story*, p. 175.

8. Interview with author, October 19, 2002.

9. *Strikeout Story*, p. 175, and *Cleveland Indians*, p. 210.

10. *Cleveland Indians*, p. 211.

11. *Strikeout Story*, p. 176.

12. *Sport Magazine*, August 1951, p. 34.

13. *Cleveland News*, September 8, 1956.

14. Bob Broeg, *Superstars of Baseball* (South Bend, Ind.: Diamond Communications, 1994), p. 138.

15. *Sporting News*, July 19, 1940.

16. *Crybaby Indians*, p. 40.

17. *Strikeout Story*, p. 181.

18. *Crybaby Indians*, p. 45.

19. Bill James, *The Bill James Guide to Baseball Managers* (New York: Scribner, 1997), p. 106.

20. Interview with author, October 18, 2002.

Chapter 8

1. Undated newspaper clipping found in Feller File in the *Sporting News* archive.

2. *Strikeout Story*, pp. 195–96.

3. Ibid., p. 198.

4. *Sporting News*, May 1, 1941.

5. Lawrence S. Ritter, *The Glory of Their Times* (New York: William Morrow, 1985), p. 322.

6. *Sporting News*, May 1, 1941.

7. *Strikeout Story*, p. 200.

8. *Now Pitching*, p. 111.

Chapter 9

1. *Sporting News*, May 7, 1942.

2. *Strikeout Story*, p. 208.

3. *Sporting News*, June 4, 1942.

4. Ibid., August 27, 1942.

5. *Strikeout Story*, p. 208.

6. Details of *Alabama*'s operations are taken from *The Dictionary of American Fighting Ships* unless otherwise indicated.

7. *Sporting News*, January 28, 1943.
8. *Strikeout Story*, p. 210.
9. *Sporting News*, January 21, 1943.
10. *Strikeout Story*, p. 211.
11. *Sporting News*, June 22, 1944.
12. *Strikeout Story*, p. 213.
13. Ibid., p. 214.
14. *Sporting News*, January 6, 1945.
15. *Sporting News*, January 18, 1945.
16. *Sporting News*, July 26, 1945.

Chapter 10

1. *Cleveland News*, February 26, 1945.
2. Interview with author, October 18, 2002.
3. A September 1957 article in *Baseball Digest* by John Holway deals with this issue, although Holway's conclusions can be duplicated by anyone with access to a baseball encyclopedia and a calculator.
4. *Strikeout Story*, p. 222.
5. *Sporting News*, January 17, 1946.
6. *Cleveland News*, March 15, 1946.
7. *Baseball Magazine*, February 1946.
8. *Sporting News*, February 14, 1946.
9. *Strikeout Story*, p. 226.
10. Ibid., p. 229.
11. Conversation quoted in Donald Honig, *Baseball When the Grass Was Real* (New York: Coward, McCann, and Geoghegan, 1975), p. 260.
12. *Now Pitching*, p. 129.
13. Frederick Turner, *When the Boys Came Back: Baseball and 1946* (New York: Henry Holt, 1996), p. 204.
14. *Sporting News*, September 25, 1946.
15. *Baseball Digest*, September 1946.

Chapter 11

1. Mark Ribowsky, *Don't Look Back: Satchel Paige in the Shadows of Baseball* (New York: Simon and Schuster, 1994), p. 203.
2. *Now Pitching*, p. 138.
3. Art Rust, Jr., with Michael Marley, *Legends: Conversations with Baseball Greats* (New York: McGraw-Hill, 1989), p. 50.
4. Press release from Bob Feller's All-Stars, found in archives of *Sporting News*.

5. Buck O'Neil, with Steve Wulf and David Conrads, *I Was Right On Time* (New York: Simon and Schuster, 1996), pp. 179–80.

6. Ibid.

7. John Holway, *Josh and Satch* (Westport, Conn.: Meckler, 1991), p. 188.

8. Glenn Stout and Dick Johnson, *Jackie Robinson: Between the Baselines* (San Francisco: Woodford Press, 1997), p. 67.

9. *Sporting News*, October 30, 1946.

10. *Sporting News*, November 6, 1946.

11. *Sporting News*, October 30, 1946.

12. Undated newspaper clipping, quoted in Jules Tygiel, *Baseball's Great Experiment: Jackie Robinson and His Legacy* (New York: Oxford University Press, 1997), p. 76.

13. *Legends*, p. 48.

14. *Now Pitching*, p. 141.

15. *Ebony*, May 1949.

16. Interview with author, October 19, 2002.

Chapter 12

1. *Sporting News*, January 29, 1947.

2. *Newsweek*, June 2, 1947, p. 77.

3. *Saturday Evening Post*, April 19, 1947, p. 170.

4. *Newsweek*, June 2, 1947, p. 76.

5. *Sporting News*, June 11, 1947.

6. *Sporting News*, August 27, 1947.

7. *Sporting News*, August 13, 1947.

8. *Sporting News*, November 5, 1947.

9. *Josh and Satch*, p. 196.

10. *Don't Look Back*, p. 242.

11. Ibid., p. 253.

12. Ibid.

Chapter 13

1. *Sporting News*, February 18th, 1948.

2. *Sportfolio*, April 1948.

3. For a detailed and superbly written account of the '48 race, see David Kaiser, *Epic Season: The 1948 American League Pennant Race* (Amherst: University of Massachusetts Press, 1998).

4. *Cleveland News*, April 21, 1948.

5. *Sporting News*, May 19, 1948.

6. *Now Pitching*, p. 153.

7. *Sporting News*, July 21, 1948.
8. Ibid.
9. *Cleveland Plain Dealer*, August 29, 1948.
10. *Now Pitching*, p. 157.
11. Ibid., p. 164.
12. *Baseball Digest*, November 1948.

Chapter 14

1. *Sporting News*, October 27, 1948.
2. Ibid., February 16, 1949.
3. *New York Sun*, February 8, 1949.
4. *Cleveland Press*, February 9, 1949.
5. Ibid., July 29, 1949.
6. *Sporting News*, November 9, 1949.
7. *Cleveland News*, November 23, 1949.
8. *Sporting News*, January 25, 1950.
9. *Sporting News*, April 19, 1950.
10. Ibid., June 14, 1950.
11. Ibid.
12. Ibid., June 28, 1950.
13. *Now Pitching*, p. 183.
14. Ibid., p. 186.
15. *Baseball Digest*, September 1951.
16. *Cleveland Plain Dealer* and *Detroit Free Press*, July 2, 1951.
17. UPI wire service story, July 2, 1951.
18. *Cleveland Press*, July 3, 1951.
19. Ibid.
20. *Sport Magazine*, October 1951.
21. *Sporting News*, August 22, 1951; also *Cleveland Plain Dealer*, August 14, 1951.
22. *Sporting News*, August 29, 1951.

Chapter 15

1. *Sporting News*, October 31, 1951.
2. *Toronto Globe and Mail*, October 11, 1951.
3. *Sporting News*, January 30, 1952.
4. *Sporting News*, April 2, 1952.
5. *Sporting News*, September 3, 1952.
6. *Now Pitching*, p. 190.
7. *Sporting News*, December 3, 1952.
8. *Cleveland News*, February 5, 1953.

9. *Sporting News*, February 11, 1953.

10. Western Union telegram to G. Taylor Spink found in *Sporting News* archives.

11. *Cleveland News*, August 1953.

12. *Sporting News*, February 3, 1954.

13. *Sporting News*, November 11, 1953.

14. Wes Singletary, *Al Lopez: The Life of Baseball's El Señor* (Jefferson, N.C.: McFarland, 1999), p. 171.

15. *Sporting News*, January 12, 1955.

16. *Sporting News*, March 30, 1955.

17. *San Francisco Examiner*, March 26, 1955.

18. *Sporting News*, May 11, 1955.

19. *Cleveland Press*, August 16, 1955.

20. *Des Moines Register-Tribune*, September 27, 1955.

21. *Sporting News*, December 28, 1955.

22. *Chicago Daily News*, March 14, 1956.

23. Ibid.

24. Interview with author, October 19, 2002.

Chapter 16

1. *Sporting News*, February 13, 1957.

2. *Sporting News*, March 13, 1957.

3. *Sporting News*, May 22, 1957.

4. *Boston Globe*, July 26, 1957.

5. *Cleveland Press*, July 10th, 1957.

6. Transcript, "The Mike Wallace Interview," August 4, 1957.

7. *Sporting News*, November 20, 1957.

8. *Sporting News*, August 14, 1957.

9. *Sporting News*, February 5, 1958.

10. Undated newspaper clipping in *Sporting News* archive.

11. *Denver Post*, April 13, 1958.

12. *Sporting News*, June 3, 1959.

13. *Los Angeles Mirror*, August 22, 1960.

14. Arnold Rampersad, *Jackie Robinson: A Biography* (New York: Alfred A. Knopf, 1997), p. 362.

15. *Sporting News*, January 31, 1962.

16. *Miami Herald*, May 15, 1962.

17. *Sporting News*, August 4, 1962.

18. *Now Pitching*, p. 207.

19. Ibid., p. 215.

20. Interview with author, October 18, 2002.

21. Marvin Miller, *A Whole Different Ball Game* (New York: Birch Lane Press, 1991), p. 7.

22. *Cleveland Press*, August 19, 1965.

23. *Sporting News*, August 9, 1969.

24. Ibid.

25. Ibid.

26. Ibid.

27. Al Campanis made an infamous appearance on *Nightline* in the late eighties when he said that blacks "may lack the essentials" to work in front offices. It cost him his job as the Dodgers' general manager and helped set the stage for greater attention to minority candidates in the future.

28. *Sporting News*, August 9, 1969.

29. AP wire dispatch, August 15, 1970.

30. *Peoria Journal-Star*, July 2, 1983.

Chapter 17

1. 1941 quote, found in numerous sources.

2. Lawrence S. Ritter, *The Glory of Their Times* (New York: William Morrow, 1985), p. 317.

3. *Chicago Daily News*, undated clipping found in *Sporting News* archive.

4. Brent Kelly, *Baseball Stars of the 1950s* (Jefferson, N.C.: McFarland, 1993), p. 96.

5. *New York Times*, September 17, 1951.

6. *Boston Globe*, June 3, 1954.

7. Eugene McCaffrey and Roger McCaffrey, *Players' Choice* (New York: Facts on File, 1987).

Chapter 18

1. *Sporting News*, February 26, 1958.

2. "Hitting Bob Feller," *The National Pastime*.

3. *Cleveland Plain Dealer*, July 23, 1952.

4. Undated newspaper clipping from 1953, found in *Sporting News* archive.

5. William Marshall, *Baseball's Pivotal Era: 1945–1951* (Lexington: University of Kentucky Press, 1999), p. 343.

6. Donald Dewey and Nicholas Acocella, *The Biographical History of Baseball* (New York: Carroll and Graf, 1995).

7. *Sport Magazine*, August 1951.

8. *Cleveland Press*, January 19, 1952.

INDEX

ABOUT THE AUTHOR

JOHN SICKELS writes about minor league baseball for ESPN.com. He is the author of the annual *Baseball Prospect Book* and seven editions of the *Minor League Scouting Notebook*. Sickels also holds a master's in European history from the University of Kansas. He lives in Lawrence, Kansas.

FELLER, BOB

B - FEL

Sickels, John

Bob Feller.